D0851883

HARMONY

By
HEINRICH SCHENKER

Edited and annotated by
OSWALD JONAS

Translated by
ELISABETH MANN BORGESE

THE MIT PRESS
CAMBRIDGE, MASSACHUSETTS, AND LONDON, ENGLAND

Original edition published by
The University of Chicago Press, Chicago, Illinois

Copyright © 1954 by The University of Chicago

First MIT Press paperback edition, October 1973
Second printing, July 1978

Printed in the United States of America

Library of Congress Cataloging in Publication Data

Schenker, Heinrich, 1868 -1935.
  Harmony.

  Translation of Neue musikalische Theorien und
Phantasien, 1. Bd.
  1. Music—Theory. 2. Harmony.
MT40.S2912 1973   781.3   73 -3082
ISBN 0 -262 -69044 -6

INTRODUCTION

The book presented here in its first English edition was published in its original almost half a century ago. Why, one might wonder, did it take all this time to bring it before the public again? It should be pointed out, first of all, that a similar fate, if not worse, has befallen other books as well. C. P. E. Bach's *Essay,* for example, which is, beyond doubt, one of the most important books ever written on music theory, was grossly neglected for almost two hundred years, to be reissued, in a complete edition, only quite recently. This new edition is in English translation (by W. J. Mitchell), and it is deplorable that the work is still unavailable in its German original.[1]

This fact, which reflects fairly well the whole situation in which our musical culture finds itself today, may offer a general explanation, not an excuse. The particular circumstances at the root of the case presented here will appear more clearly as we go on with this Introduction.

Heinrich Schenker published his *Harmony* anonymously in 1906, under the most unusual title, "New Musical Theories and Fantasies—by an Artist." The title itself was to indicate the author's intention of finding artistic solutions to artistic problems rather than any concern for commonplace theoretical discussions. This volume was the first in a long series and marks the beginning of a lifelong development, which was concluded only with the last volume, *Free Composition,* published thirty years later—a few months after the author's death. In this sequence of works, interspersed with a good number of other publications, Schenker revealed his theories as they developed. Each volume represents a step forward, based on an ever growing artistic experience. This process, however, entailed certain difficulties. Some concepts were still immature when first published and found their final and clear expression only in a subsequent volume. Furthermore, certain parts of the work, though each one of them constituted an essential basis for subsequent constructions, would, in certain aspects, be obsolete when the later work appeared.

1. A facsimile-print edited by Lothar Hoffmann-Erbrecht has since been published (Leipzig: Breitkopf & Härtel, 1957).

Schenker's doctrine thus was in a continuous process of growth and development; and the author, always occupied with the completion of new work, was never in a position of even considering the revision of older works. This provides a partial answer to our original query. One need only consider, in addition, the unquestionable difficulty of the subject matter as such, aggravated by the author's recalcitrance toward any form of belletristic presentation, and his attitude, on the other hand, of ruthlessly standing his ground, no matter whether this put him into shrill contrast with all his contemporaries; and it becomes obvious that he soon was to find himself in a state of total isolation. What else could be in store for an author who dedicated, in the face of his contemporaries, his monograph on Beethoven's *Ninth Symphony* "to the memory of the last master of German music—Johannes Brahms"? Owing to its undoubtedly original and comprehensive manner of presentation, the book itself was well received and widely perused. This fact, however, did not modify in the least the negative attitude widely held toward the author personally—paradoxical as this may seem. Indeed, it can be said that Schenker's works were read and studied more than some care to admit and more than one would expect, in view of the personal attacks on the author and, on the other hand, the conspiracy of silence that greeted his work.

In the long run, however, neither hostile attacks nor silence could subdue the need for a more objective grappling with the problems. This was true with regard to Schenker's work, as it is true with regard to any important intellectual movement. And at no time has there been a more urgent need for a basic reorientation than just now. We are passing through a period admittedly submerged in experiments, with all basic concepts thrown into a state of hopeless confusion. There are many who, consciously or unconsciously, have set out to find a solution; who are groping for a clarification of the basic problems of art, a clarification which is essential for an understanding of the fundamentals of music as art. Of course, there are also those who still try to escape reality and to circumvent the answers. There are also those who know Schenker's theories only from secondhand sources, which are responsible for a number of misunderstandings.

Both categories of musicians may be skeptical with regard to Schenker's work, and they will ask whether and why Schenker should be considered the man to bring the needed clarification. It is up to the writer of this Introduction to give a convincing affirmative answer to these questions in the following pages. It is legitimate, however, to quote here an opinion whose complete impartiality must be beyond any suspicion. In December, 1936, when Schenker's name and work were blacklisted for political reasons, an article appeared in the *Allgemeine Musik Zeitung* under the title, "Can We Still Listen to Music?" Whether the author, Hans Jenkner, proceeded from defiance or unawareness of the circumstances is beyond my judgment. Whatever his motives, he deserves to be rescued from oblivion.

Naturally, laymen as well as experts will raise the question as to whether it is probable that Schenker, of all men, is the one who was destined to wrest from music her secrets. To this one might answer: The level of Schenker's thinking on the art of music is higher than that of most other people. He has listened more intensely and has perceived her law. Creative composers have fulfilled the law without ever grasping it rationally (with the one exception of Brahms, the Great Reticent). The revelation of the wonderful natural law regulating the flow of music in its totality is tantamount to an acoustic perception of the moral law. Thus theory comes to be more than the teaching of forms; it becomes perception of first causes. . . . This work, created by a man who is faithful to art, indicates to us the way to regeneration.

Roger Sessions once described Schenker's *Harmony* as "certainly unsurpassed and perhaps unequalled in its sphere." The book is of the greatest importance, if only because it contains many of Schenker's ideas in their embryonic stage. It is natural, on the other hand, that the author at that time was still largely under the influence of conventional concepts, from which he broke away during later stages of his development. For these reasons it seemed advisable to provide the work with a running commentary which should forestall the danger of possible misunderstandings and misinterpretations. It also should forestall attacks against Schenker on the ground of certain more or less speculative and challengeable ideas which the author himself repudiated in his subsequent work. Such ideas are expressed, for example, in the chapter on the "mystic number five."

This chapter, its content often misunderstood and distorted, has been a target of much unfavorable criticism (§§ 11, 15, 17, 113). The chapters on seventh-chords (§§ 52, 99 ff.) and on modulation (§§ 171 ff.) were completely remodeled in Schenker's later work. All this is noted at the proper places in the running commentary.

We have left the illustrations used by Schenker throughout the work as nearly as possible in their original form; even in those cases where Schenker himself, in a later stage of his development, probably would have read fewer scale-steps and more voice-leading for a proper analysis. We have added, however, an Appendix to this Introduction in which a number of illustrations are presented in the form which, according to all probability, Schenker would have given them in a later stage; and we have added the necessary explanations for this hypothetical development.

If Schenker's *Harmony* is to serve as a practical introduction to his whole work, this Introduction has to fulfil two tasks. First, it should give a brief account of the general situation in which musical theory found itself at the time when Schenker began his work and should expose any widespread errors which he had to face. Second, it should give a synopsis of the development of Schenker's theories in his later works.

Before embarking on this twofold enterprise, we should like to anticipate one of the main objections to Schenker's work. It has been said time and again that his theory is too "narrow," too "lopsided," since it does not offer any key to the understanding of modern music or music written after, say, the time of Brahms. This objection should be rejected on the ground that Schenker's theory is deeply rooted in the principles of tonality as he found them elaborated in the works of the great masters from Bach to Brahms, fulfilling an almost millennial development of music as art.[2] One may even say that, for Schenker, tonality is the *conditio sine qua non* of music as art; and the proof of this hypothesis constitutes the content of his teachings. If Schenker has succeeded in proving that tonality is the foundation of

---

2. Recently an attempt was made to offset this objection by applying Schenker's ideas to modern music and its interpretation: *Structural Hearing* by Felix Salzer (New York: Charles Boni, 1952). Such an attempt was possible only through misinterpretation of Schenker's basic theories, first of all his concept of tonality, and therefore is doomed to fail.

the musical masterworks—though his concept is essentially different from the ordinary one—the burden of proof is now on those who claim that there are other foundations, as strongly rooted in the laws of nature, for music as an art to rest upon.[3]

The chief merit of Schenker's early work consists in having disentangled the concept of scale-step (which is part of the theory of harmony) from the concept of voice-leading (which belongs in the sphere of counterpoint). The two had been confused for decades. Schenker's operation wrought a complete change even in the external aspect of the teaching of harmony, in that he banned from his handbook all exercises in voice-leading and relegated them to the study of counterpoint.

The significance of this undertaking cannot be fully grasped except in the context of its historical setting. We have to consider here briefly the development of musical theory since the end of the eighteenth century. This survey will also help to clarify the meaning of Schenker's two basic concepts, "prolongation," and "compositional unfolding," or *Auskomponierung*.

According to the theory of prolongation, free composition, too, is subject to the laws of strict composition, albeit in "prolonged form." The theory of *Auskomponierung* shows voice-leading as the means by which the chord, as a harmonic concept, is made to unfold and extend in time. This, indeed, is the essence of music. *Auskomponierung* thus insures the unity and continuity of the musical work of art.

The core of music theory as it had developed and was taught in the eighteenth century was voice-leading. The study of theory was divided into two parts: the study of strict counterpoint and the study of figured bass ("thorough bass" or "continuo"). The rules guiding the former were derived from the epoch of vocal music. They were codified by Joseph Fux in *Gradus ad Parnassum* (recently reprinted in part in an English translation). In this work Fux undertook an analysis of the nature of intervals, a distinction between consonant and dissonant notes, and a study of the use of the latter. It was a study of voice-leading in its purest form, totally free of any considerations of harmony. More than anything else, it was a body of rules for the

3. Cf. Appendix II, below.

training of the ear. In this sense counterpoint has attained universal validity. But it never could lay claim to the teaching of advanced composition, although this may have been the original intention of *Gradus ad Parnassum;* in this respect Fux was still too deeply under the influence of the vocal epoch.

The development of figured bass was somewhat different. Following the development of instrumental music, it showed more flexibility and freedom. It remained, however, a discipline of voice-leading and never degenerated to a mere juxtaposition of chords. In this sense, the study of figured bass served as a preparation and introduction to the study of composition. Bach, indeed, went so far as to call it "*the* school of composition." Since the composers of that time never executed the details of their compositions but left it to their interpreters to fill in the upper voices in accordance with the numerals, figured bass became a most efficient conveyer of general musical education; for anyone who wanted to play music had to have an adequate theoretical preparation. The study of figured bass was the obligatory gateway to any musical performance. Piano playing "for its own sake" and without general musicianship was utterly unthinkable at that time. The dependence of performance on theory is indicated by the very title of C. P. E. Bach's treatise, *Essay on the True Art of Playing Keyboard Instruments,* which is a codification of the rules of figured bass at the acme of their development (1762).

If the theories of counterpoint and figured bass had remained the basis of teaching during the following generations, musical history might have taken a different course. This, however, is history of the might-have-been. In 1722 Rameau discovered the principles of harmony and developed them in his *Traité d'harmonie.* In this work he revealed the function of harmonic steps and inversions. He demonstrated that the harmony of a triad does not change when the root is transferred from the bass to another voice. The concept of the harmonic step as such may have enriched musical theory, though it should be remembered that the inversion of intervals had already been well known to the school of strict counterpoint. But the use to which Rameau put this concept certainly created confusion and was baneful to the further development of music theory. Rameau's concept was much too narrow. This may be due to the fact that he was totally unaware of the new trends in German music. Perhaps his theory was adequate for an understanding of his own music, which assumed almost identical meaning of chord and scale-step; it most certainly was inadequate if applied to the finesses of voice-leading in the works of Bach as understood in the theories of C. P. E. Bach's *Essay*. Rameau did not even suspect the possibility that voice-leading could be the means for the "compositional unfolding" of wider harmonic areas. For him "chord" and "scale-step" were identical. He reduced any simultaneity of tones to its supposed root position and rent the artful texture of voice-leading into strips of more or less closely related chords. The chord, endowed by voice-leading with its full meaning and contextual logic, now was to stand in isolation, generally without reference to what preceded and what followed. The bass line, meaningful as the *Auskomponierung* of a chord—a blessing that had accrued to composition from instrumental music and figured bass—was weighted down, note for note, by the burden of the "ground bass," which inhibited and finally arrested its motion. All the life of music congealed. Thus the same year, 1722, which brought forth the first volume of Bach's *Well-tempered Clavier,* with its miracles of voice-leading, also heralded the decay of musical theory and practice.

In broadest terms, Rameau's great error was to interpret harmonically, or vertically, a bass that was composed horizontally, according to contrapuntal principles. The possibility of *Auskomponierung* was totally overlooked. The bass line of a thorough-bass composition represented a happy attempt at horizontal construction. The upper voices, whose movement was directed by the continuo numerals, moved along similar horizontal lines. To reduce this living bass line to the so-called "ground bass" was the fundamental error of Rameau's doctrine.

To illustrate further: the continuo numerals indicated the movement and progression of the upper voices, not a chordal structure of harmonic steps. Thus we read in Bach's *Chorale Melodies with Figured Bass:*

The indication *8-7* leaves no doubt that Bach wanted the seventh to descend in passing from the octave. The indication *8* cannot be explained otherwise; for any other interpretation would render this indication superfluous. The numerals indicate a movement, a specific movement—not, indeed, a "dominant seventh-chord." Likewise, the numerals (*b*) indicate a slow turn; a chordal interpretation would be equally meaningless. Kirnberger writes in his *Art of Pure Composition* (1774), I, 30: "The genesis [of the essential dissonances] can be reconstructed as follows:

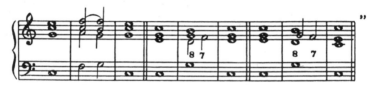

Rameau's theory was introduced into Germany by Marpurg, who translated D'Alambert's brief Introduction to the works of Rameau. The reception was cool. It was, indeed, so skeptical that it is hard to see how Rameau's prestige and influence could have survived it. Bach and his circle of friends remained completely negative. Emanuel Bach wrote to Kirnberger, who was a faithful pupil of Sebastian Bach and, at that time, engaged in a controversy with Marpurg: "You may announce it publicly that my father's principles and my own are anti-Rameau." Kirnberger himself, in *The True Principles of Harmonic Practice* (1773) has the following passage: "Rameau has stuffed his theory with so many inconsistencies that I am just wondering how it could have come to pass that there are Germans who fall for it and even fight for it. We always have had among us the greatest harmonists, and their treatment of harmony certainly could not be explained by Rameau's propositions. Some have gone so far as to throw doubt even on Bach's treatment of chords and their progressions rather than admit that the Frenchman could be in error." And in his *Pure Composition* (I, 248) Kirnberger writes: "Rameau himself has not grasped the simplicity of harmony in its true purity; for he occasionally mistakes passing notes for fundamental ones." This latter observation already reveals a distinction between voice-leading and a merely "harmonic conception."

Art precludes any approach by short cuts or oversimplifications; and the danger of oversimplification inherent in Rameau's theory was recognized even in France. No lesser critic than Rousseau expressed his alarm as early as 1752, and his comment anticipates the conditions in which the teaching of harmony finds itself in our day: "The study of composition, which used to require about twenty years, now can be completed in a couple of months; musicians are devouring the theories of Rameau, and the number of students has multiplied. . . . France has been inundated by bad music and bad musicians; everybody thinks he has understood the finesses of art before having learned as much as the rudiments; and everybody tries to invent new harmonies before having trained his ear to distinguish between right and wrong ones." This passage could have been written today.

In Germany, however, strict composition was still the basis of teaching. Our masters still applied themselves to the study of C. P. E. Bach's *Essay,* not to that of Rameau. Haydn said of C. P. E. Bach that he owed him everything. The *Essay* and Fux's *Gradus* were the foundations of his own teaching and later also of Beethoven's.

The fate of music was sealed when figured bass, once fallen into disuse practically, became obsolete also in theory as a method of instruction. Owing to the lack of alternatives, it was still adhered to formally; but its essence was completely falsified by Rameau's theory of the ground bass. From this amalgamation of voice-leading and harmonic steps there arose our own "harmony" as a rigid theory of "chords." For a while, tradition survived. There is no doubt that Mendelssohn, for example, was instructed in the old style. C. P. E. Bach and Quantz had left some traces of their work in Berlin. But Brahms had already complained that, before being able to do anything constructive himself, he had first "to unlearn everything" he had learned; and his dictum—"even Schumann did not learn anything any more . . . . nor did Wagner"—gives cause for alarm. "You would not believe," he wrote to Riemann, "what I had to suffer from incompetent textbooks." Riemann, on the other hand, was naïve enough to propose to dedicate to Brahms his own *Harmony,* which, indeed, he did, much against the latter's desire.

It is small wonder that, in the long run, the consequences of an instruction restricted to the teaching of chords began to show in the style of composition. Composers began to think only "vertically" and to write accordingly. The great ones among them were fully aware of this danger. In his critique of the "Waverley Ouverture" by Berlioz (1839), Schumann wrote: "Often it is only a series of empty sound effects, of lumps of chords thrown together, that seems to determine the character of the piece." And Delacroix noted in his diary a conversation with Chopin, during which the latter told him: "It has become customary now to learn chords ahead of counterpoint, which means, ahead of the sequences of notes by which the chords are formed. Berlioz simply sets down the chords and fills the interstices as best he can."

By also reducing merely passing chords to "fundamental chords," Rameau destroyed all continuity. The bass line had itself been a result of *Auskomponierung,* and this had been achieved by means which belonged in the sphere of counterpoint, such as passing notes or neighboring notes. It now lost its meaning and continuity. The theory of the ground bass was tantamount to the destruction of contrapuntal thinking, which it replaced by the so-called "harmonic" way of thinking. It rested on false premises. The reduction of a passing chord to a fundamental one divested it of its logic and distorted the perspective of the value it possessed as a passing chord and derived only from that position. In response to the need for a more meaningful standard of evaluating notes, there arose the so-called "theory of functions," which reduced all chords simply to tonic, dominant, or subdominant. This attempt was to no avail either. It was bound to fail because it overlooked the possibility that identical chords have different meanings according to the context in which they move. The concept of the "secondary dominant" (*Hilfsdominante*), likewise, could not lead very far because it applied only to the relations between two neighboring chords. It could never bring about a synthesis of the whole. In what concerns the appreciation of the great masterpieces of music, all that could be learned by these methods was to drag one's ear from the perception of one chord to that of the next. As a consequence, the energy necessary for a broader understanding was lost.

The overemphasis on the vertical was bound to arouse a reaction. The pendulum, however, had swung too far in one direction for the countermotion to stop at the center of reason and moderation. The opposite extreme was to be reached in the theory of "linear counterpoint" and the school of "linear composition" it engendered. All the thinking and writing now was "horizontal," without any regard to the natural laws of harmony, to whose unfolding any sequence or simultaneity of notes must be subordinated. Only where the horizontal serves the unfolding of harmony can vertical relations be integrated into a whole. Justice can be done to the bass line only when it is understood in its double function: within the large structure of tonality, it must be the bearer of harmony; at the same time, however, it must be so led as to express, through and beside the pillars of harmony, a continuity of melodic unfolding.

Heinrich Schenker has shown the correct relationship between the horizontal and the vertical. His theory is drawn from a profound understanding of the masterpieces of music which his genius not only interpreted but, so to speak, created anew. Thus he indicates to us the way: to satisfy the demands of harmony while mastering the task of voice-leading.

"In contrast to the theory of counterpoint, the theory of Harmony presents itself to me as a purely spiritual universe, a system of ideally moving forces, born of Nature or of art." With these words, on the very first page of his Introduction to *Harmony*, Schenker embarks on his long journey. He immediately arrives at a considerably broader concept of the scale-step, at least ideally. For its practical application to the understanding of the masterpieces, a host of ex-

periences, was still needed. A glance at the wealth of examples offered in *Harmony* should be sufficient, however, to make it clear how
far even his early concept of the scale-step deviates from the usual
one (examples 120, 121, 124, 130, and 201 should be noted in particular). Here his concept of "step" is already no longer identical
with the concept of a mere chord. It has rather become the artistic
expression of an ideal chord, a chord given by nature. The task of
the artist, then, is to fashion this raw material and to endow it with
form, according to the laws of art.[4]

The chord is a simultaneity. To use a metaphor, it has a dimension
in space; and the nature of music, which flows in time, demands its
translation into a temporal sequence. This process, called by Schenker
"compositional unfolding" or *Auskomponierung*, is clearly understood in *Harmony*, Schenker's first major work (§§ 115 ff. should
be noted in particular in this connection). It could find its final expression, however, only after an incursion into the field of counterpoint, since the goal of creation in time, of *Auskomponierung*, can be
reached only via voice-leading. Basically, the development of our
occidental music begins from an understanding of nature and an
interpretation of its relations to man-made art. It is marked, stage by
stage, by the conquest of the necessary means of expression, i.e.,
voice-leading. Metaphorically, one could say that this philogenetic
development was recapitulated ontogenetically in Schenker's progressive stages of interpreting the masterpieces. The final aim was to
reach a balance between the two components of any musical structure: the "vertical" of the chord and the "horizontal" of voice-
leading.

Before proceeding with this exposition, however, we should consider Schenker's use of one more artistic means. It embodies the
law of repetition, and its primary expression in musical composition
is the motif. The opening paragraphs of this book, with the commentary notes, will provide the reader with an adequate interpreta-

---

4. One of these laws, essential for the creation of any art, is the law of abbreviation, for
man to grasp nature in its infinity. In this sense Schenker's restriction with regard to series of
overtones has a foundation in reason. Unfortunately, he tied it up too closely with his considerations of the "number five," and instilled into it an overdose of speculation and mysticism
(see above, p. vi).

tion of this phenomenon. We may therefore restrict our observations here to those of its aspects which must be considered as a significant advance in the development of Schenker's theory. Again, a detour over the theory of counterpoint was obligatory, as voice-leading was a decisive factor also in this respect.

In § 7 of *Harmony* Schenker says that the "cancellation of parallelisms" constitutes an "exception." The motif for him is something more or less unalterable, which can be identified only if its notes are maintained in their original form. He does not yet suspect the existence, in the background, of forces strong enough to fix what is essential, even where the externals of a motif are subjected to change. Only as he developed his theories on counterpoint and strove to reconcile them with the principles of free composition could he discover those basic laws which apply, with equal validity, both to strict and to free composition. He took up the concept of "prolongation" (see Appendix I). He proved that whatever notes or chords are to be understood as passing in strict composition retain this function also in free composition, albeit in a prolonged or extended context. Thus Schenker came to understand that any melodic development, in the external aspect of a work of art, can be reduced to some simple principle of counterpoint, such as passing notes, neighboring notes, etc.

It is obvious that those notes or chords which are passing between diatonic intervals and, so to speak, constitute the lifeblood of the whole composition also penetrate the motif, whose recurrence or repetition may now be established even where its notes are not reproduced faithfully and its content and meaning are presented in an externally altered form. It was these recurrences which led Schenker to the concept of the "primordial line," or *Urlinie*. This concept was probably the one which provoked the most violent objections on the part of Schenker's critics, mainly for the reason that he could not find a final and unequivocal formulation for it until a later stage in his development. We shall soon see why this must have been so. The *Urlinie* concept was, nevertheless, of decisive importance for the development of his theory. It was significant in two ways.

First of all, certain external phenomena of composition now could be reduced to simple contrapuntal passing notes (as pointed out above, in connection with the concept of "prolongation"). The laws of strict composition thus acquired effectiveness and validity also in free composition, although in expanded and veiled form. Counterpoint thereby came into its own and was freed from the common prejudice according to which it was nothing but a traditional matter of instruction without practical value, except, perhaps, for the composition of fugues or other "academic" exercises.

Second, the *Urlinie* led, in turn, to a clearer, though more specific, understanding of the concept of *Auskomponierung*. For it demonstrated the unfolding of a harmonic idea or interval into a melodic, horizontal line. This unfolding was achieved by a contrapuntal device, the passing note.

It is true, as we said above, that the *Urlinie* concept had not yet found its ultimate and precise formulation. In particular, its application was still restricted to the upper voice and had not yet been adjusted to the bass. Nevertheless, even at that early stage of Schenker's development, the concept was by no means as vague as claimed by his critics.

$$\text{III}^{♭7} \quad \text{VI} \quad \text{I}^{♮3} \quad \text{IV} \quad ♭\text{VII (V)} \quad \text{I/IV} \quad \text{V} \qquad \text{I}$$

In one of his earliest presentations of the *Urlinie,* with reference to the E-flat minor prelude of the *Well-tempered Clavier*, Book I (*Tonwille* [1922]), Schenker is quite precise in pointing to the *Auskomponierung* of the interval of a third, which he recognizes to be far more significant than an "arbitrary" linear concept. (In subsequent writings, this kind of *Auskomponierung* is called *span*. The span varies according to intervallic differences. Thus there are third-spans, sixth-spans, etc).

In broad terms, Schenker's concept of the *Urlinie* signifies his departure from simple "foreground" hearing to a perception of the forces operating in the "background" of a piece of art. The mere fact that his theory begins from the observation of the simplest foreground phenomenon, the "motif," should be sufficient to ward off the accusation of "constructionalism" which has been so frequently leveled at him. The discovery of the "background" and its hidden connections was essential to the perception of the continuity of a work of art: points separated in time could be heard and understood as belonging together, because they constituted the initial and concluding points of an interval, rooted in nature and grasped as a unity. Such points were linked by the passing notes, familiar from the study of counterpoint, and were severed, at the same time, by the manifold and expansive alterations of the foreground. It is obvious that Schenker did not stop at the perception of slightly altered motivic repetition. Further penetration revealed to him the existence of still greater complexes of repetition in the background. The reader may be referred here to the first four examples in Appendix I (A1–A4) which attempt a reconstruction, in the light of Schenker's later theories, of Examples 2, 11, 12, and 14 of the *Harmony*. A comparison between his early definition of the motif as "an association of ideas intrinsic in music" (*Harmony*, § 2) and his later presentation of those background repetitions in which our masterpieces abound (*Free Composition*, § 254) will illustrate most dramatically the distance covered by Schenker's intellectual journey. (Note also the arpeggios in bars 1–4 and 9–10 in Fig. 8, as presented by this editor in Appendix II. The arpeggios in question are marked by beams.)

The discovery of the *Urlinie* signified the introduction of the "horizontal" into Schenker's theory. This horizontal, however, moves within definite intervals and is therefore to be distinguished sharply from that other "horizontal," which, derived from the so-called "linear principle," has recently invaded musical theory and practice. Owing to its origin in the contrapuntal concept of the passing note, it further signified a clarification of the concept of dissonance. "Dissonance is always in passing, never a harmonic aim." This quotation is the title of Schenker's essay in the second *Yearbook* ([1926], p. 24), a classic, which defines most precisely the nature of dissonance and its origin. It is true that in *Harmony* Schenker still clings to the "chordal" concept of the seventh-chord; but even here some anticipations of his later concept can be traced, as indicated in the commentary notes. This later concept, however, could find its final formulation only in counterpoint (see §§ 10, 52, and, particularly, 55 and 99). Incidentally, it may be pointed out that even the examples quoted earlier from Bach and Kirnberger should give an approximate idea of the derivation of the dominant seventh-chord.

In so far as the *Urlinie* was a horizontal concept, it presented itself as a "sequence." This sequence, however, was composed of rather short units, at least initially. The units were short for the simple reason that the passing dissonances were pressing toward their respective goals and, as "motor forces," resisted any slowing-down. In spite of the various transformations to which the foreground motifs may be subjected, those brief recurrent units in the background are sufficiently strong to unify the "idiom" of the whole composition (see Bach's Prelude in E-flat minor, as quoted above). The basic problem, however, still remained unsolved. How was it possible to integrate these units into one unity comprehending the whole? How was it possible to create a truly organic whole, to transform a mere addition of sequences or juxtapositions into a hierarchy of compositional values?

To anticipate the answer: the relation of the *Urlinie* to the whole was modified by a new concept grasping the *Urlinie* as a part of a "primordial composition," or *Ursatz*. This concept created the necessary balance between the vertical and the horizontal (see above, p. xiv; also § 19, n. 21). Again, a long stretch of road had to be covered by Schenker to reach this final goal. The bass line in its double function (see p. xiv) as sustainer of the harmonies as well as of their connecting melodic progressions (arpeggios or passing notes) had to be brought into agreement with the upper voice. It became clear in this process that passing notes which were dissonant within the context of the bass line and passing notes which were dissonant within the context of the upper voice could be consonant in their relationship to each other. The dissonance thus appeared, passingly, as a consonance. Temporarily the urge toward its tonal goal could be relaxed, and a new chordal region was thus procured for *Auskom-*

ponierung. The dissonance was, so to speak, arrested and transmuted into a region of consonant sounds. As such, it was hierarchically subordinated to the original setting, where it appeared as a passing dissonance. The units thus were integrated into a hierarchy, i.e., a *stratification* of primary and subordinated parts.

A passing dissonance in the upper voice could be arrested and transmuted, furthermore, by having the bass skip to an interval which would be consonant with the passing note. We shall briefly examine here the most common instance of this phenomenon, with the bass skipping to the fifth:

The passing note *d* in the upper voice, within the *third-span e–d–c* of the *c* major diatonic scale, is accompanied by a *G*, obtained by a skip in the bass voice from *C*. The two voices meet in a fifth-interval, which now may be expanded into a dominant-chord and interpreted as such. This probably constitutes the most common example of the expansion of musical content. A dominant-chord obtained by this process is called a "divider" (*Teiler*) in Schenker's terminology. The divider chord, in turn, may be extended by passing notes of its own; and thus there is practically no limit to the possibilities of further transmutations, except by the aim of intelligibility. What applies to this "divider chord" obviously applies to any other consonant chord obtained by this process. The note which is to be transmuted may be passing within a third (see example), i.e., a *third-span,* or within any other interval: *fifth-span, sixth-span,* etc. The particular *span* in question will present, hierarchically, the next higher *stratum* or order, which, in turn, may be subordinated to the next higher span, until we reach the ultimate one, which spans the unity of the whole composition. This ultimate and supreme unity, which sustains the unity of the whole, represents, in its *Ursatz* form, the *Auskomponierung* of one single chord, the bearer of tonality. It is obvious that Schenker's concept of tonality differs widely from the customary one. For Schenker, tonality is the fashioning and expression in time of one single chord as given by Nature and extending in space. This concept is not changed by the fact that the subordinate *strata* may acquire, by the use of chromatic devices, some autonomy: Schenker calls this process "tonicalization" and describes it as early as *Harmony* (§§ 136 ff.). On the contrary, "tonicalization" restores to the work of art the needed contrast and color, which music was bound to lose in the process of systematization (cf. § 18). "Tonicalization," however, affects only the subordinate *strata*—the *middle ground,* in Schenker's terminology—or the surface phenomena of a composition—its *foreground.* It never takes place in the *background,* the ultimate *stratum* expressing the whole. Accordingly, Schenker later on rejected the concept of *modulation* in its strict sense, although in *Harmony* this concept is still retained. However, this work already contains some amazing premonitions, hinting at the later concept of *stratification* (see §§ 82, 86, 88, and 155, 157, with their corresponding notes). One almost feels tempted to draw a comparison between this theory of the strata and its effects, on the one hand, and the concept of perspective and its effects, on the other. In both cases "spatial depth" has been reduced to a surface or line.

The fragmentary example below and the entire "Little Prelude in F Major" by Bach, as reproduced in Appendix II, may further illustrate this concept. The former, the second theme of Mozart's Sonata in F, is presented as Example 7 in *Harmony.* In this connection, one more of Schenker's terms—*interruption*—needs to be clarified; furthermore, a few words ought to be said about the graphic method of its interpretation, to the elaboration of which Schenker dedicated much time and effort. This graphic presentation often attains such a degree of precision that it could dispense with any explanatory text.

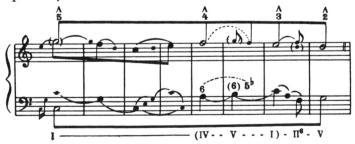

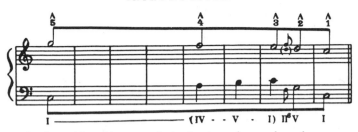

I ———————————————— (IV - - V - I) II⁶ V   I

Schenker offers this example in § 5 in order to show how repetition takes place not only on a small scale within the motif but
within a somewhat larger complex; in other words, how repetition
engenders the form of antecedent and consequent. It is true that
Schenker here deals merely with repetition as such, without going
into its musical foundation. But the principle of repetition rests primarily on psychological premises, and it is up to the composer's force
of conviction to demonstrate its cause and shape its musical effect.
A most powerful urge to repeat is created by initiating a certain
movement whose starting and concluding points may be unequivocally presumed by the listener, then to interrupt this movement at
the crucial moment—say, just before the concluding step. A tension
is thereby created which can be relaxed only by a repetition, this
time without interruption, running its full course to a satisfactory
conclusion. Before Schenker, such a phenomenon of tension (bar 8)
would have been called a "half-cadence," i.e., only the bass voice
would have been considered in the explanation of the interruption.
Schenker's theory has added the melodic, horizontal, factor. The
"melody"—the fifth-span—demands its full course. The note *d*, at
which the movement is interrupted, is a passing note. Just at the
moment when this *d* is pressing toward its goal, supported by a G
in the bass voice, which transmutes it into a consonant fifth, the
fifth of the dominant-chord, it is arrested. The span is interrupted. In
a wider sense, the melody, too, has been led to a half-cadence.

Bars 9–16 show the completed fifth-span, supported in the bass by
the arpeggiated chords of a C-cadence. This is the *Ursatz* form of this
part of the composition. Schenker, in analogous cases, would use the
term "figurative *Ursatz*" form, because the part in question constitutes only one *stratum* of the whole sonata. The *Ursatz* is graphically
indicated by those half-notes which are connected by beams, as well

as by numerals: the Arabic numerals with carets indicating the diatonic notes, the Roman numerals indicating the notes sustaining the harmony in its *Auskomponierung* in the basic steps: I–V–I.

The graphic presentation of the antecedent (bars 1–8) shows some detail. In the first four bars, the third-span *g–e* is indicated by quarter-notes connected by beams, in contrast to the half-notes, which belong to a higher stratum. Every note of the third-span, in turn, is provided with a newly unfolding third-interval (see the slurs in the graphic presentation). The third and last unfolding introduces a *d,* passing within the lowest *stratum.* The whole process is accompanied by bass arpeggios of a lower stratum. In bar 2, the *g* leads the upper voice into a passing dominant; the *d* in the upper voice (bar 3, third beat) is transmuted by the bass *G* (divider) into a consonance. The *f* in the upper voice first appears as consonant in bar 5 but returns in the next bar as dissonant, as in a prepared suspension in syncopated counterpoint.

Example A11 (Appendix II) demonstrates the effects of *Ursatz* and *stratification* on a whole piece of composition. It would have been tempting to present here a larger work, say, a sonata or a fugue. This, however, would exceed the scope of this Introduction, which represents merely an attempt to facilitate the understanding of this book and to present a summary outline of Schenker's later development.

A masterpiece of music is, in Schenker's conception, the fulfilment of a primary musical event which is discernible in the background. The process of composition means the foreground realization of this event. This explains the boundless wealth and power of the masters and the improvisational effects in which their works abound. The composer, his balance centered unconsciously or instinctively in the *Ursatz,* can wander unerringly, like a somnambulist, and span any distance and bridge any gap, no matter what the dimension of his work.

With the *Ursatz* concept, the circle of Schenker's system is closed: it opened, in *Harmony,* with the quest for a pattern in Nature for music as art. It closed with the discovery of the primordial chord and its artistic re-creation through the process of *Auskomponierung.*

CHICAGO 1954   OSWALD JONAS

In contrast to other books on music theory, conceived, one might say, for their own sake and apart from art, the aim of this book is to build a real and practicable bridge from composition to theory. If this aim is good and worth while and if the way we chose to reach it is well chosen, this book should be self-explanatory, and the advantages of its approach should result clearly even without a prelude of diffuse preannouncements. There are some points, however, which need preliminary clarification.

The critique of current methods of teaching as offered in §§ 90 ff. implies two consequences. First, all exercises in voice-leading, which so far have constituted the main material of textbooks, had to be banned from the teaching of harmony and relegated to that of counterpoint. Second, it became impossible, accordingly, to follow the standard practice of dividing the book into a theoretical and a practical part. In contrast to the theory of counterpoint, the theory of harmony presents itself to me as a purely spiritual universe, a system of ideally moving forces, born of Nature or of art. If in a sphere so abstract any division in the usual sense could be imposed at all, it had to be drawn along somewhat different lines. The theoretical part now presents, so to speak, all matters of topographical orientation, such as tonal systems, intervals, triads and other chords, etc. The practical part, on the other hand, describes their functioning, the moving forces of the primordial ideas of music, such as progression of harmonic steps, chromatic alteration and modulation, etc.

I should like to stress in particular the biological factor in the life of tones. We should get used to the idea that tones have lives of their own, more independent of the artist's pen in their vitality than one would dare to believe.

This whole work is guided by this exalted concept of the vitality of tones in the reality of the work of art. Every verbally abstracted experience or proposition is therefore illustrated, without exception throughout the work, by a living example from the great masters themselves.

I will refer several times (§ 84 and *passim*) to a work on counterpoint which is in preparation. There are three factors which might have induced me to present, first of all, a theory of voice-leading and only subsequently the more abstract theory of harmony. A logical and natural disposition of the whole material mediated in favor of such an order, supported, second, by the historical priority of counterpoint over harmony and, third, by my own concept of the relation between the two as it will result from these pages. Nevertheless, I thought it preferable to begin with the harmony. Any delay, however small, in initiating the needed reforms seemed to me to be counterindicated by the very factors just enumerated. For that same reason I shall also hasten the publication of a supplement, under the title, "On the Decadence of the Art of Composing Music: A Technical-critical Analysis," which should reinforce the ideas here expressed and facilitate their practical utilization. And only then shall I proceed with the publication of my *Psychology of Counterpoint*.

In closing, a few words ought to be said to clarify the meaning of § 9, which rejects the derivation of the minor triad from the series of undertones. From this theory Riemann quite legitimately drew the conclusion that, in reality, the root of the minor triad is to be assumed to lie above, whereas the bass voice represents the fifth. This very conclusion leads the whole theory *ad absurdum*. For if art, in its becoming and being, is to be explained by theory and not vice versa, theory has to accept the fact that composers at all times have followed the principle of basing harmonic progression on the roots in the bass voice and that they have proceeded to do so with equal verve in both major and minor modes and without any regard for the occurrence of minor triads. This argument, taken from a purely artistic angle, would stand, even if the acoustic phenomenon of the undertone series were proved more scientifically than is the case today. The problem, in essence, is the following: Considering that at least two components of the minor triad—the root and the fifth—are in no way contrary to the series of overtones; considering also that, from an artistic and psychological angle, the treatment of the minor triad is quite analogous to that of the major triad, would it seem advisable, in view of such determining factors, to remove the minor triad from so firm a concept as the overtone series, merely on account of its minor third, and to force it into the much more dubious concept of the undertone series? In this case all three components of the minor triad would have to stand on the shaky ground of a hypothesis, and, furthermore, the assumption of the root in the upper voice would violate the artist's instinct and practice of harmonic-step progression.

PART I

THEORETICAL APPLICATION

DIVISION I

Tonal Systems: Their Origin and Differentiation with Regard to Position and Purity

SECTION I

The Origin of Tonal Systems

SECTION II

The Differentiation of the Tonal System with Regard to Position and Purity

DIVISION II

Theory of Intervals and Harmonies

SECTION I

Theory of Intervals

TABLE OF CONTENTS

SECTION II

Theory of Scale-Steps

SECTION III

Theory of Triads

SECTION IV

Theory of Seventh-Chords

SECTION V

The So-called Dominant Ninth-Chord and Other
Higher Chords

TABLE OF CONTENTS

PART II
PRACTICAL APPLICATION

DIVISION I
Theory of the Motion and Succession of Scale-Steps

SECTION I
On the Psychology of Contents and oj Step Progression

SECTION II
On the Psychology of Chromatic Alteration

SECTION III
Some Corollaries of the Theory of Scale-Steps in Free Composition

TABLE OF CONTENTS

DIVISION II

Theory of the Progression of Keys

SECTION I

Theory of Modulation

SECTION II

The Theory of Modulating and Preludizing (§§ 181–82)

PART I

THEORETICAL
APPLICATION

SECTION I

The Origin of Tonal Systems

CHAPTER I

THE NATURAL TONAL SYSTEM (MAJOR)

§ I. *Music and Nature*

All art, with the exception of music, rests on associations of ideas, of great and universal ideas, reflected from Nature and reality. In all cases Nature provides the pattern; art is imitation—imitation by word or color or form. We immediately know which aspect of nature is indicated by word, which by color, and which by sculptured form. Only music is different. Intrinsically, there is no unambivalent association of ideas between music and nature. This lack probably provides the only satisfactory explanation for the fact that the music of primitive peoples never developed beyond a certain rudimentary stage. Against all traditional and historical notions, I would go so far as to claim that even Greek music never was real art. It can only be ascribed to its very primitive stage of development that Greek music has disappeared without leaving any traces or echoes, while all other branches of Greek art have been preserved as inspiration and paradigm for our own arts. It seems that without the aid of association of ideas no human activity can unfold either in comprehension or in creation.

§ 2. *The Motif as the Only Way of Associating Ideas in Music*

But whence should music take the possibility of associating ideas, since it is not given by nature? Indeed, it took a host of experiments and the toil of many centuries to create this possibility. Finally it was discovered. It was the motif.

The motif, and the motif alone, creates the possibility of associating ideas, the only one of which music is capable. The motif is a primordial and intrinsic association of ideas.[1] The motif thus substitutes for the ageless and powerful associations of ideas from patterns in nature, on which the other arts are thriving.

§ 3. *Music Becomes Art*

Music became art in the real sense of this word only with the discovery of the motif and its use. Fortified by the quiet possession of a principle which was subject no longer to change or loss, music could now subordinate those extrinsic associations, such as, e.g., of word or dance, from which it had benefited for brief moments in the past. Through the motif, music could finally be art, even without a pattern in nature, without, however, giving up those other inspirations which convey, so to speak, second hand or indirectly, other associations from nature.[2]

§ 4. *Repetition as the Underlying Principle of the Motif*

The motif is a recurring series of tones. Any series of tones may become a motif.[3] However, it can be recognized as such only where

[1. During a later stage of his development Schenker would hardly have defined the motif as an association of ideas *intrinsic* to music. It is undeniable that the motif introduced into music the principle of repetition in its pure form. This had already happened during the epoch of imitative music. But the only principle intrinsic to music is the chord as presented by Nature in the overtone series (cf. below § 8, and *Free Composition*, "The Background of Music"). According to Schenker, music was elevated to the rank of an art only by the unfolding of the chord in *Auskomponierung* and the theory of *Auskomponierung* constitutes the essential part of Schenker's theories (cf. Introduction).]

2. We shall discuss elsewhere the manifestations of those secondary, extrinsic associations in music, especially in program music.

[3. It should be added that this "series of tones" itself must not be irrational but, if it is to be comprehensible, must be derived from Nature by means of *Auskomponierung*. Cf. Schenker's own note to § 88: "The idea of the triad comprises a longer series of tones; its own unity bestows on them, despite their length, a unity easy to grasp." Cf. also § 115 and Example 116.]

NOTE.—All notes inclosed in brackets are the editor's; those without brackets are Schenker's original notes.

its repetition follows immediately. As long as there is no immediate repetition, the series in question must be considered as a dependent part of a greater entity, even if later on, somewhere in the course of the composition, the series should be elevated to the rank of a motif.

Only by repetition can a series of tones be characterized as something definite. Only repetition can demarcate a series of tones and its purpose. Repetition thus is the basis of music as an art. It creates musical form, just as the association of ideas from a pattern in nature creates the other forms of art.

Example 1 (2).[4] Mozart, Piano Sonata, A Minor, K. 310:

Allegro maestoso

Example 2 (1).[5] Beethoven, Piano Sonata, op. 22:

[4. It should be noted that the simple arpeggio of measure 1 appears, in its repetition in measure 3, in a state of "diminution" effected by neighboring and passing notes, i.e., in a state of *Auskomponierung*.]

[5. Schenker indicates here only the simple motivic repetition of measures 1 and 2. I should like to add, however, that during a later stage of his development he probably would have gone further in indicating also the less obvious repetitions whose perception arises from Schenker's theory of the "background" and which have "liberated music from the hampering effects of imitation" (*Free Composition*, p. 162; also, Examples 119 and 120 quoted there. More generally, the study of this chapter on "diminution" [§§ 251–66] of *Free Composition* is absolutely basic for the correct understanding of Schenker's theories). In the present example, the arpeggio *d–f–d* in measures 1–2 signifies a brief breath-taking, in preparation for the deep melodic breath pervading the following four measures. Incidentally, in this paragraph Schenker already alludes to "freer forms of repetition and imitation," thus anticipating his later theories. In his own working copy he noted a number of "difficult examples of repetition."] See Appendix I, Example A1.

NOTE.—The numbering of the examples differs from the ones in the German edition; for reference purposes the old numbers are added in parentheses.

Man repeats himself in man; tree in tree. In other words, any creature repeats itself in its own kind, and only in its own kind; and by this repetition the concept "man" or the concept "tree" is formed. Thus a series of tones becomes an individual in the world of music only by repeating itself in its own kind; and, as in nature in general, so music manifests a procreative urge, which initiates this process of repetition.

We should get accustomed to seeing tones as creatures. We should learn to assume in them biological urges[6] as they characterize living beings. We are faced, then, with the following equation:

In Nature: procreative urge → repetition → individual kind;

[6. The "biological urges" of tones express themselves in a kind of "egotism," as further explained in the chapter on "tonicalization" (§ 136), and in the impulse to procreate overtones. The principle of repetition, on the other hand, is of a purely psychological nature. It is inherent in the artist, not in the tones as such. It should be mentioned, furthermore, that rhythm plays a particular role in effecting repetition. Schenker here merely hints at its importance. Rhythm, however, is one of the main elements through which and in which the urge to repetition can express itself, from the humblest beginnings of music (already familiar to primitive peoples) to its supreme maturation and transformation as art (*Free Composition*, §§ 285 ff.).]

In music, analogously: procreative urge → repetition → individual motif.

The musical image created by repetition need not be, in all cases, a painstakingly exact reproduction of the original series of tones. Even freer forms of repetition and imitation, including manifold little contrasts, will not cancel the magical effects of association.

It should be added, furthermore, that not only the melody but the other elements of music as well (e.g., rhythm, harmony, etc.) may contribute to the associative effect of more or less exact repetition and thus to delimiting the individualities of various patterns.

Example 3. Beethoven, Piano Sonata, op. 90, First Movement:

The upbeat to the first bar (marked by the first bracket) consists of an eighth-note followed by an eighth-rest. Under the second bracket this upbeat is repeated without any change; under the third and fourth brackets, however, the upbeat shows certain contrasting changes: the eighth-note is transformed into a full quarter-note, emphasized, in its fourth recurrence, even by a *portamento*.

Example 4. Beethoven, Piano Sonata, op. 90, Last Movement:

This example demonstrates most strikingly how a rhythmic motif can arise without reference to melody or form. The genius of the composer here manifests itself in the clear and formal separation of subject from transition (bar 6 in our example). The subject, however, in concluding, engenders a purely rhythmical motif which, so to speak, radiates through that separation into the transition, where it experiences its obligatory repetitions.

Example 5. Haydn, String Quartet, G Minor, op. 74, No. 3:

In this example the association of ideas initiated in the first bar (first bracket) is carried out by the viola and the cello parts (second bracket). The two associations are separate and, in the viola part, are emphasized by a *portamento*.

Example 6. Beethoven, Piano Sonata, op. 53, First Movement:

Within the same motif and the same key (E minor), the association indicated by brackets contains a harmonic contrast, i.e., the contrast between the diatonic II, F-sharp, and the Phrygian II, F-natural.

§ 5. *Repetition as Creator of Form*

The principle of repetition, once successfully applied to the understanding of the microcosm of musical composition, now could be applied on a larger scale as well. For if the significance of a small series of tones results clearly only after it has been repeated, it should seem plausible that a series of such small series would also acquire individuality and meaning by way of simple repetition. This is the origin of the two-part form a:a; or, more exactly, a:a2.

Example 7.[7] Mozart, Piano Sonata, F Major, K. 332:

[7. With regard to Example 7, cf. Schenker, *Yearbook*, II, 11, and my Introduction.]

Example 8. Haydn, Piano Sonata, G Minor, No. 44:

The next problem was to discover the conditions under which a deviation from the strict rule of immediate repetition could be risked without jeopardizing the effects of association. If there are, for example, two members, a1 and a2, associatively linked, it is possible to insert an extraneous member b, which, so to speak, increases the tension and thereby emphasizes the effect of the repetition. Thus, apparently, there arises a three-part form. It should be stressed: "apparently." For a true three-part form should consist of three members, viz., a:b:c—a form whose application to music is simply unthinkable and is probably ruled out forever. The form a1:b:a2, on the other hand, which seems to be the only three-part form applicable to music, can be reduced ideally to the two-part form, a1:b2, on which it is originally founded. The inserted member b, however, whose function it is to delay the repetition, must be so characterized that it should not require, in its turn, a repetition for its clarification. For, in that case, we would obtain the form a1:b1:a2: b2, in other words, a four-part form with an underlying two-part basis.

This is the real meaning of the three-part or so-called *lied* form. If we now rise from the consideration of such structural details to that of larger formal units, we find that this same three-part structure a1:b:a2 constitutes the foundation also of the fugue, with its articulation into exposition, modulation, and final development; or of the sonata, with its exposition, development, and recapitulation.[8]

Even where an artist succeeds in associating his ideas or images in a still more complicated way, still the principle of repetition can be recognized as underlying even the most daring feats. Thus music has risen to the ranks of art. By its own means and without direct aid from nature,[9] it has reached a degree of sublimity on which it can compete with the other arts, supported by direct associations of ideas from Nature.

Example 9 (11). Brahms, Horn Trio, op. 40, Finale:

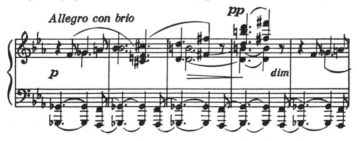

[8. Here, as in a number of other passages of his *Harmony*, Schenker builds his reasoning, first of all, on general psychological considerations, providing only subsequently its purely musical basis (cf. *Jahrbuch*, Vol. II, "The Organic Nature of the Fugue," and *Free Composition*, p. 228).]

[9. Later on, Schenker refers repeatedly to the overtone series, especially the fifth, as the "eternal hint of Nature." With respect to the "unambiguity" or "directness" of this hint, cf. Schenker's "Comments" (*Yearbook*, I, 204 and elsewhere): "Only the genius is endowed with the feeling for tone space. This feeling is his a priori, just as the concepts of space and time are a part of the mere bodily instinct of ordinary man."]

The faithful repetition, in bars 6–9, of bars 2–4 obviously should read as in Example 10.

Example 10 (12):

In bar 9, on the contrary, one element of this repetition, which should have been expected one bar earlier, has been used as a surprising inauguration of the closing part. Thus Brahms elegantly fulfilled the requirements of form, without violating in any way the principle of repetition.[10]

§ 6. *The Biological Nature of Form*

Also within the above-mentioned larger formal units, the biological momentum of music recurs in an amazing way. For what is the fundamental purpose of the turns and tricks of the cyclical form? To represent the destiny, the real personal fate, of a motif or of several motifs simultaneously. The sonata represents the motifs in ever changing situations in which their characters are revealed, just as human beings are represented in a drama.

For this is just what happens in a drama: men are led through situations in which their characters are tested in all their shades and grades,

[10. This type of connecting link, for which Brahms had a particular liking and which he employed time and again as a means of insuring continuity, is designated later on by Schenker as *Knüpftechnik* ("technique of linking"). Cf. also Example 4.]

so that one characteristic feature is revealed in each particular situation. And what is character as a whole, if not a synthesis of these qualities which have been revealed by such a sequence of situations? The life of a motif is represented in an analogous way. The motif is led through various situations. At one time, its melodic character is tested; at another time, a harmonic peculiarity must prove its valor in unaccustomed surroundings; a third time, again, the motif is subjected to some rhythmic change: in other words, the motif lives through its fate, like a personage in a drama.

Obviously, these destinies, in drama as well as in music, are, so to speak, quantitatively reduced and stylized according to the law of abbreviation. Thus it would be of no interest at all to see Wallenstein having lunch on the stage regularly during the whole process of dramatic development. For everyone knows anyhow that he must have lunched daily; and the poet could therefore omit the dramatic presentation of these quite unessential lunches in order to concentrate the drama on the essential moments of his hero's life. In an analogous way the composer applies the law of abbreviation to the destiny of the motif, the hero of his drama. From the infinity of situations into which his motif could conceivably fall, he must choose only a few. These, however, must be so chosen that the motif is forced to reveal in them its character in all its aspects and peculiarities.

Thus it is illicit, according to the law of abbreviation, to present the motif in a situation which cannot contribute anything new to the clarification of its character. No composer could hope to reveal through overloaded, complicated, and unessential matter what could be revealed by few, but well-chosen, fatal moments in the life of a motif.[11] It will be of no interest at all to hear how the motif, metaphorically speaking, makes its regular evening toilet, takes its regular lunch, etc.

11. Incidentally, it seems to me that the cyclical compositions of our days (as well as the so-called "symphonic poems") are largely failures precisely for this reason. On the one hand, they indulge in all too many unessential situations which do not reveal anything worth hearing; on the other hand, the choice among possible situations is made so awkwardly that the motif is never given a chance for a full manifestation of all its character traits. The composers of our generation, as well as of the next, will have to go to the school of the great old masters if they want to relearn the art of describing the fate of a motif succinctly and through a strict choice of really essential fatal moments.

§ 7. *The Cancellation of Parallelism as an Exception*

While repetition is an inherent and inviolable principle of music as art, yet there may arise situations of such a peculiar nature that the composer may feel constrained to deviate from the norm and to get along without repetition.

Obviously, it would be impossible to give an exact description of such exceptional circumstances and their causes. It is up to the artist to decide when and whether the existing milieu, i.e., the material already evolved or foreboded, will permit him to steer that exceptional course.

The liberation of music, in the midst of a situation bound by parallelism, from the coercive pressure of the principle of repetition which is inherent in art, exercises a peculiar charm. It is this charm of the unaccustomed, this fascination of a procedure, so to speak, contrary to art, which incites the artist to deviate from the norm. In such situations, music re-evokes, if only fleetingly, the memory of that primordial or natural phase of our art which preceded the discovery of the motif as intrinsic association of ideas, limiting itself to the use, however meager in its yield, of extrinsic association through motion or word (dance or song). It is easy to understand, accordingly, why music, on such occasions, assumes a rhetorical, declamatory character, with verbal associations lurking ghostlike behind the tones —words, denied by an inscrutable fate their realization and complete expression; words, however, speaking to us the more penetratingly and the more mysteriously. Such a situation is illustrated by the piece quoted in Example 11.

Example 11 (13).[12] Beethoven, Piano Sonata, op. 110, Last Movement:

[12. It goes without saying that the principle of repetition is still effective even here, albeit in a "veiled" form. Cf. n. 4 above. Cf. also Schenker's commented edition of Sonata, op. 110. See Appendix I, Example A2.]

In spite of its length, it remains almost entirely free of parallelisms. Significantly, Beethoven entitled this piece "Arioso" (Arioso dolente), thus indicating quite clearly the hidden existence of words. It should be remembered, however, that the whole piece (transposed to G minor) is repeated later in the composition, i.e., that the composer submits, though belatedly, to the principle of repetition.

Example 12 (15). Ph. Em. Bach, Sonata, D Minor:

This is one of the most daring passages in C. P. E. Bach's work. The composer moves far ahead, even changing key in order to introduce new ideas, while, on the other hand, he is satisfied with a most humble motivic association, repeating a few notes (content of the first bracket) on a few subsequent occasions (subsequent brackets) which might as well do without them (see Appendix, Example A3).

The principle of repetition is disowned (as far as possible) especially in the transition and cadencing parts of a composition. Haydn, whose work bristles with such ingeniously conceived liberties, remains inimitable in the application of this rhetorical art, a legacy from C. P. E. Bach. The asterisks in the following examples indicate those passages where the motivic content is, so to speak, unexpectedly pushed forward.

Example 13 (17). Haydn, Piano Sonata, E-Flat Major, No. 49:

Example 14 (18). Haydn, Piano Sonata, B-Flat Major, No. 41 (see Appendix, Example A4):

§ 8. *Problems Involved in the Formation of Tonal Systems*

Thus the motif constitutes the only and unique germ cell of music as an art. Its discovery had been difficult indeed.[13] No less difficult, however, proved to be the solution of a second problem, viz., the creation of a tonal system within which motivic association, once discovered, could expand and express itself. Basically, the two experiments are mutually dependent: any exploration of the function of the motif would, at the same time, advance the development of the tonal system, and, vice versa, any further development of the system would result in new openings for motivic association.

It is true that in founding the tonal system the artist was not left by Nature as helpless as in discovering the motif. However, also in this respect, it would be erroneous to imagine Nature's help to be as manifest and unambiguous as that afforded by her to the other arts. Nature's help to music consisted of nothing but a hint, a counsel forever mute, whose perception and interpretation were fraught with the gravest difficulties. No one could exaggerate, hence, the admiration and gratitude we owe to the intuitive power with which the artists have divined Nature. In broad terms, mankind should take more pride in its development of music than in that of any other arts. For the other arts, as imitations of Nature, have sprung more spontaneously—one might even say, more irresistibly—from the innate human propensity to imitate.

This hint, then, was dropped by Nature in the form of the so-called "overtone series." This much-discussed phenomenon, which constitutes Nature's only source for music to draw upon, is much more familiar to the instinct of the artist than to his consciousness. The artist's practical action thus has a much deeper foundation than his

[13. It should be kept in mind, however, that man's imitative instinct, after all, is no less "natural."]

20

theoretical understanding of it. The acoustician, on the other hand, knows how to describe this phenomenon exactly and without flaw. He gets on slippery ground, however, as soon as he tries to apply this knowledge to an understanding of art and the practice of the artist. For, in most cases, he lacks any artistic intuition, and his conclusions with regard to art necessarily remain disputable. It is fortunate, under these circumstances, that the artist, whose grasp is firmer by instinct than by reason, continues to be guided by the former rather than by the latter, considering also that, in so far as there is conscious reason involved in the process, it is not the artist's but the acoustician's which is neither enlightened nor corrected by any kind of artistic intuition.

It is our purpose here to interpret the instinct of the artist and to show what use he had made and is making unconsciously of Nature's proposition; and how much of it, on the other hand, he has left, and probably will ever leave, unused.

These pages are addressed, in the first place, to the artist, to make him consciously aware of the instincts which so mysteriously have dominated his practice and harmonized it with Nature. In the second place, they are addressed to all music lovers, to clarify for them the relation between Nature and art with regard to tonal systems. Incidentally, however, the acousticians may also be pleased to learn the considered opinion of an artist endowed with intuition on a matter anticipated instinctively by his fellow-artists centuries ago.[14]

§ 9. *The Overtone Series: Conclusions To Be Drawn from It with Regard to Tonal Systems*

Let us assume *C* as root tone and erect on it the well-known series of overtones.

Example 15 (19):

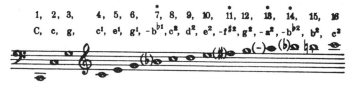

[14. Cf. nn. 1–5, above.]

It should be noted that the partial tones 7, 11, 13, and 14 are marked with a minus sign. These minus signs are to indicate that the pitch of these partial tones is, in reality, somewhat lower than the b-flat^1, f-sharp^2, a^2, and b-flat^2 of our tonal system. From this picture it is easy to deduce Nature's tendency to form ever smaller intervals by the successive divisions of a vibrating body. In their usual form of presentation, these intervals are the following:

$1:2$ = Octave
$2:3$ = Fifth
$3:4$ = Fourth
$4:5$ = Major third
$5:6$ = Minor third
$\left.\begin{array}{l}6:7 \\ 7:8\end{array}\right\} =$ Two progressively diminishing intervals leading from the minor third to the next following interval, the major second
$8:9$ = Large major second
$9:10$ = Small major second
$\left.\begin{array}{l}10:11 \\ 11:12 \\ 12:13 \\ 13:14 \\ 14:15\end{array}\right\} =$ Five intervals, all smaller than $9:10$, each one smaller than the preceding one, forming a transition to the next interval, the minor second
$15:16$ = Minor second, etc.

It should be noted that between the minor third ($5:6$) and the large major second ($8:9$) there are only two extraneous intervals which our art does not employ and which, therefore, bear no names. Between the major second and the minor second, on the other hand, we find five such nameless and unusable insertions.

From this common notation of the overtone series, which is based on certain premises, we can derive for our tonal system not only the major triad, $C:g:e^1$ ($1:3:5$), but also the minor triad, $e^2:g^2:b^2$ ($10:12:15$)—unless we prefer still another derivation from nature, which, however, is so complicated as to be monstrous. We can derive, furthermore, the fourth F of the C-scale and, finally, the seventh of our system as indicated by the seventh overtone.

§ 10. *Critique and Rejection of These Conclusions*

Even if we assumed that the way of notation and the criteria underlying it were both correct, the derivation of our seventh from the seventh overtone would not fit into the scheme as presented above, unless we let ourselves be guided by wishful thinking and a biased interpretation of the phenomena.

Such an interpretation, on the one hand, would violate Nature by the teleological assumption of a design with regard to our system in general and to the seventh in particular. It would rest, on the other hand, on a misconception of the seventh overtone, which under any circumstances must be smaller than the minor third 5:6, as is evident even from the foregoing scheme. Since the seventh of our tonal system and the seventh overtone do not coincide in reality, this interpretation must thus be satisfied with an "approximate" coincidence between the two.

It is more relevant, however, that the other derivations are also mistaken, with the one exception of the very first one, the derivation of the major triad. To forestall any misunderstanding, I should like to use an analogy: Let us look, for example, at a spreading-out genealogical tree, like the one representing the Bach family:

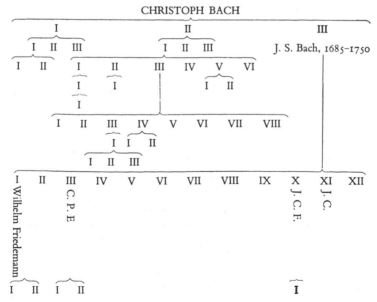

This chart indicates, no doubt, both a sequence and a simultaneity of generations; and the latter is even more striking to the eye than the former. It would be wrong, nevertheless, to yield to the visual impression and to ascribe to the simultaneity of generations a greater importance than is inherent in the real meaning of this chart. Basically, generation in Nature reflects itself in ascending or descending lines, not in side lines of brothers and sisters. The latter are rather a concept of our mind. They are descendants so far as they are creatures of Nature. They are, simultaneously, also brothers and sisters, in so far as they are creatures of our mind. It is obvious that Nature bears no responsibility for the world of our ideas; and the conceptual fraternal relationship is, in this sense, alien to Nature.

Nature's position is exactly the same with regard to the overtone series. Here also, procreation or generation proceeds according to a sequence of divisions, resulting to us in the numbers 1, 2, 3, 4, etc., i.e., the vibrating body vibrates in two halves, three thirds, four fourths, and so on. This division must not be confused with any simultaneity of intervals, just as we must not confuse, in the analogy of the genealogical tree, descendants and brothers. Also with regard to the overtone series, we must eliminate the appearance of simultaneity and see it for what it is: a postulate of our limited conception; and we should, instead, strictly concentrate our attention on the descendant series of overtones.

This view permits us, even at this stage of our investigation, to eliminate the so-called "fourth" (commonly noted as $3:4$), the minor third ($5:6$), the large major second ($8:9$), the small major second ($9:10$), and the minor second ($15:16$); for in no way can they be recognized as straight descendants of our basic tone.

Furthermore, we must reject any conclusions drawn from these false premises, as, for example, the supposed derivation of the minor triad from the minor third.

The seventh overtone, finally, represents a new overtone, resulting from a further division. It is born of Nature's procreative urge, without any forethought for the seventh of our tonal system.[15]

[15. The alleged identity of the seventh overtone with the seventh of our tonal system is disproved, furthermore, by another fact. According to practical experience, the seventh clearly characterizes the chord in which it occurs as dominant, i.e., it indicates a backward motion or "involution," which is contrary to Nature. Cf. Schenker's discussion of the "procreative urge" of tones in § 13; also p. 90, n. 4.]

§ 11. *No Overtone beyond the Fifth in the Series Has Any*
Application to Our Tonal System

In reality, the artistic relation between the overtone series and our
tonal system is as follows: The human ear can follow Nature as
manifested to us in the overtone series only up to the major third as
the ultimate limit; in other words, up to that overtone which results
from the fifth division. This means that those overtones resulting
from higher subdivisions are too complicated to be perceived by our
ear, except in those cases, where the number of divisions is a com-
posite which can be reduced to a number representing the lowest,
perceivable, order of division by two, three, or five. Thus six can be
recognized as two times three or three times two; nine as three times
three; ten as five times two, etc., whereas the overtones, 7, 11, 13, 14,
etc., remain totally extraneous to our ear.

It would exceed the scope of this chapter to describe the physio-
logical organization of the ear and to investigate why it is capable of
reacting only to the first five simple divisions while rejecting the
others. Analogously, it would hardly be possible to determine how
and why our retina reacts only to certain light vibrations in a certain
way; for just as any sound is composed of an infinite sum of overtones, so any light consists of an infinite series of component colors
which we are unable to perceive individually. Without trying to
penetrate these secrets of physiology, I should like here merely to
state that eye and ear orient themselves within these limitations set by
Nature. Our daily experiences make us sufficiently aware of the limitations of our visual perception. Let us consider a practical example
particularly close to our field of investigation: the system of musical
notation. The five-line structure of the staff reveals a wise accom-
modation to the demands of the eye. One need only imagine a system
of six or seven lines to realize immediately that the eye would find it
difficult to make a speedy and sure decision as to whether a note is
located, for example, on the fourth or on the fifth line. We need not
expatiate here on the historical derivation of the five-line staff from
the range of the human voice. However, it is gratifying to observe.

the concurrence of several quite heterogeneous elements in bringing about a certain result.[16]

To return to our problem of acoustics: it should be clear now what is meant by my observation that it may be a wonderful, strange, and inexplicably mysterious fact, but a fact, nevertheless, that the ear can penetrate only up to the fifth division.[17]

§ 12. *The Prevalence of the Perfect Fifth*

The first consequence to be drawn from our new approach is that the fifth, *g*, is more powerful than the third, e^1, as the former, resulting from the third division, precedes the latter, which results from the fifth division. It is not due to chance, therefore, but in accordance with Nature's prescription, if the artist always has felt, and still feels, the perfect fifth to be more potent than the third. The fifth enjoys among the overtones, the right of primogeniture, so to speak. It constitutes for the artist a unit by which to measure what he hears. The fifth is, to use another metaphor, the yardstick of the composer.

§ 13. *The Major Triad in Nature and in Our System*

Our major triad is founded on these two tones, the fifth and the third. It should be noted, however, that Nature's version of the major triad is more ample than the ohe usually applied in music. The natural version of the major triad is shown in Example 16.

Example 16 (20):

It is perhaps not without interest to note that the opening of the first movement of Beethoven's *Ninth Symphony* reveals this piece of Nature, albeit with a concealed third, C-sharp. Another illustration is offered, in the same symphony, at the beginning of the *Alla marcia* in the last movement. Here the third, to be performed by the clarinet,

---

16. The self-styled "reformers" of our system of musical notation probably never thought of that.

[17. The argument might have been more convincing if it had been restricted to a consideration of the generally valid and essential law of abbreviation rather than extending to the "mysterious" number five, a concept that is bound to remain more or less doubtful.]

is assigned the high place destined for it by Nature; the fifth is implicit.

In the concluding passage of Chopin's Prelude No. 23, on the other hand, almost at the end, a seventh-chord is built on the tonic by the addition of the seventh *e*-flat. Instead of hearing in this chord a true seventh-chord, I feel inclined to interpret it as a poetic-visionary attempt to offer the association of the seventh overtone—the only attempt, to the best of my knowledge.[18]

Example 17 (21). Chopin, Prelude, op. 28, No.23:

It is, however, one of the obvious consequences of human limitation that, in so far as practical art is concerned, we have no further use for this ample version of the major third. Having bumped against our first limitation and having receded from the foreclosed sphere of the seventh overtone, we now recede, for the same reason, from that

[18. It is not likely that, during a later stage of his development, Schenker would have insisted on this interpretation of the *e*-flat. The improvising, fantasying mood of the Prelude might rather be discovered in Chopin's escape, in the concluding bars, from a harmonic situation much like the one found in measure 12. Rather than run for a second time through the consequences of this situation, Chopin, through this diffuse alternative, comes to an abrupt end. Schenker's posthumous work, incidentally, contains an early, most succinct note to this

passage: "Conclusion:—Also considering the earlier I/V—last attempt" ("Schluss: auch wegen der früheren I/V—letzter Versuch").]

vast space of three octaves in which the birth of the major triad took place. The range of the human voice as determined by Nature is restricted, all too restricted (comprising, on the average, hardly more than twelve or thirteen tones). Constrained to make use of this space as the only practical one, the artist had no choice but to create an image in reduced proportions of the over-life-sized phenomenon of Nature. Instinctively guided by the vocal principle, which obviously marked the beginning of musical art in general and remains a determining factor for its development also in other respects, the artist withdrew into the space of one octave.

If we let three voices now form a triad thus (Example 18),

Example 18 (22):

we have nevertheless complied with the demands of Nature. For we have followed the most potent overtones 3 and 5 to obtain a consonance whose character is obviously determined by them.

Beyond a consideration of this reality of the three voices, I would recommend, however, that we conceive any so-called "major triad," much more significantly, as a conceptual abbreviation of Nature. Fundamentally, all art is abbreviation, and all stylistic principles can be derived from the principle of abbreviation, wherever perfection is to be reached in accordance with Nature. Thus the lyrical poet abbreviates his emotions; the dramatic author abbreviates the events of his plot; the painter and sculptor abbreviate the details of Nature; and the musician abbreviates the tone spaces and compresses the acoustic phenomena. Despite this abbreviation, Nature in her beneficence has bestowed on us the possibility of enjoying the euphony of the perfect fifth even if it does not occur exactly in the second octave, which is its natural abode; likewise we are able to enjoy the euphonic major third without waiting for its appearance, as scheduled by Nature, in the third octave.

Obviously, every tone is possessed of the same inherent urge to procreate infinite generations of overtones. Also this urge has its analogy in animal life; in fact, it appears to be in no way inferior to the procreative urge of a living being.

This fact again reveals to us the biological aspect of music, as we have emphasized it already in our consideration of the procreative urge of the motif (§ 4). Thus every tone is the bearer of its generations and—what is most relevant for us in this connection—contains within itself its own major triad, $1:5:3$.

§ 14. *The Prevalence of the Fifth-Relationship among Tones as a Consequence of the Prevalence of the Perfect Fifth*

The consequences for the relations of the tones among one another are of the greatest importance. To the question: Which two tones are most naturally related? Nature has already given her answer. If G has revealed itself as the most potent overtone emanating from the root tone C, the potency and privilege of this close relationship is preserved also in those cases where, in the life of a composition, C meets G as an independent root tone: the ascendent, so to speak, recognizes the descendant. We shall call this primary and most natural relationship between two tones the *fifth-relationship*.

If the fifth-relationship is the most natural relationship between two tones, it will also remain the most natural if applied to more than two tones. Thus the sequence of tones in Example 19 shows a relationship of fundamental and permanent validity.

Example 19 (23):

If we attribute to each of these tones its due share of potent overtones (5 and 3), the full content of this sequence appears in Example 20.

Example 20 (24):

To forestall any possibility of misunderstanding, I wish to re-emphasize, however, that each one of these tones is to be considered as a root tone with equal value; i.e., it is in no way implied here that the third note D be identical with the ninth overtone of C, or that the sixth note B should pretend to coincide with the fifteenth over-tone of C, etc.

§ 15. *Contradictions between the Basic Character of Each Tone and the Demands of Their Mutual Relationships*

The artist now was faced with an immensely difficult task. He had to reconcile in one system all those urges inherent in the individual tones—the very qualities by which they are characterized as root tones—as well as their mutual relationship.

In solving this problem, the artist availed himself, first of all, of the privilege of abbreviation; and he compressed Nature's infinite expanse into the narrow space of an octave. Nothing further needs to be said on this point, which was adequately covered in § 13.

Second, this very limitation constrained the artist to abbreviate further the raw material offered to him by Nature. If he did not want to lose sight of his point of departure, he had to restrict himself to the use of only five tones above the C. Here, again, human perception has wonderfully respected the limit imposed by the number five.[19]

By far the most difficult problem, however, was the taming of the contradictions which became rampant at the moment in which the artist adopted only as many as six tones for his use. On the one hand, he was faced with the egotism of the tones, each of which, as a root tone, insisted on its right to its own perfect fifth and major third; in other words, its right to procreate its own descendant generations. On the other hand, the common interest of the community that was to arise from the mutual relations of these tones demanded sacrifices, especially with regard to the descendant generations. Thus the basic C could not possibly coexist in the same system with the major third

[19. Again, more emphasis should be put on the principle of abbreviation than on the "number five." The lower fifth, F, obtained through the process of inversion, constitutes, so to speak, the anchor securing the system against unlimited drifting into the more remote upper fifths. The lower and the upper fifths establish the C as the center of the system, a phenomenon which constitutes the very basis of cadencing (cf. § 17).]

C-sharp, which was postulated by A in its quality as a root tone. The major third of E, G-sharp, came into conflict with the second root tone, G, etc.

§ 16. *Inversion as Counterpart to Development*

How could this situation be changed? How could the necessary abbreviation be operated?

Fortunately, the artist chanced on a new invention which helped him solve the problem. Nature had proposed only procreation and development, an infinite forward motion. The artist, on the other hand, by construing a fifth-relationship in inverse direction, falling from high to low, has created an artistic counterpart to Nature's proposition: an involution, which initially represented a purely artificial process, a phenomenon extraneous to Nature; for Nature does not know of any returns. It is nevertheless comprehensible that Nature, so to speak, has accepted *ex post facto* this falling fifth-relationship, which we shall call *inversion*. For, in the end, this falling fifth-relationship flows into the natural rising fifth-relationship; and if the latter were not given a priori by Nature, the artist would not have been able to create its mirrored reflection. Through and behind the counterpart of the falling inversion, our ear thus can perceive the original rising fifth-relationship. This inversion created a tension of high artistic value, a powerful incentive to the composer.

An analogue can be found in the sphere of language. The sentence "Father rode his horse through the woods" makes a different impression from the other possible versions of that same sentence: "His horse rode father through the woods," or "Through the woods father rode his horse." The two latter versions differ from the original one by a nuance of tension. The natural way of proceeding is first to introduce the subject of our statement, and then to explain what it is all about regarding that subject. But wherever this natural order is not strictly demanded by particular circumstances, aesthetic reasons may induce the writer to prefer a different order, engendering an effect of tension. He may begin his statement with an action ("rode his horse") or with an incidental adverbial clause ("through the woods") and, as we are accustomed to learn in good natural order, first of all, *who* is being talked about and only then what he is doing, the unaccustomed inversion of this order arouses in us a state of curiosity and tension. The belated introduction of the subject finally resolves the tension; but tension undoubtedly has been created first. What could we not have thought of during that brief moment of tension! "Who rode his horse?" friend? foe? stranger? acquaintance? etc.

The situation is somewhat different in those instances of daily conversation in which we are no longer conscious of this tension, since we have become accustomed to making use of such inversions without thinking much about it, for good reasons or for none.

In music the same tension takes the following form: If we hear, for example, the tone G, our first impulse is to expect the prompt appearance also of D and B, the descendants of G; for this is the way Nature has conditioned our ear. If the artist subverts this natural order, if he proceeds, e.g., with the lower fifth C, he belies our natural expectation. The actual appearance of C informs us, *ex post facto,* that the subject was not G but rather C. In this case, however, it would have been more natural to introduce the C first and to have it followed by G.

The tension created by this kind of inversion is of the greatest importance in free composition. Inversion takes two forms: (*a*) melodic inversion; extends horizontally; applies to the melody as such; and (*b*) harmonic inversion; extends vertically; applies to harmonic step progression.

In the following pages some examples are offered. For clarity's sake, the examples of inversion are preceded by others, showing a normal development.

a) MELODIC INVERSION

Examples 21 and 22 show normal melodic development from fundamental tone to fifth.

Example 21 (25). Haydn, Piano Sonata, A-Flat Major, No. 46:

Example 22 (26). Mozart, Piano Sonata, F Major, K. 332:

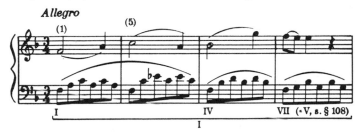

Examples 23 and 24 show melodic inversion from fifth to fundamental tone.

Example 23 (27). Mozart, Piano Sonata, B-Flat Major, K. 333:

Example 24 (28).[20] Brahms, Rhapsody, B Minor, op. 79, No. 1:

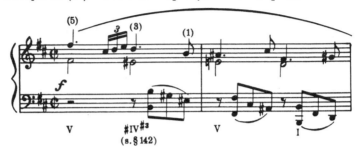

V   #IV#3   V   I
(s. § 142)

b) HARMONIC INVERSION

Examples 21, 22, and 23 show a harmonic development initiated by I. Inverted harmonic development takes off from any other degree and moves on from there to I.

Example 25 (29). Beethoven, Piano Sonata, E-Flat, op. 31, No. 3:

[20. Examples 21–24 would be covered by the concept of *Auskomponierung*, which Schenker developed later (cf. Introduction).]

Example 26 (30). Schumann, "Warum," op. 12, No. 3:

Example 27 (31). Ph. Em. Bach, Piano Sonata, F Major:

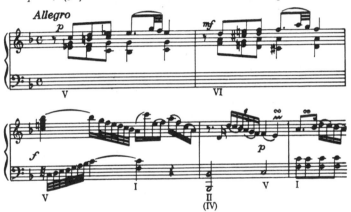

In all three examples harmonic progression develops from one of the fifths of the rising sense (II or V) rather than from the tonic. Example 27, developing from the dominant fifth, is further complicated by an unusually daring combination based on the dominant V. All three examples, however, have one element in common. They introduce the tonic without too much delay. In Example 28, on the contrary, the composer keeps us in suspense for as many as eight full bars; and only at that point does he introduce the real key of the composition and its tonic. This is done on purpose and certainly enhances the rhapsodic effect intended here by the composer. In what concerns the key of the first eight bars, it remains ambivalent whether in bar 1 we are faced with B-flat major (III–IV), or G minor

(V–VI), or even E-flat major (VII$^{♭5}$–I); bar 5, likewise, could be attributed to: D major (III–IV); B minor (V–VI), or G major (VII$^{#5}$–I). In so far as the remaining bars are concerned, the keys are indicated in the example itself.

Example 28 (32).[21] Brahms, Rhapsody, G Minor, op. 79, No. 2:

[21. Cf. Appendix, Example 5.]

G: VI V   (I) —— V

We shall have to come back to these matters later. Here we should like merely to indicate that it is in this craft of combining development and inversion, in this variability and wealth of contrasts, that the true master reveals himself and manifests his superiority vis-à-vis minor talents.

Returning now to the series of tones following *C* in a natural, rising fifth-relationship, we see that its artistic inversion reads as follows:

Example 29 (33):

Compressed into the space of one octave and restricted to the use of the mysterious 5, the up and down of the fifth, in the natural direction of development and in the opposite direction of inversion, presents itself as follows:

Example 30 (34):

FIFTHS ABOVE:
1 2 3 4 5   5 4 3 2 1

I V II VI III VII   VII III VI II V I

§ 17. The Discovery of the Subdominant Fifth as a Consequence of Inversion: Its Adoption into the System

This inversion of the fifths, leading in a fivefold descent down to the tonic, entailed a new consequence: The artist, face to face with the tonic, felt an urge to apply inversion once more, searching, so to speak, for the ancestor of this tonic with its stately retinue of tones. Thus he discovered the subdominant fifth F, which represents, metaphorically speaking, a piece of the past history of the tonic C.

As compositional practice confirmed the good artistic effect of inversion in general, the inversion from the tonic to the subdominant fifth in particular became well-established. There thus arose the need of assigning to this tone a place in the tonal system.

To illustrate further the effect of this particular inversion, we shall quote here some passages from J. S. Bach. He had a particular predilection for this method. It was almost a rule for him to anchor his tonic, right at the outset, by quoting, first of all, the subdominant and then the dominant fifth, and only then to proceed with his exposition.[22]

Example 31 (35). J. S. Bach, Well-tempered Clavier, I, Prelude, E-Flat Minor:

22. Such openings do not present action or development of any kind. Hence it is quite superfluous to burden them with an excess of sentimentality, usually indicated by over-abundant expression marks, as has been done by some of Bach's editors, e.g., by Czerny in his edition of the *Well-tempered Clavier*.

Example 32 (37). J. S. Bach, Organ Prelude, E Minor:

Example 33 (38).[23] J. S. Bach, Partita, D Major, No. 4, Sarabande: .

The system of the tone *C*, then, represents a community consisting of that root tone and five other root tones whose locations are determined by the rising fifth-relationship. One more root tone, the subdominant fifth, was added to this community and represents, so to speak, its link with the past. The whole system, accordingly, takes the following form:

Example 34 (39):

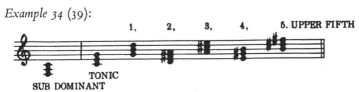

[23. With regard to Examples 31–33, it might have been simpler merely to state that Bach establishes his key with the help of the first cadence.]

What is usually called a "fourth" is thus, in reality, and considered as a root tone, a fifth in descending order. As we have seen, it can be derived from the artistic process of inversion. It would be as superfluous as it would be inartistic to reduce this tone to the proportion 3:4 (see § 8).

On the other hand, the mysterious postulate of the number five, which seems to be inherent in our subconsciousness, would violently protest against any conception of the above series as beginning with F. We would have to cope, in this case, with a series of six rising fifths, which seems to be beyond our comprehension.

§ 18. Final Resolution of the Contradictions and Foundation of the System

Having finally regulated the number of tones, their rising development, and their falling inversion, the artist could now face the task of defining quite precisely the sacrifices which each tone had to make if a community of tones was to be established usefully and continued stably.

In particular: If F and F-sharp were conflicting, the latter, as major third of the second fifth in rising order, had to yield to the former, whose superiority was warranted by its root-tone character and first by its position as fifth in falling order. C-sharp, the major third of the third fifth in rising order, likewise had to yield to the tonic C; G-sharp, as the major third of the fourth fifth in rising order, to the dominant fifth G; and, finally, D-sharp and F-sharp had to give way to D, the second fifth in rising order, and F, the first fifth in falling order, respectively. In other words, the content of the more remote fifth in rising order, beginning with the second, was tempered and adjusted to the content of the tonic and its dominant and subdominant fifths.

All that remains to be done is to project the resulting system into the space of an octave, following the order of successive pitches. This projection, however, does not reveal optically the principle of fifth-relationship.

Example 35 (40):

§ 19. *Some Comments on Certain Aspects of the System*

Thus appears the C-system, in its most common form. But just because this form has become an everyday occurrence, I should like to urge every music-lover to keep present in his mind those amazing natural forces and artistic impulses which lie hidden behind it.

Particularly, the extraneous character of the subdominant fifth F should be perceived clearly in this system. This tone should be considered as the representative of another, more remote, system[24] rather than as an organic component of the C-system, which, according to Nature's intention, originated from a series of rising fifths alone. The most important consequence arising from this fact is the relation between F and B. Within this system, which otherwise consists all of perfect fifths, the collision between B, the fifth fifth in rising order, with F, the fifth below the tonic, creates, owing to the extraneous character of the latter, a diminished fifth—the only one occurring in the system; and, consequently, its inversion constitutes the only occurring augmented fourth, the so-called "tritone." The phenomenon of the tritone can thus be explained quite naturally and without any tour de force. Any other explanation would constrain us to resort to rather complex and abstruse psychological arguments. Cherubini, for example, in his *Theory of Counterpoint and Fugue* (Example 27), ventured the following explanation:

> We have now to demonstrate how and why the tritone expresses a wrong harmonic relationship. What is said here applies to multiple as well as to two-voice counterpoint; and I shall expatiate here somewhat on this explanation lest I should have to return to it later.
>
> To demonstrate the cause of the false relationship, I shall choose the harmonic triad on G, followed immediately by the triad on F.

[24. The lower fifth cannot be considered as a representative of another, more remote system. On the contrary, it constitutes the step which art had to take to reach the possibility of "Art," i.e., of a system (cf. n. 19). Schenker clarifies this point in this very § 19. Furthermore, he writes in *Counterpoint*, II, xiii: "No key at all could have been established, unless the way of pure nature was abandoned, and the natural sequence of perfect fifths was adulterated with the admixture of the artificial, false, diminished fifth interval between the VII and the IV step."]

Example 36 (41):

TRITONE

The wrongness of this relationship is immediately obvious:

1. If the first triad is considered as part of the C-major system, it would naturally strive for a resolution in a C-major or A-minor triad, not in the subdominant F.

2. If this same triad is considered as part of the G-major system, the triad of F would be quite extraneous to it; for the concept of G-major excludes the idea of F, and includes that of F-sharp.

3. Analogously, if the second triad is considered as part of the C-major or F-major system, it would postulate, in the one case, the triad on G as a sequent; and, in the other case, a B-flat instead of a B. Thus F and B are in open conflict, and the resulting relationship cannot be but wrong.

It also follows that any harmonic progression including in one step an F and in the next a B, or vice versa, gives rise to the false relationship of the tritone.

There is another consequence. Whenever the process of inversion is continued below the subdominant, the diminished fifth is inevitable, as schematically indicated here:

I–IV–VII–III–VI–II–V–I

dim.
fifth

On such occasions the diminished fifth has the important function of channeling the process of inversion away from the sphere of falling fifths back into the realm of rising fifths; and it is only the fact that the subdominant is followed by the diminished fifth *B*, and not by the perfect fifth *B*-flat, which could lure us to continue the process of inversion into yet lower regions of falling fifths, extraneous to our C-system—it is only this fact that makes us fully aware that we are moving within the C-system at all. In the sequence IV–VII, the very process of inversion reveals most clearly the extraneous character of the subdominant fifth. To use an analogy from the field of ethics, the wrongness of the relation resulting from this sequence, i.e., the diminished nature of the fifth, could be considered an atonement of music for the prevarication of inversion, a technique imposed upon it artificially and without regard to Nature.

It would be no less wrong to consider the "sixth" *A* as nothing but a true sixth, since, as a root tone, it is the third fifth in rising order. It would be neither artistic nor otherwise fertile to engage in a frantic search for its origin in the higher regions of overtones, whence to descend to the opinion that, since there is no such origin, the thirteenth overtone could be accepted, at least, as the godfather of our sixth.

These considerations apply, by and large, also to the so-called "second" and "seventh," in so far as they must be considered root tones and should be heard as the second or the fifth fifth in rising order.[25]

A correct and conscious perception of the development of these fifth-relationships, away from the root tone in both directions, rising centrifugally and falling centripetally, is of paramount importance for the artist. In perceiving the tone *B*, we have to feel its way from *C*, passing through *E*, *A*, *D*, and *G*. In hearing the tone *E*, we have to feel the way traversed through *A*, *D*, and *G;* similarly, the routes of *A* and *D*, which led through two or one tone down to *C:*

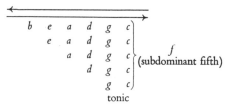

It is through this gate of the fifth-relationship that Nature re-enters inadvertently and faces the artist, claiming her rights; and all at once

[25. Schenker's emphasis on the twofold function of the steps within the system is of the greatest importance. They function as "root tones," i.e., harmonically, the distance from the point of departure being measured by rising fifths; and they function as elements of the "melody," or as passing notes within the scale, i.e., contrapuntally. This unity and mutual adjustability of the horizontal and the vertical account for the perfection of our tonal system and its superiority over the church modes (cf. §§ 26 ff.). The concept of this unity constitutes the basis of Schenker's later idea of the *Ursatz*. Cf. his note to § 48 and, later, his *Free Composition*, § 18.]

we see all those thirds and fifths, which the artist has sacrificed, come back to life, as if to protest against the unnatural coercion of the system. Here they are again, the F-sharp, C-sharp, G-sharp, and D-sharp, and here the artist reconciles, on a higher level, his system with Nature, who appears to be lying in ambush constantly in order to lavish her bounties on him, even against and beyond his intention. With this apparent rupture of the system and return to Nature, we shall deal more explicitly in the chapter on chromatic alterations, which are rooted in just that tendency (see §§ 133 ff.).

Conventional theory, too, is aware of, and able to describe, the C-system as we have just explained it. It would be erroneous, however, to conclude from this fact that conventional theory has grasped the real essence of the matter. The system was, rather, taken over mechanically from an earlier time in which it had been taught as one among others—unfortunately, without much psychological insight. Both past and present are equally far from grasping the coherence between art and nature as manifested in the C-system. Our modern era, however, is more progressive in one respect: it has begun to search for explanations in the phenomena of nature. But we have seen how the joy of this first discovery has seduced modern theorists obstinately to insist in deriving everything (e.g., the fourth, the sixth, the seventh, the minor triad, etc.) from Nature. No one would have even as much as suspected that a considerable part of the system belongs to the artist as his original and inalienable property: e.g., inversion and its consequences, as the first descending or subdominant fifth, and the outcome of the system; and that the system is to be considered, accordingly, as a compromise between Nature and art, a combination of natural and artistic elements, though the former, as the beginning of the whole process, remain overwhelming in their influence. It is our task here to present whatever merits the artist can justly claim.

CHAPTER II

THE ARTIFICIAL TONAL SYSTEM (MINOR)

§ 20. *The Identity of Our Minor Mode with the Old Aeolian System*

Medieval theory proposed to the artist the following systems:

Example 37 (42):

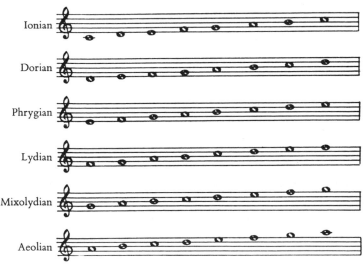

This theory rests on a misinterpretation of yet older theories, especially the Greek; and if modern theory has abandoned four of those six systems while preserving only two, it has done so unconsciously and without being aware of its own reasons. It is the sad lot of theory in general that so often it is occupied with itself rather than with following art in a spirit of sympathy. Thus the artist was left alone, guided only by his own instinct and experience, in accomplishing the reduction of those many systems to only two. Without being consciously aware of it, he continued the old Aeolian system in our so-called "minor mode," while perpetuating the old Ionian system in our major mode.[1]

It may be of some interest that Johann Sebastian Bach in his manual on thorough bass (reprinted in Philipp Spitta's biography of Bach as Appendix XII to Vol. II) expressly states the identity of the minor mode with the Aeolian system and conceives it, accordingly, as possessing a minor third, sixth, and seventh, i.e., forming minor triads on the tonic, the dominant, and the subdominant.

We are faced, then, with a surprising situation: While the theoreticians have not the slightest idea why the artists have preserved in their minor mode the Aeolian, of all systems, rather than, say, the Dorian or the Phrygian, the artists, on the other hand, have been moving freely within the Aeolian (minor) system for centuries, albeit instinctively and without racking their brains as to the reason.

Thus it is my task to analyze here the practical reasons which induced the artist to co-ordinate with the Ionian (major) system, of all the other older systems, just the Aeolian.

§ 21. *The Artificial Character of the Order of Rising Fifths in Minor*

It should be kept in mind, first of all, that those principles—the fifth-relationship between the system's root tones, the laws of evolution and involution and all their consequences—which we have examined in some detail with regard to the major mode, apply with equal validity to the minor system. In so far as those principles are concerned, the major and the minor modes behave in absolutely identical ways. The sequence of rising fifths, for example, is the same in A minor and A major. This sequence, in the minor mode, is in no way disturbed by the fact that the second fifth in rising order already finds itself in the "wrong" relationship to the third fifth $(B:F)$, al-

[1. An additional proof for the origin of the minor mode from the Aeolian system is provided by the fact that in those compositions which, by-passing the third, lead directly to the dominant, we generally find a *Auskomponierung* of the minor triad on the dominant, which is transformed into major only later on, for the purpose of regaining the leading tone and returning to the tonic. Cf. Beethoven, Sonatas, op. 31, No. 2, and op. 90. Cf. also Schenker, *Free Composition* § 89: "Diatonically, the divider chord on the dominant in minor introduces a minor triad, whose minor third is transformed into major only for the purpose of cadencing." Cf. also §§ 23, 45, 131, 139.]

ready discussed, in contrast to the major mode, where the diminished fifth occurs only between the VII and IV steps.

The following chart (cf. § 19), with only the names of the notes modified, thus applies to the minor as well as to the major mode:

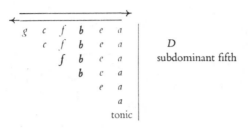

g	*c*	*f*	*b*	*e*	*a*	
	c	*f*	*b*	*e*	*a*	*D*
		f	*b*	*e*	*a*	subdominant fifth
			b	*e*	*a*	
				e	*a*	
					a	
				tonic		

Example 38 demonstrates an exhaustive application of inversion in a minor mode. The transition from measure 2 to measure 3 shows the inversion I–IV, followed, in measure 3, by the inversion IV–VII, leading—according to § 19—to the fifth fifth in rising order. The following measures bring a descent, fifth by fifth: VII–III–VI–II–V, down to the tonic (I).

Example 38 (43):[2] Brahms, Intermezzo, *B*-Flat Minor, op. 117, No. 2:

Andante non troppo e con molto espressione

[2. Cf. Appendix I, Example 6.]

This analysis has three corollaries. First, it proves the inner necessity and inevitability of the principles summarized in the opening paragraph of this section; second, it proves that the principle of step progression in the minor mode is not at all original but has been transferred artificially, nay, forcibly, from the major mode, out of this necessity. And it proves, third, that for this very reason the natural major mode is no doubt superior to the minor mode.

§ 22. *Contrasts between Major and Minor Modes*

If we now compare the relations of the tones in the minor with those of the major mode, even a superficial glance will discover a discrepancy with regard to the third, sixth, and seventh intervals, which are major in the major (Ionian) and minor in the minor (Aeolian) mode.

Example 39 (44):

This difference gives rise to a further one, in that, contrary to the major mode, the minor mode shows minor triads on the dominant and subdominant as well as on the tonic.

Example 40 (45):

It is these differences which oppose the major and minor modes as veritable antitheses.

§ 23. *The Melodic and Motivic Reasons for This Artificial Contrast*

Any attempt to derive even as much as the first foundation of this system, i.e., the minor triad itself, from Nature, i.e., from the overtone series, would be more than futile. But even if we were to assume that the minor triad really rests on the proportions 10:12:15 of the overtone series, which, it must be granted, produces these partials in this sequence, yet the system as a whole could not be explained without the help of artificial elements—disregarding, for argument's sake, the fact that those overtones, owing to their remoteness, have little effect on our ear, even though the number of divisions by which they are created is, in each case, the multiple of a prime number (1, 3, 5). We still would have to explain why the artists chose a system which, not only on the tonic, but also on the dominant and subdominant, offers minor triads with minor thirds.

49

The explanation becomes much easier if artistic intention rather than Nature herself is credited with the origin of the minor mode. Only melodic, i.e., motivic, reasons could have induced the artist to create, artificially, the minor triad as the foundation of the system; and in my opinion it was merely the contrast to the major triad that incited him to fashion his melos accordingly.

The following example may elucidate how these same motivic considerations, which, first of all, led to the creation of the minor triad itself and subsequently encouraged the formation of minor triads also on the dominant and the subdominant, thus completing the minor mode in its present shape.

Example 41 (46). J. S. Bach, *Well-tempered Clavier*, I, Fugue, D Minor:

The subject, thus put down, is possessed of an inherent urge toward the dominant to complete its nearest and strongest stage of development. It is true that such a development would leave the composer free to conceive quite naturally a major triad on the dominant, *A*, and to answer the subject, accordingly, in the D major key.

Example 42 (47):

Bach's instinct, however, urging him to preserve, at least for the time being, the minor character of his subject, rejects all other considerations. During the epoch of polyphonic composition it seemed natural to the artist to contrast his subject, at least during the first part of the fugue, merely by transposing it by a fifth, i.e., to answer it in the key of the dominant while maintaining its identity in all other respects. To complicate this contrast further by subjecting his theme to essential changes with regard to intervals and harmonies would have seemed to him much less natural. At any rate, he sensed that both processes had different effects; he recognized clearly which of the two was more natural, and he preferred to conform to Nature by keeping the exposition of his fugue clear of elements which would find their place more appropriately in a later phase. Thus the exposition remained exposition, the development was what it should have been: each part was in its right place and carried its right meaning. Thus the fugue attained its functional structure and its own style.

Exigencies of motivic development and exposition have brought a remedy not only in the case of the fugue but also in other forms, including those of free composition. Such a remedy was found in conceiving the dominant of the Aeolian system as a minor triad, just like its tonic.[3]

For motivic purposes it was enticing for the artist to have at his disposal three analogous minor triads on the tonic, the dominant, and the subdominant. As already indicated, the collective artistic instinct could not, and cannot, be deterred from this concept in practice. How it could have come to pass, on the other hand, that the theoreticians are still so helpless vis-à-vis the minor mode—recognizing it at one time in this guise:

Example 43 (48):

at another, in that:

Example 44 (49):

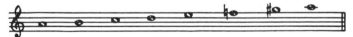

and, at still another, in a mixture of both:

Example 45 (50):

—we shall have occasion to examine later on. We shall also have to come back to the secondary question: Why are the theoreticians so

[3. Cf. n. 1.]

confused when they try to derive from Nature this system which they themselves so arbitrarily created?[4]

§ 24. *The Artificial System as the Claim of the Artist*

In this sense, the minor mode springs from the originality of the artist, whereas the sources, at least, of the major mode flow, so to speak, spontaneously from Nature.

§ 25. *The Occurrence of the Minor Mode among Primitive Peoples Does Not Disprove Its Artificial Character*

One may ask whether the above characterization of the minor mode is not belied by the well-known fact that many primitive peoples seem to take to the minor much more easily than to the major mode.[5] If the minor mode occurs among primitive peoples and seems even better developed among them than the major and preferred to the latter, this fact alone—so one might argue—should suffice to prove that the minor mode, too—that is, its perfect fifth and minor third—must be somehow rooted in Nature, and perhaps even more solidly so than the $1:3:5$ of the major mode.

It is often assumed that savage primitive peoples are closer to Nature and have firsthand, and therefore more reliable, information regarding her intentions than do the more cultivated peoples. This

[4. Cf. §§ 42 and 45.]

[5. It might be added here that the minor mode undoubtedly is to be credited to the artist and derived from his experience—a point sufficiently stressed by Schenker himself in § 23. This fact, however, does not preclude the other one, that the minor mode has constituted, and still constitutes, one of the many scales customarily used by primitive peoples. The various forms which the minor mode has assumed within our tonal system are easily explained by the lack of the leading tone, which, whenever needed, had to be borrowed from the homonymous major scale. Schenker's later explanation (§§ 42, 45), which involves the concept of "combination," is to some extent supererogatory.

The employment of the leading tone, however, caused the appearance of an augmented second, introducing a step progression which, from the melodic point of view, was undesirable. This interval had to be smoothed by also borrowing from the major mode the sharping of the VI step. In descending, the need for the leading tone usually was nonexistent, and the Aeolian scale could thus reassume its original form.

Regarding the use of the minor mode among primitive peoples, cf. the correspondence between Brahms and Billroth (*Billroth und Brahms in Briefwechsel* [Berlin and Vienna: Urban & Schwarzenberg, 1935], pp. 479–86), where Brahms, supporting his thesis with an extensive and carefully selected statistical material, tries to prove that the use of the major mode prevails unquestionably not only in classical music but also in folk songs.]

assumption, valid though it may be in most cases, remains nevertheless an arbitrary hypothesis.

Especially in the field of music such a hypothesis is gratuitous. The primary musical impulses of man should be considered in comparison with songbirds, e.g., canaries, much more than under the aspect of artistic intention. The songbird knows of no diatony, no fixed point of departure, no absolute pitch, no connection between determined tones. All he knows is a chaos of tones, a slurring and gargling and irrational trilling, which is deeply rooted in his animal emotions, especially in the erotic impulse. Primitive man, likewise, fashions but a chaos of indeterminate tones in accordance with his nature. Whether he is in love or arousing himself to a warlike mood, whether he dances or yields to his grief—no matter what emotion comes into play—the tones thus evoked are vague and approximate, whether taken individually or in their context. While it is easy to recognize the psychologic relationship between tones and emotions, it is much more difficult to find in them even as much as a trace of an order. And yet this very indefiniteness must be considered as a first groping step toward real art. It is one of the mystifying features of our art that its truth is not penetrated any more easily for having its roots in Nature! Today we know that the major mode has been, so to speak, designed and recommended by Nature; and yet we needed hecatombs of artists, a universe of generations and artistic experiments, to penetrate the secrets of Nature and attain her approval. For the way by which we could approach Nature was merely our auditive sense, which had to make its choice between the valid and the invalid all by itself and without any assistance from the other senses. Therefore, the difficulties in the path of artistic progress were very real ones, and, at any rate, they could be overcome only by an accumulation of experiences.

If art is considered as a final and correct understanding of Nature and if music is seen moving in the direction of art so defined, I would consider the minor mode as a steppingstone, perhaps the ultimate one or nearly so, leading up to the real and most solemn truth of Nature, i.e., the major mode. Hence the preference of primitive peoples for the minor mode; hence, also, the legitimacy of the prophecy that they will soon adopt the use of our major, if any possibility of further development is ordained to them by Destiny, whose attention verily is not restricted to music when she metes out life or destruction to whole tribes and cultures.

We shall have occasion later on to see even more clearly how deeply rooted in the artist, too, is the feeling for the major mode as *ultima ratio*—how every passage in minor yearns to be resolved into major, and how the latter mode absorbs into itself nearly all phenomena.[6]

6. Cf. the reproduction in the minor mode of the order of rising fifths as originally established in the major mode (§ 21).

CHAPTER III

THE OTHER SYSTEMS (CHURCH MODES)

§ 26. *The Church Modes—Defective from the Point of View of Motivic Exigencies*

We have, thus far, reached two major conclusions:

1. The motif has introduced into music the possibility of associating ideas, an element which is essential to any art and which, accordingly, could not be withheld from music in the long run unless music was to be bereft of any possibility of development and growth.

2. The artist's motivic endeavor led quite spontaneously to the establishment of the major and the minor modes, since both show, in their decisive points—the tonic, the dominant, and the subdominant—an even temperature, major or minor, and are therefore particularly suitable for the development of motivic problems.

We shall now examine, from the angle of even harmonic distribution, the other systems, already enumerated in § 20, viz., the Dorian, the Phrygian, the Lydian, and the Mixolydian systems. It should be noted that both the Lydian and the Mixolydian systems form major triads on the tonic, which approximates them to the Ionic, i.e., the major system. The Dorian and Phrygian scales, on the contrary, are characterized by minor triads on the tonic, which relegates them to the sphere of the Aeolian system or minor mode. If, however, we include in the scope of our scrutiny not only the tonic but the dominant and subdominant as well, we discover, alas! a rather disturbing irregularity with regard to the major or minor character of the scales under consideration (Table 1).

And, what is even more disturbing, in the Phrygian and Lydian scales we are faced with the emergence of diminished triads, on the dominant in the former, on the subdominant in the latter—situations totally alien to both the major and the minor systems.

It should result clearly enough from what has been said in § 23 that such irregular configurations of the I, V, and IV steps are most inappropriate for the development of motivic intentions or, at any

TABLE 1

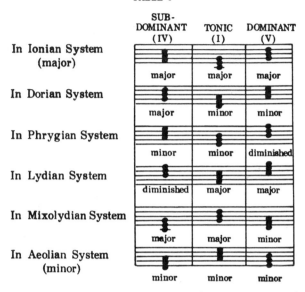

	SUB-DOMINANT (IV)	TONIC (I)	DOMINANT (V)
In Ionian System (major)	major	major	major
In Dorian System	major	minor	minor
In Phrygian System	minor	minor	diminished
In Lydian System	diminished	major	major
In Mixolydian System	major	major	minor
In Aeolian System (minor)	minor	minor	minor

rate, that they would engender situations far too unnatural for any style to cope with. For, whatever may be the problem under consideration, the style will demand, under any circumstances, an orientation toward what is most natural, most simple, and as concise as possible.

The nature of the fugue certainly would be violated—and the fugue, in my opinion, has been historically the touchstone of all these motivic-harmonic experiments—if the subject, introduced in major on the tonic, were to be transposed into minor in the immediately following answer on the dominant, as would happen in a Mixolydian composition; or if, as would be the case in Dorian, the subject, barely touched off in minor on the tonic, would already find itself transformed into major on the subdominant. I am disregarding here those other, even more difficult, cases in which the motif, conceived in major or minor but developed in the Phrygian or Lydian system, would fall all of a sudden into the Procrustean bed of the diminished triad, a position which would be altogether insufferable.

It may suffice to imagine Bach's theme, quoted in § 23, developed within the diminished triad of the Phrygian dominant:

Example 46 (51):

We immediately realize the resulting difference and visualize how difficult—nay, how unnatural—would be the transition from the mood conveyed by the minor mode to that aroused by a diminished triad.[1]

For a correct understanding of the artist's intention it should be noted that what is natural takes precedence over what is less natural, i.e., what is particular or individual or special. This principle applies to the art of music as it does to all other arts and to life in general.

Hence the artists, preferring what is natural to what is special, have come to prefer those systems which insured to them the possibility of natural development, viz., they have come to prefer the major and the minor modes. Thus the conclusion is justified that the other systems, covering only specific situations, could not, in the long run, persist independently.

§ 27. The Gravitation of the Other Systems toward the Major and Minor Modes

Not only did the four systems discussed earlier prove inferior to the minor and major modes, or even unusable from the point of view of motivic exigencies, but the close approximation to those two preferred systems turned out to be baneful to them also in some other respects.

If, in the Dorian mode, the *B* was merely replaced by a *B*-flat, immediately an Aeolian scale was constituted, albeit transposed to *D*. Was not that a dangerously close approximation?

---

1. Fux, in his famous *Gradus ad Parnassum,* taught, accordingly (p. 128), that in a fugue in the Phrygian mode, "the first cadence is to be concluded on the sixth, although in the previous example and in all other keys the first cadence is to lead to the dominant. For the development of the melody, at the moment in which the melody is joined by the third voice demanding the major third, would lead into regions too remote from the original key. This would entail a vicious harmony from *mi* toward *fa*, which, considering the immediately following *f,* would be offensive to our ear" (from the German of Lorenz Mizler [Leipzig, 1742]).

If chance or intention would introduce a ♭ before the *B* in the Lydian, was it not the Ionian system that resulted, if only transposed to *F*?

And if, to avoid the diminished fifth, the *F* of the Phrygian scale was sharped, it was but the Aeolian system that emerged. Likewise, the sharping of the *F* in Mixolydian introduced the Ionian system on *G*.

Probably the unnaturalness of those systems often vexed and tortured our ancestors; for it is an open secret that the singers were given license, which was sanctioned even by the theorists,[2] to introduce, on their own responsibility, those ominous *B*-flats and *F*-sharps, as the case may have required, in the respective works of Dorian, Phrygian, etc., composition.

In practice it seems that the major and minor modes thus have defeated the other systems everywhere, and the reader of old scores is well advised to investigate carefully whether here or there a sharp or a flat was intended implicitly, where it was not stated explicitly, by the composer, whereby the passage under consideration would be changed into Aeolian or Ionian. The editors of old scores have taken the quite justifiable habit of indicating or suggesting such alterations with a small ♭ or ♯ above the text.

§ 28. *Significance of the Church Modes as Experimental Steps of Practical Art*

Nevertheless, I am far from denying the rightful and real existence of those systems, despite their unnaturalness. Historically, they constituted inevitable stages of development. They have furnished the most convincing proof for the fact that systems and theories, constructed on paper arbitrarily or by dint of some misunderstanding

2. Cf. the discussion regarding the third species of simple counterpoint in Fux, *Gradus ad Parnassum*, p. 79:

"ALOYS: Why did you use, on several occasions, the ♭, a sign alien to the diatonic mode in which we are now working?

"JOSEPH: I noticed that otherwise there would emerge a vicious relationship between *mi* and *fa*. Also, I think I have not violated the diatonic mode; for those ♭'s are not conceived as essential but as incidental and due to dire necessity.

"ALOYS: You are right; and for this very reason also sharps have to be used occasionally; but the moment and the way they are to be employed calls for good judgment."

of history, are soon led *ad absurdum* by the practical experiments of the artists. On the other hand, those experiments prove that those theories, however false and arbitrary they may have been, were powerful enough to exert a disturbing influence on the artists. And who would be surprised at that? At all times there have been false doctrines, promulgated by theoreticians who were the captives of their own errors. And at all times, alas! they have found followers who would translate their false theories into practice.

In our day we can find a good number of bad compositions, especially bad symphonies, quartets, sonatas, etc., merely because the artists have yielded to superficial theories and doctrines on cyclical compositions—doctrines which are alive in the gray minds of the theoretician but not in art itself. So much talent is wasted, immolated on the altar of theory, even of the most perverse theory. Thus it was, thus it is today, and thus, probably, it is bound to be forever. It must be conceded, however—and this is somewhat of a solace—that only the more modest talents have to lean on theory to such an extent that, in the end, they have to pay for their submission to an extrinsic doctrine with their death as artists. They constitute the only medium for the propagation of false theories, and—assuming a teleology—perhaps they were created by Providence to exhaust the poison of false theories.

Hence there is no violence against the spirit of History in the assumption that the old church modes, though they had their undeniable right to existence, were nothing but experiments—experiments in word and fact, i.e., in theory as well as in practice—whence our art benefited especially in so far as they contributed decisively to the clarification, *e contrario,* of our understanding of the two main systems.

§ 29. *The Independence of Great Talent from the Deficiencies of Such Theories*

As already indicated, those experiments were often beset with unnatural, vexed, and tortuous features. It could hardly have been otherwise. The creative artist, however, as mentioned above, often escaped from that unnaturalness by switching over to the Ionian or Aeolian system by sharping or flatting the decisive tones. In so doing, he sneered at theory, often even with theory's explicit and self-satirizing permission.

But where the artist failed to make use of such remedies, two developments were possible: Either the composition turned out as unnatural and poor as the theory had been mistaken, or the composition inadvertently turned out well, in spite of the theory behind it. The first alternative needs no explanation: the compositions were preconceived badly and followed too closely a wrong theory. But how could a good composition result, one may ask, from a wrong theoretical preconception? The answer is not hard to find. A great talent or a man of genius, like a sleepwalker, often finds the right way, even when his instinct is thwarted by one thing or another or, as in our case, by the full and conscious intention to follow the wrong direction. The superior force of truth—of Nature, as it were— is at work mysteriously behind his consciousness, guiding his pen, without caring in the least whether the happy artist himself wanted to do the right thing or not. If he had his way in following his conscious intentions, the result, alas! would often be a miserable composition. But, fortunately, that mysterious power arranges everything for the best. It is in this sense that we have to distinguish clearly between the good and the bad works of that early phase of our art; the latter are to be debited entirely to a faulty theory; the former, on the contrary, turned out well solely because the talented artist could not get himself to utter an artistic untruth, even though his conscious efforts were guided in that direction.

To clarify this point, we merely need to recall certain examples of our own time, e.g., Beethoven's "Dankgesang" in the Quartet in A Minor, op. 132, in the Lydian mode. It is well known that Beethoven, during the last period of his creativeness, tried to penetrate the spirit of the old systems and that he hoped to derive much gain for his own art from a cross-fertilization with the old systems. Accordingly, he attacked his task in a spirit of orthodoxy, and, in order to banish F major once and for all from our perception, he carefully avoided any B-flat, which would have led the composition into the sphere of F major. He had no idea that behind his back there stood that higher force of Nature and led his pen, forcing his composition into F major while he himself was sure he was composing in the Lydian mode, merely because that was his conscious will and intention. Is that not marvelous? And yet it is so.

Let us have a closer look at this example, interesting to us also from other points of view.

Example 47 (54).[3] Beethoven, String Quartet, A Minor, op. 132:

[3. In the following, Schenker is demonstrating that Beethoven, while successfully achieving the effect (!) of the archaic Lydian system, reached that effect, nevertheless, by the means put at his disposal by the modern systems, viz., chromatization and tonicalization (cf. § 51, last paragraph, and § 136). Thus it is obvious that Beethoven did not prove in any way the possibility of writing in a "Lydian system," which, in reality, never existed. All he proved is the manifold and differentiated possibilities inherent in the modern systems. There is a decisive difference between using the "Lydian" mode in a purely horizontal, melodic sense and promoting it to the status of a harmonic system. The latter alternative, according to Schenker, was beyond the reach even of a genius like Beethoven.]

Basically, this section consists of four clearly differentiated, yet similar, parts, followed by a fifth part, which, however, merely serves the purpose of modulating to D major.

Each of the four parts, considered by itself, consists of two different elements, the first of quarter-notes, the second of half-notes. The number in which these elements recur is exactly the same in all four parts: Each time we find eight quarter-notes, representing, so to speak, two whole measures of four fourths, and then eight half-notes, representing four such complete measures.

The four parts differ, however, from one another in several respects. First of all, the quarter-notes each time do not compose the same motif. Even though the second, third, and fourth parts present the same motif, the motif of the first part is different—even if we disregard the varied arrangement of the different voices due to imitation. Second, each part has its own meaning with regard to form and harmonic development. Thus the first part is concluded by an interrupted cadence on the VI step of F major; the second part, modulating to C major, concludes, accordingly, on the tonic of that key; the third part, written altogether in C major (this constituting the dominant of F major), ends with a half-close, i.e., on the dominant of C major; until the fourth part, finally, leads back from C major to F major, apparently the basic key of the composition, to come to a conclusion there on the tonic. If we were to assume here a continuation of C major rather than a transition to F major, we would have to accept a conclusion on the IV step. It is quite impossible, however, to elicit, in this context, such an effect from the IV step, since the IV step naturally lacks the power to effectuate a perfect cadence (cf. § 119), while, in this particular case, the precision necessary to effect a half-close is also wanting. As far as the last, or fifth, part is concerned, it exceeds the scope of this analysis, considering its proper, although secondary, purpose, which is the modulation to D major.

The analysis proves, I think, that the composition may well be heard in F major, with a natural modulation to C major and a return from there to F major. In that case the listener need not undergo any more violence, or inflict it on the composition, than would be necessary, on the other hand, if he wanted to hear it as composed in the Lydian mode.

It could be objected that the two B's in measures 5 and 23 (first and fourth part) are incompatible with F major and can be explained only if we presuppose the Lydian system as basic key. This objection can be countered: The two B's, as they appear here, are in no way incompatible with our F major. They result from a trivial chromatic trick, which we use every day and on any slight occasion to emphasize the cadence and to underline the F major character of the composition. In falling from the II step (in rising order, second fifth from the tonic) via the V step (in rising order, first fifth from the tonic) to the tonic, the artists have always preferred to sharp the minor third, as, in general, they have liked to imitate the relationship V–I in falling from fifth to fifth, especially when dealing with the remoter fifths. We shall have to discuss this phenomenon at greater length later on (§§ 136 ff., on tonicalization). In the meantime, we should like to quote here the following example:

Example 48 (55). Beethoven, Piano Sonata, op. 7, Andante:

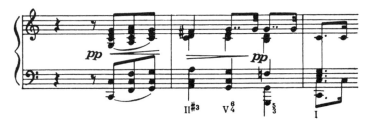

Applied to our case, this example clearly indicates that, in progressing from the II step to the V, we, too, may use a chromatic *B* on the II step of F major. This will have the result of disguising, if only temporarily, the V step as a tonic, and it is subsequently all the more effective to fall to the real tonic of F major via that alleged I in C major, which, in reality, was merely the V step in F major.

In this respect there is thus no difference at all between the above-quoted, allegedly Lydian, composition by Beethoven and the general treatment of the major or minor modes—in this particular case, of F major. The only difference is that we usually have the chromatic *B* followed by a diatonic *B*-flat—the root of the subdominant chord —which emphasizes the character of our key (cf. § 17). In other words, if we considered the piece as a regular F major composition, we would still use the chromatic *B*, there being no reason for scorning a chromatic step progression; but we would follow it up with a diatonic *B*-flat. Thus, for example:

Example 49 (56):

But for the sake of maintaining the fiction of the Lydian mode, Beethoven stubbornly abstained from using this *B*-flat in either of the two places where it would have been so gratifying to our ear. It should be noted that, accordingly, it is not the two *B*'s by themselves which give the composition its allegedly Lydian character—as we have seen, these *B*'s are of a trivial chromatic nature, and it is not necessary to trace them back to a Lydian origin—but it is rather the omission of *B*-flat in the following harmonies which distinguishes this piece from other classic compositions. Most listeners are particularly sensitive to this lack of *B*-flat, because the opportunities for introducing it are so very scarce; the second and third part, and even four measures of the fourth part, are already plainly in C major, thus offering no possibility at all of using any *B*-flat. But even if I grant, in accordance with most listeners, that their demand for a *B*-flat, as an element of the subdominant chord, is justified, it does not follow in any way that the composition must be considered as Lydian rather than as in F major, just because there happen to be *B*'s on the II step on two occasions. If it is erroneous to exclude F major on account of a chromatic *B* on the II step, the lack of the *B*-flat by itself cannot cancel the F major character of the composition either, considering that this lack is preconceived and forcibly maintained in a composition where so many other factors indicate F major as the basic key. Besides, is not the gap opened by the lacking *B*-flat—the subdominant—at least partially filled by this very II step, only with a chromatic *B* (cf. §§ 119 ff.)? Apart from the modulation and the interrupted cadence of the first part, one should also consider the key of the second subject: D major! Does not this key prove the conception of F major in the preceding section?

It is true that several other factors contribute to arousing in the listener the impression of an old church mode. Consider, for example, the chorale-like progression of the half-notes, the consistent preference given to triads, which, in most cases, even appear in their root positions (there are only very few harmonic inversions), and, especially, the strict avoidance of any chromatic progression, for which our ear has developed such an urgent demand. If the listener remembers that the old church modes, likewise, lacked the *B*-flat, he will immediately rally to the composer's desire in attributing to the composition a true Lydian mode. All this is easily understood, as it also can be understood that Beethoven himself believed in his

Lydian mode when he was merely avoiding the B-flat. And yet the author and his audience are in error if they negate their instinct, inclined under all circumstances to hearing F major, despite the lack of the B-flat, which, according to our undoubtedly well-founded practice, should have followed the B.

This example makes it quite clear that even a genius like Beethoven could not persist in the Lydian mode; that he could not impose it either on his own instinct or on ours. No matter how much effort he exerted in the attempt, the F major character of the composition is unmistakably transparent, even though we may feel disturbed by a somewhat vexed and unnatural strain. It is true that the author's intention to avoid the B-flat is particularly noticeable—an intention which, in art, unfailingly entails punishment; it is not true, however, that, in accordance with that intention, the Lydian mode is presented convincingly.

Here is one more quite recent example: Brahms, Chorale, op. 62, No. 7, which is the same as his "Song for Voice and Piano," op. 48, No. 6.

Example 50:[4]

[4. Here, too, the composer aims at reaching an archaic effect, and it must be conceded that this effect was attained. The B-flat in the second-to-last measure is no evidence to the contrary, as this tone merely serves as a means of avoiding the diminished triad—a turn frequently found in old editions of chorale compositions: Cf. Example 135, measures 7 and 8, as well as the G-natural in Example 136, measure 3; likewise, "a C-sharp certainly was used in the old Dorian system as an accidental."]

The artist here clearly aims at writing in the Dorian mode on D. This results from the mere fact that he omitted the key signature ♭ in a composition really written in D minor. Brahms, too, guided by his desire to compose in the Dorian mode (just like Beethoven, in the previous example, aiming at the Lydian) strictly avoids any B-flat— with one single exception in the second-to-last measure. Because he treats the four-part composition as a chorale and limits himself in the strictest possible way to the use of triads, which, without any exception, appear in their root position (it should be noted that there is not one single inversion in the whole composition!), the idea of an archaic mode is suggested irresistibly to the listener.

If one so desires, one may consider the afore-mentioned exception as a sufficient and complete surrender to D minor, i.e., as a testimony corroborating my conception of the matter. But since this B-flat could also be interpreted as belonging to the third half-note of this same measure, i.e., to F, as a means of tonicalizing this tone (cf. §§ 136 ff.), I rather renounce this all too cheap proof. And yet I insist: None of the *B*'s occurring in this beautiful chorale is to be derived, as Brahms believed, from the Dorian scale as such; we must substitute, rather, the following explanations.

The first bars constitute, basically, the A minor scale; hence the *B* is justified merely in consideration of that key. It is true that, with the *C*-sharp of measure 2, the composition changes to D minor. If in this D minor the IV step is presented with the third *B*-natural rather than with the diatonic third *B*-flat, the idea of D minor remains nevertheless alive in the listener. More than that, we recognize here the very *B*-natural which we employ in our daily practice in $D_{\text{minor}}^{\text{major}}$ (cf. §§ 38 ff.) and, to boot, in this same sequence, $IV^{\sharp 3}-V^{\sharp 3}$, without sacrificing in any way the identity of the D minor! That Brahms abstains from using the *B*-flat in the subsequent development (measures 10-13) is simply explained by the turn the composition is taking toward C major.

It should be noted, on the other hand—if we now pay some attention to the seventh of the Dorian system—that Brahms, without any qualms, uses the *C*-sharp as the third of his V (measures 2, 3, 4, etc.) whenever he aims at the conclusion V–I on D. Could anyone claim the *C*-sharp to be a legitimate part of the Dorian system, strictly speaking? The answer must be No. In defense of Brahms, one might recall that, even at the time of the strictest orthodoxy with regard to the church modes, such a *C*-sharp often was imposed on the Dorian system. This, however, merely proves, in my opinion, that the Dorian system never led an independent and wholly natural existence, any more than did the Phrygian, Lydian, and Mixolydian systems, and that our ancestors were already forced to remedy this unnaturalness by sharping and flatting certain individual diatonic tones. It proves, in other words, that events took the course they had to take.

Thus this example, too, demonstrates how music itself holds on to the minor mode even where the artist's intention aims at the Dorian system.

I have quoted these two rather recent examples merely to prove a much older truth: Even in olden times, when the faith in those theories held strong, many works, consciously or intentionally written in the church modes, spontaneously came out as major or minor (Ionian or Aeolian system). This happened whenever the genius of the artist was so strong that Music could use him as a medium, so to speak, without his knowledge and quite spontaneously, while other works, perhaps the vast majority, were born crippled from crippled theories, for the lack of that power which, standing behind the artist, might have saved him, despite his theoretico-practical error.[5]

§ 30. *Reasons for the Long Perseverance and Final Disintegration of the Church Modes*

One may ask why those unnatural systems were not thrown overboard much sooner. The answer is not hard to find.

First of all, they were backed up by the authority of the church, which had created them. This authority alone was sufficient, during that age, to hold its own.

Second, developments had not yet begun to emerge from the fog of experimentation, and the instinct of the artist was too beclouded as yet even to suspect the all-comprehensive significance of the Ionian and Aeolian modes.

To these factors should be added a third one—not to be under-

5. Incidentally, such a distinction seems to me practically inevitable, merely for the reason that in our time—this time of "historical monuments of music"—the signs are increasing in favor of the assumption that old works are good *eo ipso* and merely on account of their age and that they deserve to be saved and reproduced at great expense. Oh no! The committee in charge of such decisions ought to make up its mind whether it wants to represent the archivist point of view, according to which all works, no matter whether good or bad, ought to be reproduced (a point of view adopted by most museums with regard to old paintings), or whether they want to adopt the criterion of goodness or badness as decisive for the inclusion of a work into new volumes. The two points of view are different; the former is merely historico-archivist, the latter is critical besides. Accordingly, both lead to different practical conclusions. The former advocates the indiscriminate revival of all old works, the second calls for a process of sifting of the material. Each approach has its two sides: The historical approach has the advantage of strict neutrality; its disadvantage is that of misleading public opinion. Our audience, trained to trust its artists and scholars and wont to impute to rediscovered works an artistic value which alone would warrant their revival, transfers this assumption, in itself justified, to the assessment of any work. Unaware of the purely historical motivation of the revival, this audience is inclined to corrupt its own judgment, to force upon itself the conviction of the justice of its prejudice, rather than to admit a truth less pleasant. By this process, the formation of good taste suffers severely.

The critical approach, on the other hand, has the advantage of a systematic sifting of the whole material. Its disadvantage is that this sifting depends on the whim of some editors who are not in all cases as gifted and as learned as is required by the task.

rated—viz., the inertia of the artists who, for better or for worse, had wedded themselves to those theories, and composed accordingly.

Fourth and last, there may have been certain features, recurrent in the compositions of that time, which to our ancestors seemed to demand a derivation from the Dorian, Phrygian, Lydian, or Mixolydian system, whereas those same features could just as well be explained within the Ionian or Aeolian system, a possibility altogether unsuspected by our ancestors. But no one could expect this insight from that early age, considering that it is sorely lacking even today, after so many centuries and despite the fact that passages come up constantly which would be better explained by the church modes—than missed altogether, escaping both our ear and our mind! It takes a considerable dose of perversion, a respectable amount of obtuseness and corruption of taste, to ignore the screaming facts in the works of our masters, to preach, *ad nauseam,* harmony and counterpoint beyond good and evil, and to refuse to resolve the contradiction between theory and art! I much prefer those good craftsmen of yore, who, far from turning a deaf ear to the particular phenomena of their art, chose to believe in all sorts of systems, however superfluous, if only they would explain those phenomena!

In still plainer words: Is it not true that even Beethoven, even Brahms, assumed *optima fide* those B's in the examples quoted earlier to be Lydian or Dorian characteristics, no matter whether in this assumption they were right or wrong? It is likely that our ancestors may have ascribed similar turns in a similar way to the Dorian, Phrygian, Lydian, etc., systems; and this assumption perhaps provides the only proper and honest explanation for the fact that it took so long and was so hard to get rid of those systems.

But how can we explain today the following examples:

Example 51 (58). Wagner, *Die Walküre,* Act II, Scene 1:

Example 52 (59). Brahms, Chorus "Die Müllerin," op. 44, No. 5:

Die Müh-le,die dreht ih-re Flü-gel, der Sturm,der saust da-rin

Example 53 (60). Chopin, Mazurka, op. 51, No. 1:

How can we fit into a key which, beyond any doubt, is B minor an a-diatonic C-natural (fifth eighth-note, etc.) in place of the diatonic C-sharp (Example 51)?

And, likewise, what are we to make of a D-natural, instead of D-flat, in C minor, as shown in measure 3 of Example 52?

And can we really recognize, in Example 53, a perfect C-sharp minor, if Chopin uses, instead of the D-sharp, a D-natural?

Would it do to explain all these phenomena, which certainly are abnormal in a perfect diatonic frame, as merely passing notes or chords? Would anybody believe that such an assumption would relieve us from the duty of explaining their origins? Far from it. But, then, what is really going on in these examples?

Or, let us have a look at the following:

Example 54 (61). Schumann, Piano Sonata, F-Sharp Minor, op. 11, Finale:

How can we justify the unexpected intrusion (measures 2 and 3) of the dominant seventh-chord (V⁷) of E-flat major—interrupting a step progression moving in an otherwise perfectly normal A major? If the inversion from the II step (second fifth, in rising order) to the V step (first fifth, in rising order) is quite normal, as in measures 6–9, and if, furthermore, the chromatic D-sharp is employed in order to emphasize the tension normally created by this inversion (measures 4 and 5; cf. also §§ 139 ff.), what on earth shall we make of that insertion between the purely diatonic II step (in measure 2) and the II step with chromatically sharped third (measures 4 and 5)?

Do we have to assume here a true modulation to E-flat major; and on what elements would we have to found such an assumption? Or do we have to take the insertion merely for a passing chord? Or, finally, are we faced here with one of those strokes of genius which, shielding our ignorance, we like to explain away as "exceptions"?

The following example seems to raise a no less difficult problem:

Example 55 (62). Liszt, Piano Sonata, B Minor:

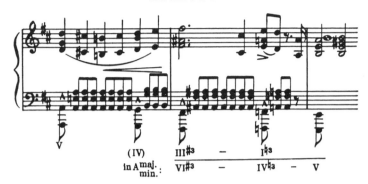

Shall we try here to muddle through with the notion of modulation (measures 5 and 6)? But what is to be done about the unquestionable fact that the basic key, D major, turns up again in measure 7? If it is thus impossible to get through on the assumption of a modulation, what explanation could be offered for a C major triad (measure 5) and an E-flat major triad (measure 6) in a composition in D major?

To quote one more example: How is the emergence of the V^7 chord of E-flat major to be explained in A minor?

Example 56 (63). Schubert, "Deutsche Tänze," op. 33, No. 10:

How are these examples to be explained?

Alas! we do not explain them at all. We do not even hear them. And if, occasionally, a sensitive listener turns up, whom such passages strike as odd and who asks for explanations, he will be fed a comfortable answer: All those instances represent unaccountable exceptions; licenses which men of genius take occasionally, etc. "Exceptions?!" "Exceptions from what?" I should like to ask. Is it true that the alleged "norm" of genius is established in manuals and lectures? Or is it not true, on the contrary, that our theory does not reach to the level of even the most primitive problem raised by a piece of art? If theory could reach but there, it would immediately understand that those examples, far from constituting exceptions, derive from the normal, most normal, process of thought of any composer. There is something humorous in the assertion of some scholars, as, for example, Spitta, that it was only Brahms, or some very few talents of more or less his caliber, who succeeded in maintaining a spiritual affinity with the old modes and were able to make practical use of them, by which they manifested their greatness. Far from it! It was not Brahms alone who thought and wrote this way, and it certainly was not this ability that accounts for his greatness. For we all write this way, and our ancestors would recognize with great pleasure their Dorian, Phrygian, Mixolydian, etc., systems in our compositions.

Faced with the examples quoted above, they would exclaim: "Is not this, basically, the very phenomenon we cultivated in the Phrygian mode?[6] The half-tone above the tonic as we find it here—whether as a passing note in the melody, as in Wagner (Example 51), Brahms (Example 52), Chopin (Example 53), or as harmonic step, as in the excerpts from Schumann, Liszt, or Schubert—is it not provided for by our Phrygian system? etc.?"

They could not understand at all how it could be claimed that we dropped their systems, since, in their opinion, we obviously are still using them in our practice.

Now what would be our answer to such questioning? Most of us would be so baffled by being told, all of a sudden, that we are still

[6. Cf. n. 11, regarding the interpretation of the Phrygian II in the minor mode (§ 50).]

writing in the Dorian, Phrygian, or Mixolydian mode that, in our surprise, we would not find a prompt answer.

I myself find it not difficult to answer, and I shall not hesitate to speak up. When we shall discuss, later on, the combination of the major and minor modes, to which discussion we shall dedicate a separate chapter, we shall discover two of the old systems as products of this combination. Note well: merely as products of this combination. In the meantime I wish to restrict my observations to the following: The artists' intuition in dropping all the old modes with the exception of our major and minor was perfectly justified. Nature's secret hints, reinforced by experiences, ever growing in scope and meaning, pleaded with the artist in favor of major and minor to the exclusion of the other modes. And even if he occasionally did things which he could not explain with the major or minor modes alone, his basic instinct for these two modes remained unswerving, nevertheless. Indeed, who would be tempted to erect new systems merely for the sake of some particular turn and despite the fact that his instinct is perfectly at peace? Is it not true that a system must be strong enough to explain, without exception, all phenomena within its range? And is not that system always to be considered the better one which covers more individual cases? The artist's instinct can be interpreted accordingly: "If the major and minor modes alone (understood correctly, of course) are adequate to evoke the charm of the so-called Dorian and Mixolydian modes, why should we burden ourselves with still more independent systems?" It was quite logical, hence, that matters went as they did, even though the reduction of those many systems took place, for the time being, in the instinct of the artist only, without being reflected in the theoretical literature.

The Differentiation of the Tonal System with Regard to Position and Purity

CHAPTER I

TRANSPOSITIONS

§ 31. *The Principle of Fifth-Relationships Applied to Transpositions*

Every system can be transposed, without any trouble, from its root tone to any other tone. All we have to do is imitate exactly the relationship between the tones as observed in the respective systems. Keeping in mind the principle of development or evolution in the direction of the rising fifths and the principle of inversion in the direction of descending fifths, we will notice at once that transposition will follow most naturally the directions of the rising or falling fifths.

§ 32. *Sharping and Flatting*

If the Ionian system is to be transposed to the first fifth in rising order, G, and if the imitation of the model is to be complete and faithful, it will be necessary to raise the seventh, F, to F-sharp.

Example 57 (64):

Likewise we are faced with the necessity of again sharping the seventh if we want to transpose the major system to the second fifth in rising order, i.e., D. This sharp hits the tone C, transforming it into C-sharp.

Example 58 (65):

In the inverse direction of descending fifths, the transposition of the system results in the flatting of whatever happens to be the fourth tone.

Example 59 (66):

§ 33. *The Analogy between the Order of Fifths and the Order of Sharps and Flats*

As these examples demonstrate, the F-sharp is introduced prior to the C-sharp, the B-flat prior to the E-flat, etc. This order inevitably follows from the faithful imitation of the intervals of the major system. Hence the axiom, the importance of which cannot be overemphasized: We may encounter an F-sharp without a C-sharp, a B-flat without an E-flat; but never the other way round: there is no C-sharp without an F-sharp, no E-flat without a B-flat. Thus the first fifth in rising order has introduced one sharp; the second fifth, two sharps; the first fifth in descending order, one flat; the second, two. The transposition to the third fifth in rising order will introduce a third sharp; the fourth, a fourth sharp; the fifth, a fifth one; etc. In other words, *there is an exact correspondence between the ordinal number of the rising or descending fifth and the ordinal number of the sharp or flat introduced by it.*

Example 60 (67):

Example 61 (68):

It will be seen, for example, that *A*-sharp is the fifth sharp to appear and points to the fifth fifth in rising order, i.e., B major. It follows, furthermore, that, whenever the tone *A*-sharp occurs, the four preceding sharps are at once to be taken for granted; likewise, that the ordinal number 5 can never belong to any sharp but *A*-sharp.

§ 34. *Double-Sharps and Double-Flats*

If we continue our climb from fifth to fifth, we will soon be faced with the necessity of raising the single-sharps, which have continued to accrue on whatever note happened to occupy the seventh place, to double-sharps. We see that, accordingly, this will give rise to a sequence of keys with double-sharps which will correspond to the sequence of the keys on the rising fifth 1–7, with single-sharps.

Example 62 (69):

To summarize, we obtain the following correspondences:

Example 63 (70):

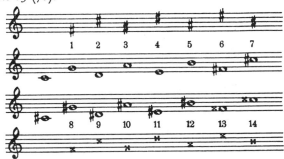

79

The same phenomenon is to be observed with regard to the flats accruing beyond the seventh fifth in descending order.

Example 64 (71):

It will be seen that, beginning with C-sharp major (C-sharp being the seventh fifth in rising order), the whole diatonic system of C major has been raised by half a tone. Likewise, G-sharp major results from raising the G major system by half a tone, and the same correspondence obtains between D-sharp major and D major, A-sharp major and A major, etc. The ordinal numbers 8–14 can be replaced, accordingly, if so desired, by the ordinal numbers 1–7, provided that key No. 8 is assumed to be half a tone higher than key No. 1. In fact, G-sharp major is the first key in the series of keys with double sharps, which series begins with C-sharp major, i.e., the C major system raised by half a tone.

This conception facilitates the process of taking one's bearings with regard to transpositions. For example, whenever a G-double-sharp occurs, all one has to do is to think of G-sharp with its ordinal number 3 in the series of single-sharps. By way of A major, as the key corresponding to the ordinal number 3, this thought will lead straight to A-sharp major, which, in the series of keys with double-sharps, likewise bears the number 3 (or 10).

The understanding of this straight correspondence between sharps and double-sharps, on the one hand, and the respective keys, on the other, is invaluable to the musician, not only when he is trying to find his way quickly through the most complicated passages, but also for a far more important consideration. Such understanding will contribute to a truly artistic insight into the functioning of even the most minute passing or auxiliary notes (cf. § 144).

The following excerpt from Chopin's Etude op. 25, No. 10, is quoted here as a paragon of overcomplicated notation (Example 65*a*). Since all that is involved is a half-close in B minor, it would have been simpler, and probably more correct, to write this passage as shown in Example 65, *b*.

Example 65 (72). Chopin, Etude, op. 25, No. 10:

If Chopin, at the beginning of this same etude, writes F-double-sharp, G-double-sharp, and A-double-sharp,

Example 66 (73). Chopin, Etude, op. 25, No. 10:

it is obvious, nevertheless, that we are not dealing here either with a true G-sharp major or A-sharp major or B-sharp major. It is equally true, however, that the F-double-sharp, followed by G-sharp, must be understood to belong to G-sharp major, strictly speaking. These two apparent contradictions are reconciled by the fact that the tone G-sharp itself, preceded by its own diatonic VII step, F-double-sharp, plays only a secondary role in this context, viz., that of a passing note between the tone F-sharp in measure 1 and the first note, B, in measure 5 of the etude.

In the field of music it is particularly important to pay attention to every phenomenon, even the least significant, and to hear every detail, even the smallest, in its cause and effect. In so doing, we will do justice not only to the artists but to music itself. It is a peculiarity of the musical art that it gives effect to several laws simultaneously and that, while one law may be stronger than the others and impose itself more powerfully on our consciousness, such a law does not silence the other laws, which govern the smaller and more restricted units of tones. He who learns to hear with the ear of a true artist, grasping the coincidences in time and space of various musical events and their manifold separate causes,[1] will save himself the trouble of having to hunt for new harmonies and to clamor for new theories, as so many do today whenever they are faced with a more complex phenomenon which defies any single explanation.

§ 35. *Transposition in the Church Modes*

It goes without saying that the method of transposition, as we have just studied it, applies equally to the old modes.

§ 36. *Equal Temperament*[2]

If we want to follow Nature, in her purity and infinity, and continue in our rise from fifth to fifth even beyond B-sharp major, which represents the key of the twelfth fifth in rising order, we must assume the existence of yet more keys, such as F-double-sharp major, C-double-sharp major, etc. The artist, however, has availed himself here, too, of the principle of abbreviation, making the twelfth fifth, B-sharp, coincide with C, which was the point of departure of our series of fifths. He thus identified artificially two tones which, in reality, are different in frequency of vibration.

Practical considerations, without which art could not have mastered the abundance of nature, led the artist spontaneously to the

---

[1. What is meant here is that the ear should learn to grasp not merely the strictly vertical connections but the horizontal of "voice-leading" as well. Cf., in this respect, §§ 53-55, especially the explanatory notes to Example 94, as well as the examples in § 79.]

[2. Cf. Sec. I, chap. I, n. 19].

adoption of this artifice. The tuning-down of the twelve fifths, and especially the downward adjustment of each individual fifth by one-twelfth of the so-called "Comma of Pythagoras" is called "equal temperament." More detailed information about this phenomenon can be found in any dictionary of music.

§ 37. *The Universal Applicability of the Method of Transposition Refutes Current Theories on the "Minor System"*

The method of transposition as described above has a most important implication, viz., the recognition that under no circumstances could there ever be a system with a G-sharp alone, or with an F-sharp and G-sharp but without the C-sharp. It should be noted that it is the existence of such a *system* which is excluded here. For this reason alone—apart from others—the systems which we today are wont to explain as "minor"—no matter whether they are conceived as a trinity or as a duality—are logical monstrosities and impossibilities; for a G-sharp, with the ordinal number 3, is simply inconceivable, unless it be preceded by an F-sharp and a C-sharp. And music knows of no exception to this law.

It may be objected that an assumption of this kind amounts to assassinating the desire for truth and truth itself—merely for the sake of applying the method of transposition in a theoretically consequent and pedantic way. Since I am able, however—as will be seen in the following chapter—fully to satisfy this desire for truth, even without admitting a single exception to the universal validity of the method of transposition, this objection will lose any point.

§ 38. *The Biologic Foundation of the Process of Combination*

I have repeatedly had occasion to show the truly biologic characteristics displayed by tones in various respects. Thus the phenomenon of the partials could be derived from a kind of procreative urge of the tones; and the tonal system, particularly the natural [major] one, could be seen as a sort of higher collective order, similar to a state, based on its own social contracts by which the individual tones are bound to abide. We are now entering another field of consideration which will further reveal the biologic nature of the tones.

How do the vitality and egotism of man express themselves? First of all, in his attempt to live fully in as many relationships as the struggle for life will permit and, second, in the desire to gain the upper hand in each one of these relationships—to the extent that his vital forces measure up to this desire.

What we call "vitality" or "egotism" is directly proportionate, then, to the number of relationships and to the intensity of the vital forces lavished on them. In other words, the more numerous the relationships cultivated by a human being and the more intense the self-expression within these relationships, the greater, obviously, is his vitality.

Now what meaning are we to ascribe to "relationships" in the life of a tone, and how could the intensity of its self-expression be measured? The relationships of the tone are established in its systems. If the egotism of a tone expresses itself in the desire to dominate its fellow-tones rather than be dominated by them (in this respect, the tone resembles a human being), it is the system which offers to the tone the means to dominate and thus to satisfy its egotistic urge. A tone dominates the others if it subjects them to its superior vital force, within the relationship fixed in the various systems (cf. §§ 18 and 20 above). In this sense, a system resembles, in anthropomorphic terms, a constitution, regulation, statute, or whatever other name we use to grasp conceptually the manifold relationships we enter. Thus the tone *A*, for example, may subject all other tones to its domination in so far as it has the power to force them to enter with it into those relationships which are established in our major and minor systems (to mention, for the time being, only these two). The vitality of the tone A will be measured by its ability to enter with the other tones not only that relationship which is determined by the major system but simultaneously those other relationships created by the minor system. In other words, the tone lives a more abundant life, it satisfies its vital urges more fully, if the relationships in which it can express itself are more numerous; i.e., if it can combine, first of all, the major and the minor systems and, second, if it can express its self-enjoyment in those two systems with the greatest possible intensity. Each tone feels the urge, accordingly, to conquer for itself such wealth, such fulness of life.

§ 39. The Various Relationships Offered to the Tone by the Old Systems

If we consider that our ancestors assumed the existence of four additional systems, it is obvious that each tone had at its disposal an astonishing wealth of possible relationships well worth its while. Imagine the immense number of always new relationships which, for example, the tone C was free to enter.

Example 67 (74):

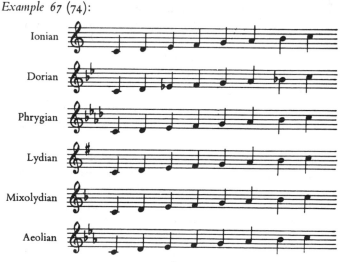

Ionian

Dorian

Phrygian

Lydian

Mixolydian

Aeolian

§ 40. *The Combination of Major and Minor as a Substitute for the Old Systems*

In dropping the Dorian, Phrygian, Lydian, and Mixolydian scales, we have *apparently* reduced the number of possible relationships into which each tone could enter, to the detriment of its vitality and egotism. This loss, however, is apparent only. The tone bravely stood its ground, and it seems it was the tone itself that urged the artist to leave the door ajar for relationships of a Mixolydian, Dorian, etc., character, even where the artist no longer believed in the validity of those systems.

We have had other occasions to admire the artist for his power of intuition; but in the present context this quality deserves all our praise: for the artist has intuited the most powerful vital urges of the tone and fulfilled them with his own artistic means. To these means I should like to apply the comprehensive term *combination*.

As already indicated, the artist was led to the discovery of these combinations by his instinct alone; for even today he is in no way aware of the fact that, through them, he created the possibility for the tone to enter those manifold relationships which were offered to it in olden times by the church modes. One might say that the artist harkened to the soul of the tone—the tone seeking a life as full and rich as possible—and in his submissiveness, however unconscious, to the tone, he yielded to its urges as much as he possibly could.

The combinations are actuated between the major and minor modes and, obviously, only within homonymous keys, i.e., between C major and C minor, A major and A minor, E-flat major and E-flat minor, etc. The combination may proceed from major to minor or from minor to major; in both cases, the same result is reached.

Properly speaking, I think that any composition moves in a major-minor system. A composition in C, for example, should be understood as in C major-minor (C $\frac{major}{minor}$);[1] for a pure C major,

---

1. This term, "major-minor mode" (or $\frac{major}{minor}$ mode) must not be confused with M. Hauptmann's "minor major" or H. Riemann's "major minor"; for these latter two indicate, in each case, only one determined mixed scale, whereas our use of the term includes the sum total of all possible mixtures or combinations.

without any C minor ingredient, or, vice versa, a pure C minor, without any C major component, hardly ever occurs in reality. The expansive urge of the tone demands the use of both systems as well as of all their possible combinations.

§ 41. *The Six Products of Combination*

As mentioned before, the major and minor modes differ only with respect to their thirds, sixths, and sevenths, these three intervals being major in the major mode, and minor in the minor mode (cf. § 22). Hence it is obvious that any combination of the two systems can affect only these intervals. If we take C major as our point of departure and introduce into this key the minor intervals, one at a time and in all possible combinations, we obtain six different scales or series, as shown in Example 68.

Example 68 (75):

§ 42. *The First Series: The So-called Melodic Minor Scale*[2]

The first series, as we shall see, has an E-flat, whereas the B-flat is lacking. But, as our experience with transpositions has taught us, no transposition can ever wrench the ordinal number 2 from the E-flat. It is illicit, accordingly, to ascribe the ordinal number 1 to the E-flat in our first series, as this would violate the law of transposition. What are the implications of this fact? The most important implication is that this series, in which we recognize the so-called "melodic minor scale" of our harmony manuals, can constitute neither a system nor the transposition of a system. It must be considered, on the contrary, as a product of a combination or, rather, as one of several equivalent products of possible combinations.

Thus the instinct of the artist, once again, was right, as against the paper systems of the theoretician, who does not understand the vital needs of the tones. The artist preserves a pure concept of the major and the minor modes, and, securely anchored in this concept, he becomes a truthful interpreter of all the forms of egotism displayed by the tones. The theoretician, on the other hand, takes the product of one single combination, which he took great pains to identify among all the other possibilities, and exalts it, with a childishly exaggerated fervor, to the status of a system. There is an enormous difference between the two concepts, that of the artist and that of the theoretician. We are not faced here merely with a question of differing nomenclatures. Artistic truth itself is in question. In other words, it is far from indifferent whether that series of tones, accessible to all of us, is designated as a system or as the product of a combination; for behind this difference in nomenclature there lurks a clash of conceptions. If we concede to one single combination the rank of a system, there is no reason at all why this rank should be denied to the other possible combinations. In that case, we might have even more than eight systems to cope with. And yet the history of the human mind should have taught us at least this, that whatever can be reached with the help of two systems should not be approached with eight or even more. If anyone should get the impression that this argument is merely dialectical, let him stick to practical art: under its aegis he would soon learn to follow the artist in the recognition that there is more

[2. Cf. Sec. I, chap. II, § 23.]

concrete value in drawing the elements for a combination from only two sources, which, however, are clear and perspicuous, than in vacillating, betrayed by instinct and intelligence alike, and in drifting, in this uncertainty, as far as to posit several answers to one single problem.

For it is merely a result of uncertainty if the minor mode, as shown in § 23, is presented, ad lib. and for your free choice, now in two and now in three different guises. *De facto,* none of these solutions is correct; and as far as the needs of the artist are concerned, theory shows a far deeper understanding when it identifies the minor mode with the old Aeolian system and presents the combinations for what they are, i.e., as mixed modes.

With regard to the first series, it should be added that it shows a minor triad on the tonic, whereas there are major triads on the dominant and the subdominant.

§ 43. *The Second Series*

The second series, likewise, results as a product of combination, for it contains an *A*-flat without *B*-flat and *E*-flat. This combination has been used frequently; for the configuration of major triads on the tonic and dominant with a minor triad on the subdominant offers the artist the possibility of rich coloring. It is significant, nevertheless, that there is not even a name for this series. The designation "minor-major" proposed by Hauptmann (cf. § 40) has not gained general recognition—at least, not for the time being.

For our purposes—i.e., for the purposes of art and the artist—it may suffice to mention this series merely as one of the products of possible combinations. We may leave it to the particular context of a composition to clarify whether we are dealing basically with a C major with the minor sixth borrowed from C minor or, vice versa, with C minor which has adopted the major third and seventh from C major. For, as I mentioned above, the combination may move from major to minor as well as in the opposite direction, from minor to major. It is only the composition itself, whose basic mode is easily established, which can convey to us the desired information.[3]

[3. In a later stage of his development Schenker probably would have noted the plagal effect, IV♭³–I, in C or the half-close effect in F (cf. § 122).]

§ 44. *The Third Series: The Mixolydian System*

The third series offers to the artist the following combination: major triads on the tonic and subdominant and a minor triad on the dominant. One glance at this series will be sufficient for anybody to recognize here the Mixolydian system, transposed to C. For the series contains the B-flat, which bears the ordinal number 1 among the flats and, accordingly, points to the ordinal number 1 among the fifth in descending order. But what tone would have C as first fifth in descending order, if it were not G? Thus the identity between this series and the old Myxolydian system is established beyond any doubt. It may suffice to state here merely that the combination between major and minor may lead to a Mixolydian result. This explains very clearly why the artists could afford to drop the old Mixolydian as an independent system.[4]

§ 45. *The Fourth Series: The So-called "Harmonic Minor Scale"*

The fourth series contains a minor third, a minor sixth, but a major seventh. This series cannot be considered an independent system any more than the first series can; for it lacks the B-flat, which under all circumstances must precede the E-flat and A-flat. The preferred designation for this series today is that of "harmonic minor scale," which, it should be noted, conveys the concept of a "system." Now, in my opinion, such a concept has no basis, nor does it have any purpose; for we can obtain the same series through the method of combination, while enjoying, at the same time, the advantage of remaining free to actuate those other combinations which the creative artist cherishes.

The artists prefer this type of combination especially when using the minor mode as their point of departure. In other words, this combination is primarily minor and only secondarily major in char-

[4. Schenker's assumption, that the Mixolydian mode was dropped because its effects can be produced anyway by the "third combined series," is somewhat teleological. The real reason is, rather, that the Mixolydian, just like our minor, lacks the leadingtone, which, if added, would transform that old mode immediately into our major. Without the leadingtone, on the other hand, the step progression G–C, i.e., I–IV in Mixolydian, will easily be mistaken for V–I of C major. Incidentally, the dropping of the Mixolydian system may afford an additional proof of the fact that the seventh of our system is in no way identical with the seventh partial, nor yet an imitation of it (cf. § 10, n. to § 13).]

acter; for it is only the major seventh which is taken over from the major mode. It seems, however, that the theoreticians were misled by the fact that this combination occurs so frequently and is used so commonly. This fact induced them to take it for an independent system. We grant that it is used frequently; but since when is use en masse, perhaps established merely statistically, to be accepted as a criterion for a system? Perhaps it could be proved by the same statistics that practical art employs the minor seventh of the true minor mode just as frequently, especially if we take into consideration the first phase of motivic development of pieces composed in the minor mode. If we were to rely merely on statistics, how could we decide this contest between the major and the minor seventh? It may be simpler to renounce the construction of a system on the basis of mere statistical frequency and to accept, despite that frequency, the concept of a combination—a combination, it must be granted, basically minor in character, as indicated by the minor triads on the I and IV steps, whereas the major triad on the V step would have been borrowed from the homonymous major mode.

The statistical frequency with which this fourth series occurs seems to me to prove, rather, that the artists have intuited the artificial character of the minor mode. We have discussed in a previous chapter the needs which led to the adoption of the minor mode; but, broadly speaking, these needs derived from artistic, purely artistic, reasoning, and Nature has not sanctioned them so fully as she has sanctioned those other needs which the artist expresses in the major mode. Thus the minor mode shows all the features of human creation, i.e., of human imperfection. Its *raison d'être* is in fully contrasting the major mode, an aim which is reached most conclusively by the Aeolian system. But this aim is merely artistic and artificial, and the instinct of the artist seems to have been unable, in the long run, to bear up under this falsity. He preferred to be inconsistent and to deny the Aeolian system rather than deny himself and his urge toward Nature, which manifests itself in music in the major mode. The major seventh, which is used so frequently in the minor mode, thus appears to us as a symbol of the victory over what is artificial (the minor mode) and of a return to Nature (the major mode)—as a symbol, to put it concisely, of the insuperable strength of the major mode.

The adoption of the major seventh from the major into the minor mode was determined, in the mind of the artist, by an additional decisive reason. As shown in the accompanying chart, the more remote fifths of a minor system are identical with the more closely related fifths of the [corresponding] major system. These coincidences are indicated in the chart by the sign ‖.

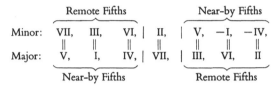

Furthermore—we shall have to come back to this point later—the listener is inclined, when hearing a fifth, to ascribe it, in cases of doubt, to a major rather than to a minor system and, second, to assume it to be less, rather than more, remote from the tonic. The minor system, in its purely diatonic form and without borrrowing the major seventh from the homonymous major system, therefore, would be misleading to our ear; for it might suggest to us that we are dealing with the major system of a different tone. Now if the composer wants to safeguard his listener against mistaking, for example, the VII step in A minor, G–B–D, for the coincidental V step of C major, all he needs to do is to avail himself of this combination, viz., to borrow the major seventh, G-sharp, from the homonymous A major. It is true that he thereby creates a diminished triad on the VII step; but he forestalls the danger of our hearing in this context a C major, a key which was not in his mind at all, and he gains the invaluable advantage of remaining unequivocally on the key he had intended, i.e., on the same A. Or take, for example, the sequence of minor triads, A–C–E and D–F–A, which could be interpreted as a sequence VI–II in C major or V–I in D minor. If the composer wants to put his D on a firm footing, if he wants to prevent the C from usurping, by virtue of the superiority of the major mode, the dominant place in the attention of the listener, he may draft the major seventh from the homonymous D major, i.e., he may actuate the combination between D minor and D major, and that danger will be forestalled.[5]

§ 46. The Fifth Series: The Old Dorian System

The fifth series reveals itself as a transposition. The presence of B-flat and E-flat indicates that we are dealing here with the second fifth in descending order. Our tonic being *C*, we are immediately referred (via *G*) to *D*, i.e., to the Dorian system. Thus we see that a combination of major and minor in the third and seventh results in a Dorian likeness!

This series has minor triads on the tonic and the dominant, whereas the subdominant shows a major triad.[6]

§ 47. The Sixth Series

The sixth series, finally, is clearly the product of a combination. While the tonic here forms a major triad, the IV and V steps yield minor triads.[7]

§ 48. An Evaluation of Our Theory of Combination with regard to the Understanding of Art

The method of combination as we have described it above has the following implication: While preserving the major as well as the

[5. Cf. § 20, n. 1. The meaning of this chart will become even clearer if it is considered in connection with the Phrygian II in the minor mode and the explanation for this phenomenon offered in § 50, n. 11. Cf. also § 145.]

[6. The use of an accidental flat on the VI step in Dorian was quite common even at a very early age. It may have served merely the purpose of avoiding the diminished triad, which otherwise might have resulted too easily (cf. § 50).]

7. The discussion, §§ 41–47, of these configurations is summarized in Table 2.

TABLE 2

The Triads of the I, IV, and V Steps in All the Combined Series

	IV	I	V
In major	Major	Major	Major
In the first series (so-called "melodic minor" scale)	Major	Minor	Major
In the second series	Minor	Major	Major
In the third series (Mixolydian)	Major	Major	Minor
In the fourth series (so-called "harmonic minor" scale)	Minor	Minor	Major
In the fifth series (Dorian)	Major	Minor	Minor
In the sixth series	Minor	Major	Minor
In minor	Minor	Minor	Minor

minor systems in their absolute purity and while equalizing the two, as demanded by our artistic purposes, not only have we obtained, by combining both systems, those series which modern theory erroneously designates as various forms of the minor system, but at the same time we have gained several additional series, two of which show the characteristics of what was formerly supposed to be the Mixolydian and Dorian systems! By this method we have not only considerably simplified theory but, at the same time, enriched it by the addition of those mixed or combined series for which our contemporary manuals on theory do not have any explanation. We can now afford to renounce those three perfectly abstruse minor systems, viz., the melodic, the harmonic, and the mixed minor system, to be satisfied with the purely Aeolian system. On the other hand, the principle of combination offers us the possibility not only of making up for the apparent loss but, even more, of comprehending, within the manifold possibilities of combining series, all the phenomena of our art.

But more important even than these advantages is, for me, the satisfaction of having been able to show by this method the working of the artistic instinct in its true essence. For how could the artist have chanced on the possibility of combination, had he not been driven to this discovery by the egotistic-expansive urges of the tone itself? Without the urge of the tone to live a full life in all sorts of possible relationships, the artist would never have been able to discover the artifice of combination.[8]

NOTE

It should be stressed, however, that, in identifying our major and minor with the old Ionian and Aeolian modes, I do not assume in any way that those two ancient systems continue to exist among us without any change as of yore. At a time which knew only the most primitive melodic problems, the concept of the harmonic "step," it

[8. In general it is only the combination III♭–III♮ that arouses the genuine impression of a true combination between the two systems. But the major third is often used merely for the purpose of gaining a leadingtone, i.e., for the purpose of modulation, and not in order to create the effect of a combination between minor and major. Therefore, Schenker designates the combination in the thirds as "combination of the first order" (cf. *Free Composition*, § 101; see also Schenker's own note to § 155).]

should be kept in mind, was not only unknown to theory but also beyond the artist's intuition. As we shall show later, it was only instrumental music, with its richer motivic demands, which could lead the artist to reinterpret, for his artistic purposes, these same scales, which had been called, until then, the Ionian and Aeolian, to understand them as an aggregation of seven basic tones arranged in the order of fifths, and to use them as "steps" under the aegis of one of them. Considering this difference, i.e., the novel practice and interpretation of the harmonic step, one may, if one so wishes, disregard the absolute identity of the scales and accept our major and minor as new systems as compared with the old Ionian and Aeolian modes. My own point of view was determined by the identity of the scales as well as by the fact that, of all the old modes, it was only these two, the Ionian and the Aeolian, which, without any external change, could fully respond to the intensification of motivic life and absorb the modern concept of the harmonic step. Likewise, in designating two of the scales obtained by the method of combination as Dorian and Mixolydian, respectively (cf. §§ 44 and 46), I took into account primarily the identity of the scales, just as in the case of the Ionian and Aeolian scale. After what has been said in §§ 8–19 on the basic requirements of a musical system, it should be self-evident that we cannot think of these scales without thinking, at the same time, in terms of harmonic steps. Only it must not be forgotten that, despite this implicit modern concept of the harmonic step which underlies the concept of system, those two series are nevertheless to be considered as products of combinations between major and minor, and no longer as independent systems, as they were considered in olden times. The reference to a II Phrygian step, especially in § 30, is based on a similar, unavoidable assumption of the concept of harmonic step in the old Phrygian system and on the identity between the second step, a half-tone above the tonic, and the second tone of the former Phrygian scale. Modern thinking simply cannot do without the concept of harmonic step; and this may account, perhaps, most plausibly for the fact that any return to the old modes in their true ancient form is barred, perhaps forever, and that even a Beethoven, even a Brahms, could not free himself altogether, as we have seen above, from the modern concept of the harmonic step and the treatment of keys and modulations resulting from that concept.

§ 49. *The Nature of a Combination as Independent of the Factor of Time*

The process of combination is not affected by the time factor; in other words, a combination may move in variable quantities. Thus it is not the number of measures which decides the momentum of a combination; for, as we shall see in the following examples, a combination may be actuated in the time of a sixteenth-note, even of a thirty-second, and only by one single element. It would be illicit, therefore, to deny the existence of a combination merely on the ground that its duration was brief.

EXAMPLES OF COMBINATIONS

Introductory note.—Besides the variability of the time factor, the combinations are so fluid and without any fixed line of separation between one type and the other that it would be difficult indeed to illustrate each individual series with an example of its own. I have decided, therefore, to group in this place a considerable number of examples, adding the necessary explanatory notes.

Furthermore, to show that the oldest masters were already quite familiar with the method of combination, I have ordered this group of examples from the historical point of view.

Finally, I should like to draw the reader's attention to the designation (maj.) for major and (min.) for minor, which should facilitate the explanation of these combinations.

Example 69 (76). Dom. Scarlatti, Sonata, D Major:

We have here a section of eight measures, extending from measure 3 to measure 10 of the example. The composer has availed himself of the method of combination in order to emphasize the underlying inner parallelism between the first four and the second four measures and to make this parallelism more attractive. This aim is achieved through the contrast between the major and the minor colors in the background of the same motif. The quantities of major and minor are equal; for the equilibrium of the combination can hardly be considered as disrupted by the last eighth-note of measure 6, which is a major seventh, G-sharp.

Example 70 (77). Scarlatti, Sonata, C Minor:

This sequence of measures constitutes the conclusion of the first part of the composition. Measures 1 and 2 contain G minor, with the major seventh, *F*-sharp, borrowed from G major (cf. § 45); measure 3 takes from G major the additional loan of the major third, *B*-natural, while the minor sixth and seventh still indicate G minor (cf. § 47). The concluding measure, finally, is in a pure G major.

This G $\frac{major}{minor}$ has a twofold effect: The transition from a combined series with prevalence of the minor mode, via a differently combined series, to a pure G major conveys a climaxing effect, well worth pursuing for its own sake. But this same sequence, furthermore, serves the purpose of modulation, viz., of leading back from G $\frac{major}{minor}$ to C $\frac{major}{minor}$, which is the basic key of the composition. The employment of the B-natural, as the major seventh of C major (second-to-last measure) prepares our ear far more efficiently for the advent of the C system than a B-flat could have done, had it been used, on this very step, as the third of the dominant, in the strict sense of a pure C minor (§ 45). At any rate, the coincidence of the B-natural as an element anticipating a different system, with the F-natural and the E-flat as elements still preserving the G minor character of the piece, is worth noting.

Example 71 (80). J. S. Bach, Partita No. 1, Allemande:

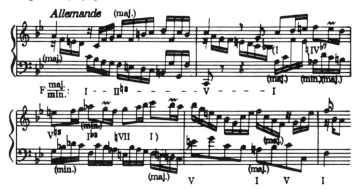

While the bass voice, at the beginning phase of the climaxing process (measure 2) still clings to the major third, A-natural, the top voice, in the following measure 3, during the process of climaxing itself, uses the minor third, A-flat, until both voices, bass and soprano, meet, in measure 4, concluding the motif on the ground of a pure F major.

Example 72 (81). J. S. Bach, Partita No. 4, Allemande:

As we see here, the cadence takes off three times—to founder each time again the rock of the deceptive cadence (V–VI). Charm, expressiveness, and variety are all enhanced by the fact that during the first two times (measures 3 and 5) the minor VI step of A minor is employed, while the third time (measure 6) it is the major VI, borrowed from A major, which takes its place. The struggle from minor to major, as manifested in this combination of sixths, is paralleled by a combination in the thirds, which, analogously, appear first as minor (measures 3, 4), finally to be transformed into major (measure 5).

It should be noted, however, that in measures 1 and 2 we have, on the one hand, the minor third, C-natural, in the soprano voice, while, on the other hand, the bass insists on the major sixth and seventh (F-sharp and G-sharp). This mixture is further combined with a pure minor, with minor sixth and seventh, in the soprano voice (first beat of measure 2). Finally, the soprano voice, too, has F-sharp and G-sharp (third beat of measure 4), thus forming the major dominant in A minor. But these same two major intervals, returning with the first beat of measure 5, probably should be ascribed to emotional rather than to harmonic reasons.

The D-sharp in the soprano voice (measure 1) and the C-sharp in measure 2 are to be considered merely as neighboring notes. They do not affect, nor are they affected by, the combination in any way.

Example 73 (82). J. S. Bach, *Well-tempered Clavier,* II, Prelude, E major:

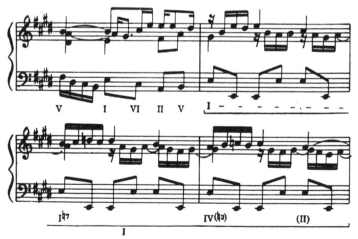

Measure 4 of this example introduces the minor triad on the sub-dominant of E major (cf. § 43). It should be noted that three elements are combined in this measure, a combination which yields a most beautiful effect: the minor third, C-natural; the major sixth, F-sharp; and the major seventh, G-sharp. This coincidence results, with the second quarter-note of this same measure 4, in the diminished fourth, C–G-sharp. What expressiveness is elicited by this interval!

Example 74 (83). Haydn, Piano Sonata, E-flat, Adagio, No. 52:

This example shows the felicitous effect of the method of combination when applied to color the middle part of the lied form (measures 3–6).

Example 75 (84). Mozart, Piano Sonata, F Major, K. 332:

This section is the continuation of the theme in C major quoted in Example 7. Together, these two examples form the second thematic complex of the first movement. As the basic key of the composition is F major, this complex is kept, as it should be, in C major.

The example shows that a larger motivic complex may also profit from the method of combination. All factors concerned draw their advantage from it: the complex as a whole, the component parts as such, and, last but not least, the tone *C*, which dominates the complex. By displaying now its major, now its minor, system, it is enabled to unfold all its wealth.

Example 76 (86). Mozart, Piano Sonata, B-Flat Major, K. 333:

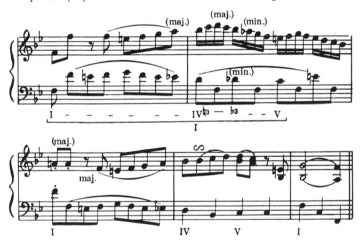

The notes *D*-flat and *A*-flat (second beat of measure 2) might be considered merely as passing notes. Such a concept would be perfectly justified by the fact that the IV diatonic step appears well established by the first beat of the same measure. Nevertheless, these notes, as minor third and minor sixth, convey the memory of the homonymous F minor, as if the minor on the subdominant were following the major subdominant to evoke the idea of this combination. The effect is the more delicate, the more fleeting and shadowy the appearance of the minor mode. The coda is kept com-

pletely free of minor-mode elements and sounds like an affirmation
of the major mode.

Example 77 (87). Mozart, String Quartet, G Major, Andante,
K. 387:

The minor-mode element in this example affects only the cadence,
the motif breathing its last. How marvelous is the effect of this
cloudlet of minor mode, appearing so quietly in the sky at the ultimate moment!

Example 78 (88). Mozart, Piano Sonata, F Major, K. 332:

This example, on the contrary, shows that the method of combination may result occasionally in harshness and disregard, even from
the hands of a Mozart. It would be difficult to deny that the second
and third beats of measure 2 have already produced just that effect.

Example 79 (89). [9] Mozart, String Quartet, C Major, K. 465: [10]

Example 80 (91). Beethoven, Piano Sonata, op. 31, No. 1:

9. If I have quoted, in the present context, quite a series of excerpts from Mozart, I have done so in order to demonstrate our master's inclination in favor of minor-mode elements in the midst of a clearly established major atmosphere. Dejection and melancholy were moods much more familiar to him than our kind of world wants to admit when imagining him as a mind forever serene and unclouded!

[10. For an analysis of this example, cf. *Free Composition*, Example 99/3, and Appendix I of this book, Example 7.]

Example 81 (93). Schubert, Piano Sonata, A Minor, op. 143:

I should like to draw the reader's attention especially to measure 18 of this example, where the minor sixth, *C*, of E minor collides with the G-sharp and F-sharp of E major, in one and the same chord.

Example 82 (95). Wagner, *Tristan and Isolde,* Act I, Scene 2:

I have marked, in this example, the step progression, in order to indicate most clearly the nature of the combination: The VI step of C minor (measures 1 and 2) is followed by the VI step of C major (measures 3 and 4). This latter harmony is further complicated by the chromatic sharping of the third (C-sharp instead of C-natural). Measure 5 resumes the minor-mode character with the minor triad on the IV of C minor, whereupon the goal of a half-close on V is reached via the altered seventh chord of the II step, D–F-sharp–A-flat–C.

If we now take a look at the solo voice, we shall notice that it does not reflect in its entirety the harmonic progression we have just analyzed. The solo voice lacks the chromatic tones C-sharp and E-natural on the VI step. In other words, this voice, considered by itself, merely moves within C minor, with the major sixth, A-natural, borrowed from C major (measures 3 and 4).

Now there was no binding reason for the composer to reflect the entire development in the solo voice. I should like to point out, nevertheless, that it could have been done. The effect would have been different. We are faced here with two alternative possibilities. In one case the harmonies, conceived in the vertical direction, appear, so to speak, unfolded in the horizontal flow of the melody; in the other case they are established merely vertically, in triads or seventh chords, without being confirmed, at the same time, in the melody. In the former case the color of the harmony penetrates the living flesh of the motif; in the latter case such penetration does not take place. The earlier examples illustrate the former technique; the example here under consideration illustrates the latter. Each alternative is motivated by its own purpose.

Example 83 (96). Brahms, Sonata for Clarinet and Piano, op. 120, No. 1:

This example shows a major triad on the subdominant of F minor (measure 3), a Dorian feature, so to speak (cf. § 46). See also the excerpt from Brahms quoted in § 29.

Example 84 (97). Brahms, Symphony III, op. 90:

Example 85 (98). Brahms, Rhapsody, B Minor, op. 79, No. 1:

§ 50. *The Phrygian II in the Minor Mode*

If we have recognized two of the old systems, the Dorian and the Mixolydian, in two of the scales produced by a combination of our major and minor systems, the question may be legitimate whether perchance the Phrygian and Lydian modes, too, lie hidden somewhere in our dual system. In fact, no turn derived from the former systems enjoys as much currency and popularity among modern composers as the formerly Phrygian II, i.e., the half-tone between the I and the II steps. We encounter it in the major triad on the flatted II step in minor in place of the diminished triad on the diatonic II. It is true that this Phrygian II can be found also in the major key; but this is to be understood in a merely figurative sense; for we would have to assume a combination, substituting a minor for the major. In the strict sense the Phrygian II must then be considered as a legitimate part of the minor, and not of the major, system, a point of view which finds its natural justification in the fact that the Phrygian mode, to begin with, is more closely related to the minor than to the major mode.

How are we to explain the Phrygian II, if the principle of combination was of no avail? Now, the flatting of the II step in minor (or also in major), together with the expansion of the diminished triad into a major triad—e.g., in A minor- *B-flat–D–F* instead of *B-natural–D–F;* or in C major: *D-flat–F–A-flat* instead of *D-natural–F–A-flat* or *D–F–A,* respectively—is not to be explained as a conscious or subconscious relapse into the old Phrygian mode. For, as we have seen, the Dorian and Mixolydian characteristics resulting from certain combinations are not due to any such relapse but rather to the immanent urge of the tone to enter all possible combinations. The so-called "Phrygian II," likewise, arises in response to motivic challenges. The only difference is that, in this case, we are facing a challenge, or a need, of the II step, i.e., the second fifth in rising order, whereas in the situations discussed in §§ 23 and 26 we were dealing with the motivic demands of the I, IV, and V steps.

As we indicated in that discussion, the motif is not always happy at the thought of possibly finding itself in the position of a diminished triad. At any rate, such a position is not to be considered as the motif's first choice. To say the least, it is not so natural as the position of a major or minor triad. This is quite obvious if we keep in mind that the diminished fifth is not a natural interval (cf. § 19) but the result of a merely artificial compromise between the first fifth in descending order, F, and the fifth fifth in rising order, B— two notes which have become acclimated, side by side, in our major diatonic system in consequence of a mere artifice, viz., the principle of inversion.

The discomfort of the diminished triad is felt as such not only when this chord occurs on the IV or the V step, as is the case in the Phrygian and Lydian modes, but wherever else it occurs. In other words, this discomfort is keenly felt also when the diminished triad falls on the II step of our minor. This explains why in most cases—unless the composer aims at evoking a very special emotional charm which may make the diminished triad outright desirable for the motif—the II step is flatted in minor (and also, by analogy, in major). For the major triad resulting from this flatting is able to comprehend the motif, and thus at least a temporary victory has been won by the motif over the system.[11]

[11. Schenker explains the use of the Phrygian II merely on the ground of motivic considerations. It should be noted, on the other hand, that our minor system already forms a diminished triad on the II step, i.e., on a step which is most important in cadencing. Since the diminished triad has an inherent tendency toward moving on to the neighboring step—in our case, the III—the II step was flatted to avoid any ambiguity in the cadence. The fact that this step, in general, was used in its first inversion (Neapolitan sixth!) is easily explained. For its use in the root position would have entailed an augmented step (B-flat–E) in the bass voice, which in most cases was better avoided for reasons of voice-leading (cf. *Free Composition*, §§ 104–5). It should also be noted that this inherent tendency of the diminished triad

Example 86 (99). Beethoven, Piano Sonata, op. 57:

Example 87 (100). Beethoven, Piano Sonata, op. 57, Finale:

From this point on, it may be justifiable to assume that the major triad on the II step in minor was resorted to for the sake of new and different artistic purposes[12] and not only for the satisfaction of motivic needs.

_____
probably accounts for the fact that compositions in minor rather tend first to the mediant before approaching the dominant. This explanation, at any rate, is far more plausible than the current one, which prattles about a "third relationship" between minor and major.|

12. The interest in tonicalization, e.g., which we shall analyze in the chapter on chromatic alterations (cf. §§ 136 ff.), provides another explanation for the Phrygian II.

In this connection also, compare the excerpts from Wagner, Chopin, and Brahms quoted in § 30. Another piece which may come to mind in this context is the English horn solo of Act III, scene 1, of *Tristan and Isolde,* a masterpiece of poetry and articulation. It is composed in an unambiguous F minor but uses, with matchless cleverness, the Phrygian G-flat now as a passing note in the melody (measure 8), now as harmonic step (measures 17–19):

Example 88 (101). Wagner, *Tristan and Isolde:*

The following example shows a curious passage from Berlioz' *Symphony Fantastique,* "Marche au supplice" (Payne ed., Eulenburg score, pp. 155 f.):

Example 89 (102).

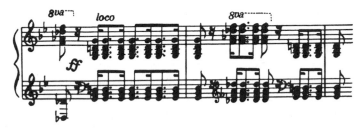

Although we are apparently faced here with a different kind of phenomenon, I prefer to include it in the scope of the present discussion; for the step progression from D-flat to G arouses in the listener, above all, the impression of the step progression ♭II–V in C minor (not in G minor)—note well, with a Phrygian II—and this impression is not canceled by the subsequent measure, which claims, in a rather brutal fashion, the V step as the tonic I of G minor, a claim which is fulfilled without true force of conviction.[13]

Be this as it may, Schumann certainly was wrong when, in reviewing the *Symphony Fantastique*, he had the following comment on the foregoing passage:

In evaluating the harmonic content, it must be granted that our symphony reveals the awkardness of its eighteen-year-old composer, who, without any ceremony, plunges headlong *in medias res*. When Berlioz wants to go, e.g., from G to D-flat, he just goes there, without any compliments.[14] One may well shake one's head in view of such recklessness. Sensible musicians, on the other hand, who have listened to this symphony in Paris, assure us that this passage did not admit of any other turn. One of the listeners went so far as to make the following bewildering statement about Berlioz' music: "Que cela est fort beau, quoique ce ne soit pas de la musique." This may be a somewhat vague description, but there is something to it. Furthermore, of such abstruse passages there are not many in the composition.

A true D-flat major, however, is out of the question here, whatever one may think about this passage in other respects.

13. This defect stems from a lack of precision with regard to the harmonic content. This, in turn, results from Berlioz' failure to unfold in any way the harmonies D-flat–F–A-flat and G–B-flat–D-natural motivically or thematically. The consequence of this failure is that these harmonies are, so to speak, suspended in mid-air, without any further confirmation, a situation which must arouse doubts in our ear.

[14. If Schumann says that Berlioz proceeds "without making any compliments," he probably intends to say what Schenker, in describing this same passage, expresses with the phrase, "suspended in mid-air, without any further confirmation or unfolding."]

Finally, the question might be raised as to whether it would not be justifiable to reinstate the Phrygian mode as an independent system, considering the supposedly Phrygian character of the flatted II step in minor. But there are several reasons militating against such a reinstatement. First of all, the usability of the II step can never make up for the resulting unusability of the V step (cf. § 26); and, since this latter step, being the first fifth in rising order, is far more important than the II, being the second, i.e., a remoter, fifth in rising order, the V step evidently has priority when it comes to a decision between the two. Second, we may observe that the composers resort to that major triad on the flatted II step only passingly and temporarily, whereas for the rest they adhere firmly to the principles imposed by the system, which clearly results from the fact that the very pieces which make use of the Phrygian element find their conclusion the more convincingly in an unambiguous minor or major mode. Finally, we have already noted certain artificial elements in the minor system and have had some trouble in upholding its independence vis-à-vis the major system, from which it is often forced to take loans (especially in what concerns the seventh). How much more difficult would it be to recognize the Phrygian system, which would have to stand on even weaker legs than the minor system itself? And why do we need an independent system merely to explain the "Phrygian II," which in most cases is explained better by the reasons analyzed in the foregoing discussion?

§ 51. *The Old Lydian System as Unusable as Ever*

The same diminished fifth was, as we have seen (§ 20), the cause for the definite rejection of the Lydian system, which notoriously had a diminished triad on the subdominant. If even in olden times the Lydian system was disowned by frequent recourse to the B-flat, which transformed the Lydian into an Ionian system, it is quite obvious that today this system must be considered obsolete and unusable. For neither can it be produced by any of the combinations of our modern systems, nor need it be produced for motivic or any other consideration.

It is true, as we shall see in our chapter on chromatic alterations, that many composers have a special liking for raising the IV step in major (but also in minor) by half a tone, in order to obtain a diminished triad; e.g., in F major the B-flat is raised to B-natural, so that the IV step yields the diminished triad B-natural–D–F, which is particularly advantageous when aiming at the V step. It is not advisable, however, to consider this chromatic B-natural as a Lydian element, as this sharping betrays too clearly the intention of a chromatic alteration, and it would not be warranted to accept it as a diatonic IV step in the frame of a system [15]

§ 52. *Far-reaching Implications of the Principle of Combination*

All that remains to be said is that the process of combination, once set in motion by the egotism of the tone, has become a principle of such immanence and compositional force that we shall have to examine with no less care its effects on intervals, triads, seventh chords,[16] etc. Originating from the life of the tone, this principle penetrates the living organism of musical composition, wherever possible, with the force of an element of Nature.

[15. Cf. Example 47 (Beethoven, op. 132).]

[16. Schenker here, however, makes a passing allusion to the "seventh-chords." This is one of the few points in which he still follows Rameau's old theories on harmony. The discovery of the origin and motivation of the "seventh-chord" in voice-leading marks one of the decisive steps in the development of Schenker's own theory. For a more detailed analysis of this point, cf. Introduction, and note to § 99.]

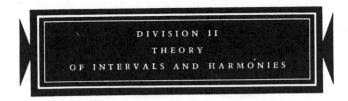

SECTION I

Theory of Intervals

CHAPTER I

THE CONSTRUCTION OF INTERVALS

§ 53. *The Meaning of Intervals during the Epoch of Figured Bass*

It is well known that the old masters of the time of the figured bass used to write out merely the bass line of their compositions while indicating with figures whatever other voices, above the bass line, they may have wished to have filled in by the performer.[1] These figures were called "intervals." If the composer wanted to indicate to the performers the use of a minor or diminished third, of a perfect or diminished octave, etc., as may have been required by chance or by the plan of the composition, he had to make a clear distinction between all the possible thirds, all the possible octaves, etc. These distinctions had to be reflected in the notation of the so-called "figured bass," which, accordingly, developed all sorts of numerals, sharps, flats, and other

[1. In the very first sentence of this paragraph Schenker points to the distinction between the theory of the thorough bass, which he relegates to the sphere of "voice-leading," and the "concepts of harmony." This distinction between "voice-leading" and "harmony" is one of the most important and meritorious aspects of Schenker's theory (cf. *Counterpoint*, I, xxiv–xxxi, as well as §§ 90–92 below and the Introduction above).]

appropriate signs. Hence it was meaningful at that time to pay special attention, for example, to the diminished octave in the teaching of theory; for the composer may have desired often enough to make use of such an interval. Thus we find the following passage in C. P. E. Bach's *Manual on Accompaniment*, chapter iii, § 20:[2]

"When the sixth goes together with the diminished octave, no other interval should be added. The octave will then descend and should be considered as a suspension resolved in the next chord. The following examples are noteworthy in this respect. In the last one we have a $^9_7$, followed by $^{\flat 8}_6$ as passing notes."

Example 90 (103):

And in the same chapter, § 22:

"The dissonant diminished sixth occurs only rarely; and it requires special skill and care. If it is used at all, it must be prepared and resolved in descending. It sounds most acceptable when accompanied only by the minor third. Never omit the necessary indication of the sharps and flats in the notation of the figured bass."

Example 91 (104):

It will be seen that it was really necessary to construct a table of intervals a priori, wherefrom the "accompanist" could learn which interval was meant by this or that figure. For any notes which perchance stood head on head were considered to form an interval. The G above the G-sharp, in Example 90, *a*) was supposed to form an interval, as was the B-flat above the D-sharp in Example 91. In what-

2. C. P. E. Bach, *Versuch über die wahre Art das Clavier zu spielen. Zweyter Theil in welchem die Lehre von dem Accompagnement und von den freyen Fantasien abgehandelt wird* (Berlin, 1762).

ever position the heads found themselves one upon the other, their relationship was fixed in figures and concepts of intervals. The rule was: "All intervals are to be measured from the bass note upward, according to the place they occupy on the staff. This distance shall determine their name, which is to be indicated by a figure" (*op. cit.,* chap. i, § 9). There was much talk about certain intervals supposed to be "most usable in harmony," and they were classified by the theorists as follows: major, minor, augmented seconds; major, minor, diminished thirds; perfect, diminished, augmented fourths; perfect, diminished, augmented fifths; major, minor diminished, augmented sixths; major, minor, diminished seventh; perfect, diminished, augmented octaves; minor, major ninths, etc. It has become a well-established custom to pass this table on from generation to generation.

§ 54. *Changing Circumstances Leading to Necessity of Correcting*
This Historical Concept of the Interval

But it is high time for this concept of the interval to be corrected and purified. For there is no need for us any longer to indicate with figures the desired arrangement of intervals. Hence it is no longer necessary to derive the concept of the interval from the haphazard position in which the heads find themselves one upon the other. Let us have a look at the following example:

Example 92 (105). Scarlatti, Sonata, D Major:

In measure 6 of this example, the $^6_5$-chord of the second step in A minor, D–A–B, coincides with the sequence C–B♭–G♯ and A in the melody of the soprano. The ear of the musician would be hurt no less than his principles if he had to interpret this casual and external coincidence of notes as "intervals," especially if he had to refer the B-flat as a diminished octave to the B-natural in the bass voice, instead of hearing this sequence of notes in the soprano merely in its relation to the following A. Most spontaneously, this sequence explains itself as a melodic paraphrase of the tone A, accomplished by the two neighboring notes, B-flat and G-sharp, the B-flat being complicated, furthermore, by a suspension, C. If the musician fulfils his first duty of thus hearing this passage, he will ascribe to the B-flat above the B-natural an effect of merely secondary importance.

Let us take another example, viz., Beethoven's *32 Variations for the Pianoforte:*

Example 93 (106). Variation IX:

Here, too, it is our foremost duty to perceive, in measure 3, the D-sharp as leading note with reference to E. It would be quite erroneous to jump from the fact of the vertical coincidence between D-flat and D-sharp to the conclusion of what would have to be called an "augmented" octave. The ear will grasp, first of all, the diminished seventh-chord, B-flat, D-flat, G, E; and if this is the spontaneous reaction of our ear, why do violence to it by searching for a relationship between *D*-flat and *D*-sharp which, in reality, is out of the question?

These examples may make it clear that, from the point of view of the artist, each note must be heard in its artistically immanent cause and effect, no matter whether our hearing is forced thereby to follow the vertical or the horizontal direction. The result may even be that one note, or even more, must be heard merely horizontally, while the vertical is to be totally disregarded; for other notes, on the contrary, the vertical concept is far more important.

Example 94 (107):

Example 94 is a restatement of the Beethoven excerpt quoted in Example 93, to which, this time, arrows have been added. The first arrow indicates the horizontal direction in which the *D*-sharp must be heard; the second one, the vertical context of the *E*. Besides the fact that it is musically more correct to hear it this way, this kind of analysis will do away with all sorts of theoretical utopias and chimeras. Especially nowadays, when everybody is so prone to fancy new harmonies whenever faced with an apparently odd vertical accumulation of notes, it is twice as essential to emphasize the duty of hearing correctly. The result will be in all cases, even in the apparently questionable ones, that, basically, we are dealing with established relationships—excepting only those cases—alas, none too rare nowadays—in which the composer himself did not know what he was writing.

§ 55. *Harmonizability as the Conceptual Prerequisite of the Modern Interval*

The reader may have understood by now that, in the present phase of our art, the concept of interval has become bound to and limited by the concept of its harmonizability.[3] In other words, the possibility of being used in a triad or seventh chord has become a conceptual prerequisite of the interval.

§ 56. *The Number of Modern Intervals as Fixed*

If the concept of interval is inseparably tied to the concept of harmonizability,[4] the consequence is that there is not, as formerly, an

[3. This term already implies the concept of "unfolding," created and developed by Schenker. It implies, i.e., the concept of unfolding the vertical or space dimension of the intervals in the horizontal or time dimension. Only consonances, i.e., the intervals contained in the triad, can be unfolded in this way. The dissonances and, in particular, the seventh-chord, owing to its dissonant character, originate in passing notes. A basic exposition of this concept can be found in Schenker's profound essay, "The Dissonance Always Consists of Passing Notes; It Never Constitutes Harmonies" (*Yearbook*, II, 24 ff.). This distinction is more implicit than explicit in the present *Harmony*; the explanations offered in § 73 likewise are kept in a negative form (cf. *Free Composition*, § 169).]

4. The Scherzo of J. S. Bach's Partita III (measure 10, second quarter-note) shows a coincidence of voices which must be considered as a special case in the literature of music. Apparently, we are dealing here with a seventh-chord which fulfils the postulate of harmonizability in accordance with the system; and yet we are forced to expel one tone from the vertical structure of tones and take this structure to be a triad.

Example 95 (108):

Originating in the following acciacatura (in Bach's usual notation):
Example 96 (109):

which means, in our notation,
Example 97 (110):

the note G-sharp seems to be forced into the sixth-chord, C–E–A, with the greatest emphasis. The composer intended thereby to enhance the sharp and capricious effect of the acciacatura, in keeping with the character of this scherzo. This proves again that we must not throw together light-mindedly in our conception whatever notes happen to be written one above the other but must always respect the compositional motivation of any phenomenon.

apparently limitless number of usable intervals, but a fixed number which cannot be increased in any way.

§ 57. *The Origin of the Intervals*

Intervals and harmonies are drawn from the selfsame source. All we have to do, accordingly, is to resort to the two diatonic systems of major and minor as well as to the compositional principle of combination, which is ever present to the imagination of the artist (cf. § 52).

§ 58. *The Number of Intervals in the Diatonic Major System*

§ 59. *The Exclusion of Any Other Interval from the Purely Diatonic System*

§ 60. *The Same Number of Intervals in the Diatonic Minor System*

§ 61. *Intervals Resulting from Combination*

[*Note:* These sections contain an enumeration of intervals occurring in the major and minor diatonic systems and their combinations. They also contain tables showing the scale steps on which these intervals appear.]

§ 62. *Total Number of Intervals Drawn from These Sources*

Adding these results to those obtained in §§ 58–61, we obtain the following sum total:

> Prime: perfect
> Second: major, minor, and augmented
> Third: major, minor
> Fourth: perfect, augmented, diminished
> Fifth: perfect, augmented, diminished
> Sixth: major, minor
> Seventh: major, minor, diminished
> Octave: perfect
> Sum total: 18 intervals

§ 63. *Advantage of This Method of Deriving the Intervals*

We are still lacking the diminished third, the diminished and augmented sixth,[5] the diminished and augmented octave—in brief, just all those intervals which we are wont to find in the standard a priori

5. With regard to the diminished third and its inversion, the augmented sixth, cf. §§ 146 ff., where this interval will be studied in the frame of the discussion of altered chords.

tables. But even those intervals which are common to the a priori tables and my own are different because of the light which is shed on them by the totally different principle of their derivation. For example, if we were to meet, in the course of a composition, an augmented second, we would have to take it, in accordance with the old concept, as one of those many usable intervals, which has made its appearance just now by some chance. My own principle of derivation, on the contrary, immediately makes it clear that we are dealing here with a combination of two homonymous modes; and, once this has penetrated our feeling, we find ourselves, so to speak, carried into the midst of the carrousel of tones; we become cognizant of what they are driving at; and our artistic understanding gains by that much. Formerly all intervals were hanging, so to speak, suspended in mid-air. It goes without saying that we cannot blame our ancestors for this situation, as their theory was nothing but a complementary phenomenon of their practice of the thorough bass. This, on the other hand, is no reason for us to adhere to that theory after having dropped long since the practice of the thorough bass. More than that, it is somewhat strange that a change has not taken place much earlier. Such a change is overdue, if only on account of the artistic intensification of musical perception which our ear has undergone in the meantime. It is true that for the mature artist there never was any danger of mishearing, for example, a Wagnerian passage, no matter how incommensurable the tones which on and off may have happened to coincide vertically. Whatever was meant to be heard horizontally, the mature artist would hear horizontally. Whatever resulted from the vertical structure he perceived as such. To put it concisely: His perception, unperturbed by the external appearances, conformed to the intention of the composer. In so far as the immature musician, or the layman, or even the theoretician is concerned, however, the conventional concept of the interval entailed great dangers. For no sooner would they spot, placed upon one another, two notes which they found entered in the conventional tables, e.g., under the heading "diminished octave," etc., than they felt an irresistible urge to dispose of this phenomenon in a manner no less superficial than those tables themselves had been: viz., they believed they owed it to the tables, as well as to the interval, to hear those two notes really together, and for the sake of this theorem they would abstain from hearing each note individually in its own context and motivation, which would have been the only correct thing to do and far more important. The situation was even worse in those cases where two notes coincided vertically in such a way that there was not even any entry for them to be found in the a priori tables. Instead of using the splendid opportunity offered by the default of the false guide to deliver themselves up to their own instinct, which certainly would have induced them to hear musically, they chose to rack their brains to find out the new meaning of this allegedly new interval, the revolution it entailed for the theory of harmony, and the importance in music history to be imputed to the genius who created this situation, allegedly for the first time. Oh, how easy is it to fabricate theory and history of music, if one's hearing is defective!

CHAPTER II

THE MEANING OF THE INTERVALS IN MODULATION

§ 64. *Locus of the Scale-Step*

The principle, just described, which derives the intervals only from the two diatonic systems and their combinations, is the source of the composer's technique of modulation, a most original feature of the musical art. If we keep present in our mind the intervals of the major and of the combined systems, we shall find that there are five major, two minor, and only one augmented second and that the major seconds are located on the I, II, IV, V, and VI steps. Using fractions, we get the following table:

$$\frac{1}{2}, \quad \frac{2}{3}, \quad \frac{4}{5}, \quad \frac{5}{6}, \quad \frac{6}{7};$$

The minor seconds are to be found on the scale steps: $\dfrac{3}{4}$, $\dfrac{7}{8}$;

Augmented second: $\dfrac{\flat 6}{\natural 7}$ (in the combination);

Major thirds: $\dfrac{1}{3}$, $\dfrac{4}{6}$, $\dfrac{5}{7}$;

Minor thirds: $\dfrac{2}{4}$, $\dfrac{3}{5}$, $\dfrac{6}{8}$, $\dfrac{(6)}{(1)}$, $\dfrac{7}{9}$, $\dfrac{(7)}{(2)}$;

Perfect fourths: $\dfrac{1}{4}$, $\dfrac{2}{5}$, $\dfrac{3}{6}$, $\dfrac{5}{1}$, $\dfrac{6}{2}$, $\dfrac{7}{3}$;

Augmented fourth: $\dfrac{4}{7}$;

Diminished fourths: $\dfrac{\natural 3}{\flat 6}$, $\dfrac{\natural 7}{\flat 3}$ (in the combination);

Perfect fifths: $\dfrac{1}{5}$, $\dfrac{2}{6}$, $\dfrac{3}{7}$, $\dfrac{4}{1}$, $\dfrac{5}{2}$, $\dfrac{6}{3}$;

Diminished fifth: $\dfrac{7}{4}$

Augmented fifths: $\dfrac{\flat 3}{\natural 7}$, $\dfrac{\flat 6}{\natural 3}$ (in the combination);

Major sixths: $\dfrac{1}{6}$, $\dfrac{2}{7}$, $\dfrac{4}{2}$, $\dfrac{5}{3}$;

Minor sixths: $\dfrac{3}{1}$, $\dfrac{6}{4}$, $\dfrac{7}{5}$;

Major sevenths: $\dfrac{1}{7}$, $\dfrac{4}{3}$;

Minor sevenths: $\dfrac{2}{1}$, $\dfrac{3}{2}$, $\dfrac{5}{4}$, $\dfrac{6}{5}$, $\dfrac{7}{6}$;

Diminished seventh: $\dfrac{\natural 7}{\flat 6}$ (in the combination);

Perfect octaves: on all scale-steps.

§ 65. Univalence and Plurivalence of Intervals

An interval is called *univalent* if it occurs on only one step of the diatonic system; thus belongs to only one key; and admits of only one interpretation. An interval is *plurivalent* if it has its locus on two or more scale-steps; belongs, accordingly, in two or more keys; and admits of two or more interpretations.

We have seen that intervals may occur on one or several scale-steps, as summarized in the following table:

A on one step only: the augmented fourth, diminished fifth, augmented second, and diminished seventh;

B on two steps: the minor second, diminished fourths, augmented fifths, and major seventh;

C on three steps: the major thirds and minor sixths;

D on four steps: the minor thirds and major sixths;

E on five steps: the major seconds and minor seventh;

F on six steps: the perfect fourths and perfect fifths;

G on seven steps: the perfect octaves.

§ 66. Deducing the Key or Keys from the Locus of the Interval

§ 67. Deducing Twice the Number of Keys from Locus of Interval if Both Minor and Major Diatonic Systems Are Included in the Scope of Consideration

§ 68. Deducing the Key from the Locus of Combined Intervals

When dealing with univalent intervals, it is particularly instructive to distinguish between the augmented fourth and the diminished fifth, on the one hand, and the augmented second and diminished seventh, on the other. Being strictly diatonic intervals, the former can be considered as univalent only with reference to their own diatonic system. From what has been said above, it should be clear enough that such intervals are to be considered as ambivalent in so far as they have one meaning each in the major and in the minor system. They are the result of a combination which, as such, encompasses both the minor and the major system. Accordingly, these intervals are literally univalent.

Thus the diminished seventh, e.g.,

Example 98 (132):

is strictly univalent and can be found only in D_{minor}^{major} as $_{\flat 6 \, (minor)}^{\sharp 7 \, (major)}$. Likewise

Example 99 (133):

can be found only as $_{\flat 6}^{\sharp 7}$ in G $_{minor}^{major}$.

§ 69. *Plurivalence of Intervals as Source of Modulation*

In our principle, according to which any interval must be derived from one of the two diatonic systems or their combinations and must therefore be harmonizable, we have thus discovered the foundation of the technique of modulation. For we have already seen that the musician can interpret the same interval in various ways. Such double interpretation of one and the same interval makes for the transition to another key, whether within the same system or in another.

§ 70. *The Use of Univalent and Plurivalent Intervals Creating Different Effects*

From what has been said so far, it will be easily understood that, in the practice of the artist, there is an essential difference between the plurivalent and the univalent intervals, with regard to both intentions and effects. The plurivalent intervals leave various ways open for reaching various keys, and the artist likes to take advantage of this situation in order to create a certain atmosphere of suspense and uncertainty. The situation, in such cases, is so uncertain that the arrival at one key or another can only be guessed, not indicated with any assurance. If, on the contrary, the artist desires to define the situation with precision and give us a sure perception of the key, he will resort to a univalent interval which, by its very nature, will exclude any other key. By combining univalent and plurivalent intervals, the artist will be able to conquer, reinforce, or give up any key; he will be able, in other words, to effect every kind of modulation and to fulfil inadvertently the basic demands of the principles of evolution and involution.

§ 71. *The Mechanics of Converting the Meaning of Plurivalent Intervals, and Its Significance for Form in the Wider Sense*

The technique of converting the meaning of plurivalent intervals is, of all artifices, the one which advances most expeditiously the tonal content of a composition. We have already noted the influence of the natural laws of development or evolution and of the artificial laws of inversion or involution on a given sequence of tones. We shall now observe how each one of the tones produced by those principles will give air to its own egotism, i.e., how it will demand both the major and the minor system and the combination of both. Each sequence of tones, likewise, will develop a sequence of steps and keys. In other words, the principles of development and inversion explain not only the sequence of individual tones but also the sequence of steps and keys. We shall come back to this point in some more detail when discussing the triads, which illustrate the mechanics of modulation even better than do simple intervals.

CHAPTER III

INVERSION OF INTERVALS

§ 72. *Inversion of Intervals*

Although the theory of the inversion of intervals forms part of the theory of double counterpoint, where it can be studied in its real effects, it is nevertheless inevitable to discuss this phenomenon also in the present context, if only in view of the inversions of triads and seventh-chords, which we shall study shortly. If an interval is inverted within the span of an octave in such a way that the highest tone is placed lowest and the lowest is put highest, we obtain the following result:

Example 100 (134):

In other words, the second is transformed into a seventh, the third into a sixth, the fourth into a fifth, the fifth into a fourth, the sixth into a third, and the seventh into a second.

In double counterpoint, intervals are inverted also in spans wider than that of an octave, e.g., within a tenth. In that case the result may be summarized in the following figures:

$$1 \quad 2 \quad 3 \quad 4 \quad 5 \quad 6 \quad 7 \quad 8 \quad 9 \quad 10$$
$$10 \quad 9 \quad 8 \quad 7 \quad 6 \quad 5 \quad 4 \quad 3 \quad 2 \quad 1$$

Or within the span of a twelfth:

$$1 \quad 2 \quad 3 \quad 4 \quad 5 \quad 6 \quad 7 \quad 8 \quad 9 \quad 10 \quad 11 \quad 12$$
$$12 \quad 11 \quad 10 \quad 9 \quad 8 \quad 7 \quad 6 \quad 5 \quad 4 \quad 3 \quad 2 \quad 1$$

The theory of counterpoint teaches some further consequences of inversion, e.g., that all perfect intervals, if inverted, remain perfect, while the major ones become minor, the minor major, the augmented intervals become diminished, the diminished augmented, etc.

CHAPTER IV

CLASSIFICATION OF INTERVALS

§ 73. *Consonances and Dissonances*

Intervals may be classified from various points of view. By far the most important angle of consideration, however, is that which divides them according to consonances or dissonances. It should be emphasized that the concept of consonance and dissonance in music must not be confused with that of euphony and cacophony. Only those intervals are to be considered as consonant which, either in their root position or inverted, can be reduced to the simple proportions 1, 2, 3, and 5 in the series of the overtones (cf. § 10). Those intervals, on the other hand, which do not fulfil this requirement are to be considered as dissonant. Accordingly, we obtain the following table:

A. Consonances
1. The prime (1)
2. The octave (2)
3. The fifth (3)
4. The fourth (as inversion of 3)
5. The third (5)
6. The sixth (as inversion of 5)

B. Dissonances
1. The second
2. The seventh
3. All augmented and diminished intervals

§ 74. *Perfect and Imperfect Consonances*

The consonances can be further subdivided into perfect and imperfect ones.

The perfect consonances are: prime, fourth, fifth, and octave.

The imperfect consonances are: the third and the sixth.

This subdivision is based on the following consideration: The perfect intervals, on the one hand, do not tolerate any alteration; or else the consonance is immediately transformed into a dissonance:

Example 101 (135):

In other words, the perfect fourth and fifth are transformed into an augmented fourth and diminished fifth, i.e., dissonances. The perfect intervals are therefore also called "pure" intervals, while the imperfect ones, on the other hand, must be further subdivided into major and minor imperfect intervals, all of which remain consonances, despite the alterations they have undergone.

Example 102 (136):

major, minor   major, minor

THIRD   SIXTH

75. The Special Case of the Perfect Fourth

Among the pure or perfect consonances, the pure fourth constitutes a special case. For in the practice of counterpoint, but only there, it may assume a dissonant character, albeit in one special and exceptional situation. We must, however, leave it to the theory of counterpoint to explain this situation and to prove the dissonant character of the perfect fourth in it.

Theory of Scale-Steps[1]

CHAPTER I

SCALE-STEPS AND HARMONY

§ 76. *The Realization of the Triad*

We have already seen in § 13 how the reality of our triad is founded on a natural association, viz., on the acoustic phenomenon 1:3:5 in the series of overtones.

But in all cases we do not need three voices to produce these consonant intervals; i.e., the concept of the triad is not tied, as one might think, to the concept of real three-phony. Rather it may be fulfilled by two voices, even by a single one. In the latter alternative, Nature as well as art[2] is satisfied if the course of a melody offers to our ear the possibility of connecting with a certain tone its fifth and third, which may make their appearance in the melody by and by.

In the folk song, for example:

Example 103 (137):

our ear will connect the first tone, G, with the B on the first quarter of measure 1 as the third of G. Likewise, it will connect that G with the D on the first quarter of measure 2 as its fifth. Our ear will establish this connection instinctively, but nonetheless in accordance with the demands of Nature. In an analogous way, it will link that first G

[1. Regarding Schenker's concept of *Stufe* (scale-step or harmonic step) cf. Introduction and § 78.]

[2. Which means: The vertical chord belongs to Nature. By unfolding horizontally, melodically, it becomes an element of art.]

with the *C* and *E* of the second half of measure 1 and thus form the concept of another triad. For our ear will miss no opportunity to hear such triads, no matter how far in the background of our consciousness this conception may lie hidden and no matter whether in the plan of the composition it is overshadowed by far more obvious and important relationships.

The harmonic element thus has to be pursued in both directions, the horizontal as well as the vertical.[3]

NOTE

The penetration of the harmonic principle into the horizontal line of the melody has its own history. It certainly would be worth while to trace this history, if only because this would facilitate the solution of many a difficult problem of music history. As is well known, it was only plain chant that was considered to be music, up until the tenth century, which saw the first attempts at polyphony. Plain chant, therefore, is particularly instructive if we want to demonstrate how musical instinct, to begin with, was totally inartistic and only very gradually condensed and rose from a chaos of fog to a principle of art. In the melodies of the first centuries A.D. we generally miss any sign of a formal musical instinct, i.e., those melodies lack the inherent urge toward the fifth and the third which was later recognized as a response to the demands of Nature herself. On the contrary, those melodies appear to have been thrown together in a haphazard and irrational fashion (cf. the discussion of primitive music in § 25), without the guidance of any harmonic or rhythmic principle. Such artistic chaos prevails not only in small melodies, where lack of space as such may have prevented any emphatic unfolding of diverse harmonic or rhythmic relations which might guide our understanding, but also in larger melodies, where such an unfolding would have been expected and obligatory.

If we take a look at the structure of a Gregorian chant, e.g., the melody of the Credo,

[3. This is more than a hint at Schenker's basic principle, the *Auskomponierung* or unfolding. For a still more explicit statement of this principle cf. §§ 115 ff.]

Example 104 (138):

we must ask ourselves a number of questions: Which tone here is the central or basic one, the first note, *G*, or the second, *E*? If it were *G*, how would we have to explain the fact that the declamation attaches so little importance to the tone *D*, which is the fifth of *G* (though used here as the fourth below)? How would we have to explain that the third below the *G*, *E*, carries much more weight than the *D* and that, finally, the melody comes to its conclusion on the *A*? If, on the other hand, we chose *E* as the central tone, what are we to make of the notes *F* and *D* in their present functions, and what of the final *A*? Or should we assume, in our search for a central tone, a third possibility? Which one?

The melody of the Gloria likewise lacks any organizational principle:

Example 105 (139):

Again, the point of departure is different from the point of arrival, and it is not demonstrable, to say the least, whether *F* is the central note, in which case the *C–F* would have to be considered to form one triad and *C–E–G* a second one, or whether we are dealing here with a series of tones dominated by *C*. The irrationality of this melody, too, may be blamed on its brevity, which could hardly harbor more than one or two fifth-relationships. The situation would be quite different if the melody consisted of a large number of tones which could give rise to several other relationships, so that, by contrast and a higher degree of differentiation, some clarity and order could be introduced into the series of notes. Considering that the mere comprehension of a wider space, of a longer series of thoughts, would be impossible without a certain articulation into several smaller interrelated groups, we might conclude that in planning a longer series of tones the composer must also have at his disposal some sort of principle, no matter whether conscious or subconscious, which would guide him in arranging his series of tones perspicuously and intelligibly. In other words, the danger of maintaining irrationality is greater in a brief series of tones than in a longer one.

But if we now take a look at a longer melody, e.g., the hymn "Crux fidelis":

Example 106 (140):

Crux fi - de - lis   in - ter om - nes Ar - bor u - na   no - bi - lis:

Nul-la   sil - va ta - lem pro-fert, Fron-de, flo-re, ger-mi-ne:

we realize that in that early phase musical instinct was so meager that one did not escape composing even a comparatively large quantity of tones in a fashion no less irrational than we had to observe in the briefer melodies. We have to accept the fact that the majority of Gregorian chants lacked any guiding principle, thus placing themselves outside the scope of art in the intrinsically musical and formally technical sense.

It was due to the suggestiveness of religion and the power of ingrown habits that such inartistic melodies could be memorized at all. Incidentally, a caveat may be in order lest we believe that the endurance of a melody (or of a work of art in general) depends altogether on its intrinsic value; for there are a good number of other suggestive forces which may contribute to the preservation of such works.

It is likely, on the other hand, that the disorderly character of those melodies often enough entailed disturbing consequences. It was difficult for the memory to preserve and transmit them correctly—whence some doubts as to the authenticity of longer melodies will always be in order. Difficulties of this kind (perhaps even more so than any other reason) may have contributed to the creation of the tonal systems which facilitated a firmer and more lasting grip on those melodies. It would almost seem to me as if we had to recognize in the old church modes—despite their unquestionable links with Greek theory—a casuistic, nay, mnemotechnical, device for orienting ourselves in melodies which lacked any other guiding principle. This may explain the well-known fact that the modes, in their original form, were concerned only with the horizontal direction, i.e., the melody, a tendency which left its traces even much later, when the technique of counterpoint had long since accustomed the ear to perceive harmonies in the vertical direction. Thus it did not seem unreasonable, even as late as in the fifteenth and sixteenth centuries, to take it for granted, for example, that a four-part composition could be written simultaneously in four different modes. For the concept of harmonic clarification, whether in the horizontal or in the vertical direction, was totally alien to the ancient system. A *cantus firmus,* for instance, like the following:

Example 107 (141):

could be accepted as Phrygian merely on account of its opening and closing note, *E,* while our instinct for harmony certainly would place it in the Aeolian system.

A long period of progressive development was needed for the artistic instinct to mature to the point where it could also reflect the harmonic point of view in the melody itself. How this came to pass —certainly in part at least under the influence of polyphony—we shall show in the following chapter.

§ 77. *The Resulting Overabundance and Threatening*
Confusion in the Tone Relationships

If our ear is thus compelled by Nature, is it not liable to be utterly confused by the abundance of potential triads? If, in the horizontal as well as in the vertical direction, each root tone seeks its fifth and its third, and each fifth responds to its root tone, where is a plan for our ear to adopt such as to establish order in this infinite sum of eternally busy relationships?

We need only recall the monodic solo for English horn from *Tristan and Isolde,* which we quoted in § 50. Fifth-relationships are established between the following sets of tones: *F* and *C,* in measure 1; *D*-flat and *A*-flat (even if, in this case, in inverted form, i.e., as a fourth) in measure 2; the eighth-notes, *D*-flat and *G, G* and *C, C* and *F,* in measure 3; and, in the same measure, the eighth-note *F* and the dotted quarter-note *B*-flat; in measure 4, finally, the *A*-flat constitutes the complementary minor third to the tones *F* and *C* introduced in measure 1; measures 5 and 6 contain completed triads, etc.

And what abundance of fifth-relationships do we not find in measures 15 ff.! Each moment of the melisma is teaming with fifths—how are we to perceive all these, and how to establish an order among them? And what if the matter be further complicated by the harmonic structure of a composition, and our ear is occupied, to boot, by the fifths and thirds of the vertical?

Now then, the artist has power enough so to order all these relationships that only a few of them are perceptible in the foreground of the composition, while the others do their work more discretely in the background. Our ear is as able and willing to follow this gradation of effects as the latter arose spontaneously in the mind of the composer. The most important device aiding both the composer and the listener to find his bearings is the concept of the so-called "scale-step."

§ 78. *The Scale-Step as Guiding Device as*
Contrasted with the Triad

But my concept of the scale-step, if it is to serve its purpose, is far loftier and far more abstract than the conventional one. For not every triad must be considered as a scale-step; and it is most important to distinguish between *C* as the root tone of a triad and *C* as a scale-step.

The scale-step is a higher and more abstract unit. At times it may even comprise several harmonies, each of which could be considered individually as an independent triad or seventh-chord; in other words: even if, under certain circumstances, a certain number of harmonies look like independent triads or seventh-chords, they may nonetheless add up, in their totality, to one single triad, e.g., C–E–G, and they would have to be subsumed under the concept of this triad on *C* as a scale-step. The scale-step asserts its higher or more general character by comprising or summarizing the individual phenomena and embodying their intrinsic unity in one single striad.[4]

NOTE

It may be of some interest to note that this abstract harmonic entity, the scale-step, had already come up in the era of pure counterpoint. We should keep in mind, however, that at that time it referred only to the fifth tone of the system, i.e., our modern dominant. Fux, for example, has the following passage on the three-part fugue in *Gradus ad Parnassum,* a work which we have already had occasion to quote:

Do you not know that a formal close must bring the major third, to be followed by the octave? A feigned close, on the contrary, brings the minor third instead of the major, and in so doing, betrays the ear, which would have expected a formal close. Thus the expectation of the listener is belied. The Italians, accordingly, have called this close *inganno.*

Example 108 (142):

[4. This paragraph also is basic for the development of Schenker's theory—the ideal significance of the scale-step and its practical realization through voice-leading, this being the meaning of the "individual phenomena" to which reference is made in the text. Cf. Example 112; cf., furthermore, § 83 and, finally, § 124 on the $^6_4$ chord on the V step.]

The formal close may be avoided, furthermore, if the major third is maintained in the upper voice while the bass proceeds to form a consonance different from the octave. E.g.,

Example 109 (143):

When there are more than two voices involved, the effect is even more gracious. . . .

You know full well that the closes in a two-part composition, by their very nature, differ from the formal closes, in so far as they are composed of the seventh and sixth, or the second and third, and are of brief duration. If you give the matter a closer look, you will find that those closes which are constructed upon the seventh and sixth or the second and third are to be considered as approximations to formal closes rather than formal closes themselves, as they give rise to a formal close when a third part is added. The following, e.g.,

Example 110 (144):

are approximations to formal closes. But if the third part is added,

Example 111 (145):

they are transformed into formal closes.

To this third part, then, which corresponds to the fifth tone of the system, Fux ascribes the effect of a definite formal close, in contrast to the mere "approximations" sensed in the sequences 2–1 and 7–8. This alone proves that the masters of counterpoint had a special feeling for the importance of the fifth tone. From there, very little is missing to reach a full understanding of this tone as a "scale-step."

Even more striking is the following construction, which, to begin with, was conceived merely in terms of counterpoint:

Example 112 (146):

This construction, as is well known, is generally considered as a precursor of our pedal point. But what is of even greater interest to us in the present context is the technique which enables a tone to gather, so to speak, a large sequence of contrapuntal parts into a unity, this being the proper function of the "scale-step."

One might even write a history of the V scale-step. The other tones of the system—with the exception of the tonic—did not encourage the concept of the scale-step, at least not to the same extent and at so early a time as did the V. The technique of counterpoint, to which the next chapter will be dedicated, provides an explanation for this fact.

§ 79. *How To Recognize Scale-Steps: Some Hints*

But how are we to recognize a scale-step if it does not coincide in all cases with the graspable phenomenon of the triad (or the seventh-chord, as the case may be)?

There are no rules which could be laid down once and for all; for, by virtue of their abstract nature, the rules flow, so to speak, from the spirit and intention of each individual composition. I shall quote, therefore, a number of examples conveying a number of hints as to how the presence of a scale-step could be recognized—without making any claim to exhaustiveness.

Example 113 (147). J. S. Bach, Organ Prelude, C Minor:

1. Our instinct justly rebels against hearing, at the asterisked place, an independent scale-step, and this despite the fact that three parts have clearly converged here into a (diminished) triad.

It was the composer himself who has indicated to our instinct the right way: for he continued the A-flat, tying it over in one of the middle voices; and by this device he makes it perfectly clear that we are not dealing here with a new scale-step but merely with a triad formed by the parallel movement, necessarily in sixth-chords, of three neighbor notes, E, G, B-flat.[5] It is more important, however, to note that even if that A-flat were not held over, the asterisked sixth-chord would have to be taken for a passing event, not a new scale-step.

Here is another example:

Example 114 (148). J. S. Bach, Organ Prelude, E Minor:

The construct, F-sharp, A, B, D-sharp, in measure 2 dissembles a seventh-chord on B, in its second inversion. Yet the E, which is continued on each second and fourth eighth-note in the bass, as well as in each third beat of the descant, prevents us from hearing that seventh-chord as such, i.e., as an independent V step in E minor. Correct hearing reveals only one scale-step here, viz., the I (E, G, B), whose root tone, E, and fifth, B, are continued, while the F-sharp and A, in measure 2, are to be considered as passing notes[6] (in thirds or tenths, respectively). This is shown by the following picture:

[5. In other words, a result of voice-leading.]
[6. This too, then, is a result of voice-leading.]

Example 115 (149):

I - - - -

A similar situation is presented by the following example:

Example 116 (150). J. S. Bach, Chaconne in D Minor for Violin Solo:

I - - - - - - -

IV - V

It is especially the *D* in measure 2 of this example, which, by following immediately upon the sixth-chord, *E, G, C*-sharp, makes it clear at once that these three notes are passing notes and do not announce at this point any VII (or V) step and that we must hear the whole deployment of harmonies in measures 1–3 as constituting only one scale-step, viz., the unfolded I in D minor.[7]

Bach's technique creates a peculiar poetic charm where he tries to soften the effect of a scale-step intentionally by holding over a tone in one of the parts, although the presence of a new scale-step may be clearly indicated by other signs, e.g., the logic of inversion and form. A sort of twilight is thus shed on the scale-step in question, as shown in the following example:

Example 117 (151). J. S. Bach, Sonata, C Major, Violin Solo:

I   VI   II   V   I

Full justice would be done to the V step only if the last sixteenth-notes had been set as follows:

[7. Here Schenker is already quite explicit about the "auskomponierte Stufe in d-moll," the unfolded I in D minor!]

Example 118 (152):

2. But even in those cases where the composer has failed to guide us by holding over a note in one of the parts, we must heed carefully whatever other hints there may be to dissuade us from identifying a triad with a scale-step.

Example 119 (153). J. S. Bach, *St. Matthew Passion*, Aria, F-Sharp Minor:

Below the asterisk we find a complete triad on C-sharp. This could very well represent the V step. The preceding and firmly established rhythm of descending fifths, I–IV–VII–III, etc., however, directs the listener most clearly to consider this triad as a merely passing configuration of three parts, which certainly does not possess the weight of a scale-step. The inversion of the fifths thus favors such a conception, quite apart from the fact that it seems superfluous to assume the presence of a V here, as the following measure already introduces this step, so to speak, *ex officio*. Each of the three parts has its own reason for passing that asterisked point. The bass voice goes through the C-sharp as a passing note between the VI, *D*, and its next goal, the IV, *B;* the suspension, *G*, in the soprano is resolved into

F-sharp, after going over *E*-sharp; the middle part, finally, follows the soprano in a parallel motion of sixths, leading from the suspension, *E*, to *A*, through *G*-sharp. The convergence of the three notes, then, must be taken for what it is: a chance product of contrapuntal movement.[8]

Rhythm, likewise, is decisive for the scale-steps in the following example:

Example 120 (154). J. S. Bach, Organ Prelude, C Minor:

In this example, too, the broad disposition of the IV and the Phrygian II (*D*-flat) in the first four measures is an inducement to conceive of each of the following measures as based on only one scale-step, in spite of the individual harmonic phenomena on each quarter-beat, which, strictly speaking, could be considered as independent steps.

[8. Here again we should like to draw the reader's special attention to Schenker's expression *kontrapunktischer Zufall*, "a chance product of contrapuntal movement."]

3. One more example:

Example 121 (155). J. S. Bach, Organ Prelude, C Major:

The third part of measure 3 seemingly forms an independent dominant seventh-chord. The immediately following measure 4, however, belies this conception. While continuing the canon technique, Bach introduces here a new counterpoint (eighth-notes) in the soprano. The independent meaning of the last three eighth-notes, which are under consideration here, is thereby canceled. For the soprano, by jumping through all the notes of the triad *C, E, G,* gives to the passage a broad and passing character, determining our conception, so to speak, retroactively. Thus the composer's own interpretation has indicated to our ear a course different from the one we were about to choose.

The meaning the composer wants to convey, which in the last example was revealed to us by the contrapuntal context, may be revealed in other cases by means of a motivic parallelism, a formal similarity:

Example 122 (156). Schumann, "Davidsbündlertänze," op. 6, No. 5:

In the second-to-last measure Schumann presents to us, in constructing a perfect cadence in D major, the sequence IV–V in quarter-notes. This fact, and this fact alone, induces us to assume the same rhythm of scale-steps in measure 3 of this example, where otherwise it would have been far from necessary to consider the dominant of A $\frac{major}{minor}$ an independent step. In a different context this construct could have remained in the background as a transitory phenomenon of passing notes. The motivic counterpart in the second-to-last measure, however, sheds, *ex post facto*, a peculiar light on it. And, considered from this more advanced point, it seems artistically more well-rounded to hear in that dominant harmony an independent step, inserted between two tonic chords, rather than a merely passing harmonic phenomenon.

4. The following example is an excerpt from Chopin's Polonaise, op. 26, No. 1:

Example 123 (157):

The listener is perfectly justified in repudiating F-sharp minor as an independent key determining the content of measure 2. This measure is to be heard rather as dissembling that key with the help of chromatic devices, while, in reality, we remain on the IV step of C-sharp minor. Now, if we reject the alternative of F-sharp minor, it becomes illicit to interpret the harmony on the second beat of this measure as a true dominant seventh-chord, because this chord would needs belong to F-sharp minor.

Thus we see how the rejection of a certain key, *e contrario*, encourages the assumption of a scale-step only, which, in turn, prevents us from considering the individual phenomena it comprises as independent scale-steps.

5. Occasionally the composer uses a way of notation which orients the reader or performer as to the composer's own feeling with regard to the scale-steps:

Example 124 (158). Chopin, Prelude, op. 28, No. 4:

Obviously, Chopin wants us to feel only the tonic all through the first four measures. This results from the fact that he studiously avoids writing D-sharp, instead of E-flat, in measure 2: thus averting even the optical appearance of the V step in E minor; and the broad flow of the I tonic remains uninterrupted. By analogy, we should feel the effect of the subdominant alone, during the next five measures, followed by the dominant in measure 10. All individual phenomena within the broad deployment of scale-steps, manifold though their meaning, considered absolutely, may be, represent passing chords,[9] not scale-steps.

6. The following example is an excerpt from *Tristan and Isolde* (orchestra score, p. 313; piano score, p. 180):

Example 125 (159). Wagner, *Tristan and Isolde:*

If, to begin with, we yield without prejudice to the impression created by the first violin, we shall note that the projection of the melody in the horizontal direction clearly results in the major triad

[9. Schenker here indicates the difference between merely passing chords, as they may result from voice-leading, and real scale-steps. His later concept of "prolongation" is here clearly anticipated, and even clearer in § 110, Example 171.]

on *F*, already within measure 1. In measure 3 we hear the last quarter-note, *F*-sharp, obviously effecting a modulation to G minor, a turn which is confirmed in measure 5, in so far as the motif of measure 1 appears to be repeated within the minor triad on G. Hence —still restricting our observations to the horizontal—one might feel induced to assume here a true G minor. The tone *E*, however, i.e., the first sixteenth of the fourth quarter-beat, creates an obstacle. In consideration of that *E*, it seems more correct to see in measures 5 and 6 the II step in F major. We are dealing, then, not with a new key but with the deployment of a scale-step, which is followed, in accordance with the principle of inversion, by the V step in measures 7 and 8. This analysis holds as long as we restrict our observations to the melodic dimension.

If we now proceed to an analysis of the vertical, we find Wagner, to put it succinctly, successfully endeavoring as far as possible to confirm in his vertical harmonies the chords he unfolded in the horizontal. I should like to disregard here the pedal point on *C*, on which all eight measures are constructed, whereas I should like to draw the reader's special attention to the content of the horn part. With the following figure:

Example 126 (160):

this part fastens measures 3 and 4 on the ground of the tonic; measures 7 and 8, on the contrary, on that of the dominant. Thus it brings the most decisive contribution toward defining precisely the respective scale-steps. It is only measures 5 and 6 which remain, so to speak, in suspense, in so far as horizontally these measures result in a II step, while the vertical (note especially the movement of the violas) constitutes a VII step. Whatever the compromise between the two dimensions here may be, it is certain that the composer, firmly anchored in this basic understanding of the scale-steps, is the more unhampered in unfolding the various parts of his composition. These, as they come and go, may form the most diverse triads and seventh-chords such as we know, in different context, to possess independent meaning and value. In this particular context, however, it would be useless to ascribe to each individual phenomenon the significance of an independent scale-step.

The following passage from *Tristan and Isolde* (piano score, p. 190; orchestra score, p. 316) corresponds, as a parallel, to the example just analyzed:

Example 127 (161):

Here, too, we are spared the trouble of hearing each individual phenomenon independently. It will be more correct, on the contrary, to explain them as mere chance products of free voice-leading. Such an interpretation becomes possible because Wagner clings, without any ambiguity, to the tonic in measures 1 and 2, to the VI step in measure 3, to the II in measure 4, returning, finally, to the I in measures 5 and 6.

§ 80. *Definition of Scale-Step Independent of Time Factor*

From what has been said so far, it should be clear enough that the time occupied by a scale-step is variable. The listener must not be deterred, accordingly, either by excessive length or by overmodest brevity, from assuming a scale-step if there are other indications in the composition which plead for such an assumption. We may recall, for example, the gigantic proportion of the E-flat major step in the Introduction to Wagner's *Rheingold* or the broad deployment of scale-steps in the Prelude to *Die Walküre,* etc.

§ 81. *Summarizing the Characteristics of the Scale-Step*

What is the result of all these observations? In our theory of intervals we have set down the principle that not every vertical coincidence of tones as such must be considered an interval. The same is true in the case of triads: not all triads have the same weight and importance. No matter what indications the composer may give to the listener—by holding over a tone, in the rhythm, by motivic parallelisms, or in other ways which defy any attempt to define them[10]—the scale-step remains, at any rate, a superior factor in composition, a factor dominating the individual harmonic phenomena.[11]

§ 82. *Identity of Step Progression and the Progression by Fifths*

The scale-steps are identical, rather, with those fifths which, as we have seen in § 16, are linked together by the principle of development or evolution in the ascending direction and inversion or involution in the descending direction and which constitute the foundation of our tonal system.

It should be noted incidentally that all the modifications to which the progression by fifths may be subject, as we shall see with some detail in §§ 125-28, apply equally to step progression.

The scale-steps, to use a metaphor, have intercourse only among themselves, and such intercourse must be kept free from interference by those triads which do not constitute scale-steps, i.e., fifths of a superior order.

Granted that the triad must be considered as one particular aspect of the scale-step, in so far as its real root tone coincides with the scale-step as we conceive it; yet a triad of this kind, if it appears *as such,* is subject to the whim of fancy, whereas that other kind of

10. For an additional indication, viz., form as indication, cf. §§ 118 ff.

[11. Cf. §'55.]

triad, which has been lifted to the rank of a scale-step, guides the artist with the force and compulsion of Nature so that he has no choice but to rise and descend on the scale of fifths as may be required by the natural course of development and inversion.[12]

A beautiful example of an almost parallel progression of steps and triads is afforded by Schubert's song, "Die Meeresstille." And yet, what a difference, even in this case, between the real phenomenon of the triad and the purely spiritual significance of the scale-steps which, behind them, inspires every form of motion.[13]

§ 83. The Scale-Step as the Hallmark of Harmony

Owing to its superior, more abstract, character, the scale-step is the hallmark of harmony. For it is the task of harmony to instruct the disciple of art about those abstract forces which partly correspond to Nature, partly surge from our need for mental associations, in accordance with the purpose of art. Thus the theory of harmony is an abstraction, inclosed in the most secret psychology of music.[14]

[12. In this paragraph Schenker has a presentiment of his later concept of *Schichten* or "layers" (cf. Introduction). It is true that, for the time being, he distinguishes only triads, composed of passing notes, and scale-steps progressing by fifths. He has not arrived as yet at the concept of *Übertragung der Ursatzformen,* "transference of *Ursatz* forms." Nevertheless, we should note the expression "The scale-steps have intercourse only among themselves." Does it not imply a clear renouncement of the so-called "harmonic analysis," which, disregarding context and continuity, attaches the label of "chord" to any simultaneity of tones and, accordingly, recognizes only juxtapositions, one chord following the other, and admits, at most, a very scant hierarchical order obtained by means of the "auxiliary dominant."]

[13. Schenker first considers the "almost parallel progression of steps and triads." Immediately afterward, however, he indicates the purely spiritual significance of the scale-step, which inspires all motion (i.e., voice-leading; see sketch of the bass line in Appendix I, Example A8).]

[14. Cf. § 78.]

CHAPTER II

SCALE-STEP AND COUNTERPOINT

§ 84. *The Lack of Scale-Steps in Strict Counterpoint*

The theory of counterpoint offers an entirely different picture. As I shall show in my forthcoming work on counterpoint, the transcendent powers of the scale-step are absent here. The ear is directed, rather, to follow the movement of two, three, or four voices from chord to chord, without any regard for the meaning of the individual chords; and such movement is pursued, above all, by means of a beautiful fluent development of the voices and the principle of the most natural solution of the most naturally conceived situations. As an illustration I should like to quote an exercise from Fux's *Gradus ad Parnassum:*

Example 128 (162):

Cantus firmus

We see here three voices in their natural flow. Each one follows its own most plausible course, motivated by various reasons, the discussion of which belongs in the theory of counterpoint; and they all unite in chords, without any intention of inducing step progression, of expressing any definite meaning.

§ 85. *The Principle of Contrapuntal Voice-leading without Step Progression Applied Also in Free Composition*

The prime principle of counterpoint as we see it demonstrated above in the frame of eleven measures—the greatest length attainable by a *cantus firmus* may extend to approximately fifteen to sixteen measures—has been adopted fully by the theory of free composition. No matter whether the style of a composition is strict or free, the parts remain duty-bound to move along as if their meaning as scale-steps counted at first for nothing. In reality, however, the tactics of voice-leading become ever freer to the extent to which, in free composition, there erupts suddenly the force of the scale-step, under whose cover the individual parts may maneuver in a less inhibited way even than in strict composition. The scale-steps then resemble powerful projector lights: in their illuminated sphere the parts go through their evolution in a higher and freer contrapuntal sense, uniting in harmonic chords, which, however, never become end in themselves but always result from the free movement.

We may remember here the examples from Wagner quoted earlier (§ 79) and compare them to Fux's exercise as quoted in § 84. Who would ascribe to the triad in measure 2 of Fux's example the meaning of a III step? Who would hear the triad of measure 3 as a VII step? Are we to understand, perchance, the following development as a progression: I, II, III, V, IV, I, V, I? Or would not the instinct of any musical person rebel against such a forced conception? And why? Obviously, for the only reason that this sequence of bass notes represents but an irrational to-and-fro, irreconcilable with the nature of step progression (cf. § 82), while the same sequence may already lay claim to the title of melody, if we disregard the lack of rhythmic organization. Furthermore, each individual triad fails to adduce any further proof for the rightfulness of its claim to this or that scale-step.[1]

Now if each individual triad fails to prove its significance as a scale-step, while, on the other hand, there exists no superior plan which, justified by its own logic, might orient us as to the step progression, whence shall we gather the courage to talk ourselves into the belief that we are faced here with scale-steps and step progression? Would this not be a falsification, a violation of our musical instinct?

If we now consider the free composition in the Wagner example, is not the situation identically the same? Must we, for the sake of a theory, search triad after triad for its meaning as scale-step—leaving

[1. Schenker here anticipates the idea of the unfolding of the bass voice. This is indicated with even greater clarity in § 88, p. 172: "Or . . . the bass voice gets emancipated."]

aside, for the moment, the pedal point—and come to the result of the following step progression, e.g.:

Measure 1: I, ♮IV⁷, V♭⁷, in F major?
Measure 3: I, VII⁷, I, II in F major; VII³ in G minor?
Measure 4: I in G minor, V in F major; I in E-flat minor; I again in F major, ♮IV, —?

I am convinced that anybody would gladly dispense with such a superficial definition of tonal events.

The analogy between the examples from Wagner and Fux is thus closer than one might have thought at first glance. Is it not equally impossible, in both cases, to conceive of the individual triads as scale-steps? In either case are not the parts urging us to deliver them from any responsibility as scale-steps in so far as each harmonic coincidence, taken individually, is concerned? In both cases, is it not the prime contrapuntal principle of voice-leading which dominates the development?[2]

§ 86. *Freedom in Voice-leading Increased in Free Composition, Owing to Scale-Step*

It might be objected that, in spite of what has been said, there is an essential difference between the two examples: Fux employs only consonant triads, whereas in Wagner's example the parts form dissonant seventh-chords as well and enter into all sorts of modulatory relations. This difference, however, is only apparent. The application, in both cases, of the principle of voice-leading, which liberates each individual harmony from the burden of having and proving the significance of a scale-step, assimilates the two quoted examples much more decisively than does the application of two different methods, viz., the employment of consonances only in the one, and of consonances and dissonances in the other, seems to separate them. In fact, Wagner's method represents a development, an extension of Fux's method, not its abandonment or opposite.[3] If both

[2. Schenker alludes here to the principle of "unfolding," i.e., the idea of the scale-steps (harmonies) which are realized, through voice-leading, in the temporal expansion of a work of art.]

[3. Free composition represents a prolongation of strict composition; the laws of strict composition retain their validity, albeit in modified form. This concept, the germ of which

methods identically result in a liberation from the concept of the scale-step, what difference does it make if in the one case only consonances are employed, while in the other both consonances and dissonances make their appearance?

§ 87. *The Physiognomy of Strict Counterpoint Explained by the Absence of Scale-Steps*

There remains the question: Why does Fux restrict himself to the use of consonant conformations, while Wagner's style includes dissonances as well?

There is an easy answer: Fux's example is but an exercise, while the excerpt from Wagner represents a work of art. Such an answer, however, must be rejected as superficial, to say the least, or as outright childish. The real explanation must rather be sought in the following: As I shall show in my theory of counterpoint, the principles of pure counterpoint can be demonstrated only on a melody suspended in strict and constant rhythmic equilibrium. Lest the problem of voice-leading be complicated by additional difficulties, the contrapuntal exercise must be constructed, first of all, in such a way as to avoid any real melodic combinations and rhythmic variety. Such combinations and varieties not only might distract from the main problem but often would, of necessity, demand exceptions to the rules of counterpoint, merely by virtue of their individual character, i.e., owing to their individual melodic or rhythmic traits. Even before grasping in its entirety the effects of voice-leading in a two-, three-, or four-part composition, we would be forced at once to concede exceptions as the individuality of the melody and rhythm might demand. It soon became obvious that this way of teaching was bound to have gravely disorienting effects. Hence the practical idea, adopted at a very early date—the historical occasion of its adoption will be discussed elsewhere—of choosing, for purposes of demonstration, a small and rhythmically rigid melody, the so-called *cantus firmus*. Its equilibrium enables the student to concentrate above all, nay, exclusively, on the effects of voice-leading. This equilibrium,

can be found here, was developed in Schenker's later theories in the concept of the "layers" of a composition (background, middle-ground, foreground). Cf. note to § 82 and *Free Composition*.]

however, would certainly be upset if the vertical coincidence of the parts resulted in dissonances as well as consonances. For the dissonant harmonies would entail a closer combination of certain measures, which would thereby stand out from the rest of the composition as a closed group, as a minor unit all by itself. Such units would, no doubt, upset the equilibrium, as we indicated earlier.[4] ☆

§ 88. *The Physiognomy of Free Composition Determined by the Scale-Steps*

Where, on the contrary, the melody is constructed freely and displays rhythmic variety, no such equilibrium is postulated. In free composition those minor units just bubble up, various rhythms compete with one another—and the principle of voice-leading has become much freer, accordingly. These newly won liberties, however, can be justified and understood only from the viewpoint of the scale-step. For it is the concept of the scale-step which has given rise to those minor units. Owing to their immanent logic of development, the scale-steps unfold the full variety inherent in free composition, in accordance with their mysterious laws. Thus they not only are responsible for the rise of free composition but, at the same time, render the technique of voice-leading both freer and more audacious. This style, accordingly, attaches to the individual chords even less significance than they had in strict composition; for the concept of the scale-step guarantees a correct understanding of all motion, from one scale-step to the next. Free composition thus has supplied an element that had been lacking in strict composition: a force, so to speak, external and superior, which would have co-ordinated the motion of chords within those, at most, sixteen bars and clarified its meaning. The scale-step now constitutes that force which unambiguously joins several chords into one unit, in whose frame voice-leading can run its course all the more freely.

Thus free composition differs from strict composition, in so far as the former possesses scale-steps, which articulate its content, and in so far as it allows for a much wider range of freedom in voice-leading. These two distinctions are intertwined, for the greater freedom in

☆ [4. Considering the current confusion in the study of strict counterpoint, the wholesomeness of this paragraph cannot be stressed too much.]

voice-leading is so clarified by the principle of the scale-step that a misunderstanding can never arise. To put it in simpler words: As compared to strict composition, free composition has a richer content, more measures, more units, more rhythm. This surplus, however, can be gained only by the force of the scale-steps. But where there are scale-steps, the motion of voice-leading is liberated. Free composition, then, appears as an extension of strict composition:[5] an extension with regard to both the quantity of tone material and the principle of its motion. What is responsible for all these extensions is the concept of the scale-step. Under its aegis, counterpoint and free composition are wedded.

What has been said so far may be further clarified, perhaps, by an analogy: Where in strict composition, we have notes consonant to those of the *cantus firmus,* we have, in free composition, the scale-step. Where, in strict composition, we have a dissonant passing note, we have, in free composition, free voice-leading, a series of intermediate chords, unfolding in free motion.

Or let us have a look at the following contrapuntal example:

Example 129 (163):

Cantus firmus

Here we are dealing with a *cantus firmus,* overarched by two contrapuntal voices. One of these voices proceeds in half-notes, the other in quarter-notes. Each one of them, considered in itself, goes a way which would be allowed even in strict composition, although each one of them brings dissonances as well as consonances. But the dissonances are formed by passing notes (the second half-note and the third quarter-note, respectively). In so far as we consider each contrapuntal voice separately, the result of voice-leading is satisfactory The situation changes as soon as we examine all three voices in their

[5. The concept of prolongation is here clearly expressed.]

conjunctions. From the point of view of strict composition, satisfactory voice-leading would require a full consonance at the upstroke, i.e., at the second half-note or third quarter-note, respectively, this being the most direct and natural postulate of three-part composition. We see, however, that in our example this postulate is disregarded. It is only the relation between each individual voice and the *cantus firmus* that is emphasized here—so much so that the required threefold conjunction cannot be reached. The example, therefore, probably exceeds the scope of strict composition and belongs in the sphere of free composition. For here the note of the *cantus firmus* is replaced by a root tone or scale-step, and each individual part is logically referred merely to that root tone or scale-step, while the dissonant relationships of the contrapuntal voices among themselves are of no consequence. This does not in any way entail a loss in clarity; for each individual part, at least, is sufficiently explained and supported.[6] Even more: far from obscuring the unitary character of the whole complex of tones, the independence of individual counterpoints results in the creation of a superior kind of complex. This very friction, which is caused by independent voice-leading, and the psychological labor required to overcome it reveal to our mind the goal of unity, once reached, in all its beauty.

If the argumentation offered in this chapter and the previous one have clarified in the mind of the reader the concept of the scale-step and of free composition, it should not be difficult now for him to appreciate the particular beauty of the following examples:

Example 130 (164). Beethoven, Diabelli Variations, op. 120, Var. XV:

[6. This phrase, "for each individual part, at least, is sufficiently explained and supported," likewise anticipates Schenker's later developments.]

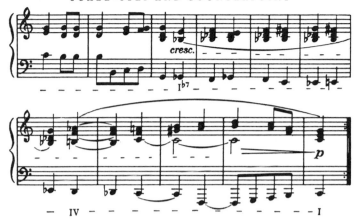

In measures 8–12 we see what kind of chords a scale-step can drive forward, in free motion, without leading us into the temptation of interpreting each chord individually. The concept of the I step as here quoted is based, incidentally, on the concept of tonicalization as we shall explain it in §§ 136 ff. But it should be noted also how the melodic line itself, in moving from *E* to *G*, as the third and fifth of the C major triad, contributes its share of the proof of this interpretation.

Turning, now, to the next example (Example 131), we should consider the voice-leading in measure 3, especially the configuration on the second quarter-note, which must be explained as based on the dominant *A*-flat chord, with reference to which all three voices, in three counterpoints, go their regular ways, paying no attention to the dissonant collision.[7]

Example 131 (165). J. S. Bach, *Well-tempered Clavier*, Vol. I, Fugue, B-Flat Minor:

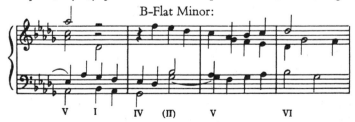

[7. Beethoven, it seems, was particularly attracted by this fugue. Nottebohm (*Beethoveniana*, II, 350) quotes from Beethoven's sketches measures 29-31 and 61-62, which were commented upon by Schenker in *Yearbook*, II, 32-33 (cf., furthermore, Example 232).]

Even more than that. The scale-step may induce the effect of poetic vision, apparently beyond the reach of any rules. Just such an effect is achieved, for example, in Beethoven's Piano Sonata, op. 81*a* ("Les Adieux"), toward the end of the first movement; or in his *Third Symphony*, in the first movement, just before the recapituation:

Example 132 (166). Beethoven, Piano Sonata, op. 81*a:*

Example 133 (167). Beethoven, *Third Symphony:*

In the first case the power of the scale-step carries that constellation of changing note on the strong beat which is so expressive and coincides, in measures 9–12 of our example, with the *E*-flat and *G* as the representatives of the I step.

The second case, if considered merely technically, may be reduced, basically, to a combination between a dominant seventh-chord and a $^6_4$ chord (measures 5 and 6), whereby the seventh, *A*-flat, is tied over. This phenomenon is quite common, the seventh appearing either as passing note or as an unprepared suspension, as shown in the following example:

Example 134 (168):

It is true, however, that in the symphony itself this basic technical idea hardly penetrates to the surface of consciousness. And this for two reasons: on the one hand, the idea is realized here, so to speak, in enlarged proportion; on the other hand, the phenomenon, which in reality should be understood as a passing note or as a suspension, seems to be unfolded here in the symphony's main motif itself, anticipated, poetically divined, expressed with matchless originality. The enlargement of the preparation, however, was possible only within a largely conceived scale-step. In other words, it was only on the basis of this enlargement that the poetical momentum could be conceived and expressed.[8]

NOTE

We have already shown that the development of the scale-step concept runs parallel with the development of content in composition. I may claim, therefore, that, historically speaking, the development of the scale-step coincides with the development of content, i.e., with the development of the melody in the horizontal direction. For the main problem of musical development is to devise the formal-technical means to obtain the greatest possible sum total of content. It does not matter what force has brought about recognition of this problem; nor does it matter how this problem has been kept burning and alive in the long run. Perhaps we are faced here with the innate playfulness of man; or perhaps it is rather an expression of the general natural law of growth, which we perceive everywhere as governing the creations of Nature, as well as of man. However this may be, the technical means for the enlargement of content had to be thought out step by step.

During the early period of polyphony (say, in the ninth and tenth centuries) the situation in this respect may have been as follows: In so far as the melody was the property of the church, the limits of its length simply could not be trespassed upon. In other words, it was

[8. Cf. *Yearbook*, III, 52.]

out of the question to extend the length of a melody, which is what ought to have been done most urgently. In what concerns the ecclesiastical jubilations and the folk songs which could be considered in this context, we lack the appropriate documentation to enable us to reach a closer understanding. It may be assumed, however, that they have contributed to the development of harmonic feeling, as manifested, for example, in the melodic unfolding of a major or minor triad or in the discovery of the Ionian and Aeolian systems themselves (cf. note to § 76)—rather than to the development of melodic length as such. In the face of the inviolability of the given melodies, our problem thus appeared insoluble, at least by any direct means. But the human spirit, driven by the urge to grow, knew how to break this impasse indirectly. Thus polyphony was invented. To the dimension given by the horizontal line, the width, another dimension, the vertical or depth, was added; and, despite the narrowness of the barriers, a new and wide space was conquered for the free play of creative imagination. Depth made up, as a felicitously deceptive substitute, for the lack of greater length. We need not recount here what pains were taken in elaborating the idea of polyphony during the following centuries, from the organum to the descant to the faux-bourdon to the creation of true counterpoint; for any music history accounts for these developments with adequate detail. It was that labor, however, as well as the first joy over the discovery, which induced the composers of that period to overlook, for the time being, the important sacrifices which were imposed on the melody by the new technique of polyphony. The first principle of counterpoint, according to which every note of the cantus must rest on a complete triad or must at least form part of such a triad, already entailed the very evil consequence that the tone of the melody was, so to speak, pulled down by the weight of the triad, which would easily enough distract the ear from following the melody in its horizontal flow. The evil grew yet larger when the expanding technique of polyphony facilitated a greater vivacity in the contrapuntal voices; for the larger series of tones which thus originated weighed yet more heavily on each individual note in the melody and dragged it down. All this resulted in a fatal and quite unwanted retardation of the melodic tempo, depriving the melody of that verve and fluidity with which inspiration and enthusiasm had no doubt endowed it *in actu nascendi*. In other words, the ear, confused as it was by the oversized and depressing weight, found it increasingly difficult to make head or tail of the melodic formations. But apart from this unfortunate situation, the melody had to undergo, in addition, the harm resulting from a screaming disproportion; for the most humble harmonic content of its own line was contrasted by the overabundance of harmonies in the vertical direction. The following excerpt may serve as an illustration:

Example 135 (169). J. P. Sweelinck, Psalm 1:

During the first nine measures the melody of the cantus (soprano) follows the path prescribed by the major triad on E-flat; and the same thing occurs during the next nine measures. Incidentally, the cantus does not succeed, even in the remaining thirty-nine measures, in exceeding the limits set by this triad. Now while it is gratifying to see that, even at such an early date, the melody is already able to unfold a harmonic concept so unambiguously, the paucity of result—to wit, one single triad—is nevertheless striking. What a lack of proportion there is between this orphaned major triad, on the one hand, and, on the other, the sum total of manifold triads attached to the individual tones of the melody! Without any further explanation it must be obvious to anybody that this abundance of chords is bound to retard the inner momentum of the melody. But it should be noted also—and this is even more important—to what extent the harmonies suffer from a lack of purposiveness, each harmony becoming a purpose unto itself and expressing, behind the melody, which is by far the most important element, things of which the melody knows nothing. What, for instance, has the melody to say in reply to the D-flat, ventured in the vertical direction, in measures 7 and 8? How can this triad, D-flat, F, A-flat, become plausible if the melody fails to participate in it with the decisive interval? And is not there a striking contrast between the fact, on the one hand, that the cantus beautifully unfolds its one triad and the fact, on the other hand, that the vertical counterpoint does not in the least unfold its many triads but brings them up, instead, merely as by-products of voice-leading? But how is it possible to use a triad, which remains enfolded in itself, to make plausible another triad, which, in turn, does not get unfolded? Thus also the sequence of triads lacks logical proof to the extent that each individual triad lacks such proof (cf. § 85); in other words, the harmonic system as such, i.e., as an independent new element, is as yet quite undeveloped, even though certain sequences may, perchance, sound plausible to some extent, as, for example, the very first four measures, which remind us of the modern step progression I–IV–V–I, and even though, by and large, the forcefulness of the text may carry the listener, at least initially, over any inadequacy. The author does not care to prove, by his technique of composition, what should be the relations, for example, between the harmony D-flat, F, A-flat in measures 7 and 8, and the harmonies which precede and follow it. For harmony, to him, is merely a by-product of voice-leading and nothing more.[9] The harmonies remain

[9. The D-flat in measures 7–8 serves the purpose of avoiding the diminished triad; the same holds for the G in Example 136; and Schenker makes this point on that occasion. But it also applies to the B-flat in the second-to-last measure of Example 50 (cf. note to Example

unconfirmed and unproved, owing to this overemphasis on voice-leading; and it is this fact which, for the time being, prevents the rise of a system on an independent harmonic basis. This much, however, is clear: In so far as our main problem, viz., the widening of musical content, is concerned, this technique does not aid our art. The very opposite technique was called for: one that would confirm the vertical harmony in the horizontal line of the melody as well. Such a technique, however, presupposes a larger amount of melodic content. The content of the composition must be rhythmically articulated and variable, unfolding now this, now that other, triad, if it is to manifest clearly its two dimensions and free them of that unfortunate disproportion from which the example from Sweelinck suffers to such a degree. Incidentally, we saw in the excerpts from Beethoven and Brahms quoted in § 29 that the technique here described, which results in an overburdening of the vertical to the detriment of the horizontal dimension, cannot create an adequate impression of plausibility or logic even where it is supported by the modern concept of the scale-step and of the disposition of the whole. Owing to the scarcity of content, these concepts, obviously, could not be deployed in the two examples just referred to, while in the example from Sweelinck, as in older works in general, they are completely lacking (cf., further, the notes to Examples 82 and 89). It may be noted incidentally that this very technique has led to the teaching of counterpoint as it has been generally adopted today (cf. § 85).

Here is another example:

Example 136 (170). Hans Leo Hassler, "Lustgarten":

Ach,Fräulein,zart,ach,Fräulein,zart,du bist mein Herz und Le - ben,

50). In Example 135, the contrast to the melody is particularly sharp where the latter (measures 7–9) runs its course, quite clearly, within the scale of E-flat major. If the bass voice had countered this development with D♯ (measure 8)–E-flat (measure 9), this would have been more logical (cf. the quotation from Schenker's *Counterpoint* in the note to § 19).]

Hassler, who composed at a later date (this work is of 1601), already leads his melody in a way that fully satisfies the demands of a modern system. Witness the clear unfolding of the triad on the tonic A in the first measure; the well-reasoned application of the subdominant D at the third beat of measure 2; the logic, furthermore, of the melodic descent from that subdominant D to the note G-sharp, which, if considered merely in the horizontal context, represents the diminished triad of VII, which takes the place of the dominant itself (cf. § 108) and constitutes a felicitous counterpart to the preceding harmonies I–IV. Despite this far-reaching correspondence to our system and our feeling for what is right, we are nevertheless suddenly faced with a harmony on G (first quarter-note of measure 3), which, from the harmonic point of view, does not fit at all into the A major system, at least not in the form in which we find it here. This is not to deny that Hassler's way of putting it best satisfies the requirements of voice-leading, in so far as it is this G which allows a fluid progression of all four voices and averts the tritone D–(E)–G-sharp in the bass voice, as well as the diminished triad on G-sharp (G-sharp, B, D). It would be arbitrary to assume that in leading his bass voice the author had in mind a Mixolydian A (cf. § 35); but what does it profit harmony, one might ask, if the interests of voice-leading are served and its own interest remains unsatisfied? If the composer had wanted harmony to come into its own as an independent and thus coequal factor, this could have been achieved only by an endeavor of the melody to confirm and prove, on its part, the triad G–B–D, which presupposes a more comprehensive melodic content. Even if Hassler's solution yielded a satisfactory effect, this is in no way a conclusive argument against the validity of the general postulate that the harmonic content of the horizontal line and that of the vertical must maintain sane proportions. This applies especially where the narrow scope of a chorale, chorus, etc., is exceeded and the associative power of the text has to be dispensed with. The irreversible consequence is that the principal element in music, even after the addition of the vertical dimension, remains the horizontal line, i.e., the melody itself. In this sense the vertical dimension is secondary (this, incidentally, corresponds to historical

chronology). Basically, perhaps, it is the mission of harmony to enhance the planning of ample melodic ideas and, at the same time,
to co-ordinate them. It may be conceded, finally, that in that same
melodic context we moderns, too, would have wanted to use that
incriminating G. But, guided by the principle of chromatization
which itself stems from a harmonic conception, we would have
introduced that G, at any rate, prior to the third beat. This would
have resulted, more effectively, in presenting the subdominant D as if
it were a tonic.

Toward the close of the period of vocal music, the result of this
development may have been as follows:

The horizontal and the vertical are engaged in a battle. At any
rate, there is a grave lack of proportion between the quantity of
harmonies in both dimensions—too much in the vertical, too little
in the horizontal. Often enough the conflict between the two dimensions is caused by the fact that the genius of voice-leading, far from
agreeing with the genius of harmony, rises to an absolute despotism
over the latent laws of harmony.

These latter, however, considered by themselves, i.e., on their
own ground, manifest an irrationality, often resembling that which,
during the early centuries, characterized the melody itself (cf. note
to § 76). It is obvious that such irrationality in the harmonic sphere
must, on its own account, press for a solution. The growing influence of the harmonies, however, penetrates ever more profoundly,
ever more securely, into the melody itself; and under this equilibrat-
ing pressure the old systems, governing only the horizontal dimensions, must crumble (cf. § 30). Their disavowal becomes a matter no
longer avoidable. But while practically no progress has been achieved
in what concerns the ancient problem of enlarging the scope of the
melody, this problem has not lost any of its pungency and impulse.
To make musical works longer, composers adopt the palliative of
simply repeating the melody, time after time. Another method, well-
known to any student of music history, consists in stretching the
melody. While this may enrich the possibilities of contrapuntal
techniques, it entails the evil consequence, alas! of distorting the
melody past recognition. Only in rare cases—and always within a

very narrow scope—may an almost perfect form originate from this technique. Such a felicitous case is presented by the following little *lied* by Hassler, excerpted from the same opus as Example 170:

Example 137 (171). Hans Leo Hassler, "Lustgarten":

What a beautiful E minor! The more striking is it that Hassler himself—God knows for what reason—took this piece to be in E Dorian (witness the two sharps)! The soprano initiates the melody with the dominant, B, i.e., forming a melodic inversion (cf. § 16).

The first three measures clearly establish an $E \frac{minor}{major}$; and the harmonic progression, though in this example it is also a by-product of voice-leading, resembles a half-close IV–V (cf. § 120). In the following three measures the idea of combination (with E major) inspires the course, so expressive, of the melody: B, C-sharp, D-sharp, and E, while at the same time the tone E, reached by the soprano in measure 5, forms, in accordance with the principle of inversion, the tonic replying to the dominant initiated in measure 1. What a beautiful disposition! The first part is then concluded by a modulation toward the key of the dominent (B minor), which is also manifested, quite clearly, in the melody itself: witness the melodic progression from the F-sharp down. The B major triad, concluding the first part, serves, for the sake of the repetition, as dominant of the main key as well. Hassler still clings unmistakably to the new key at the opening of the second part, which results most clearly, again, from the melody (measures 10 and 11). Even the two following measures, 12 and 13, belong in B minor—at least in so far as the melody is concerned—and it is only the minor triad on E in measures 13 and 14 that restores the main key, whereby the melodic progression A–D in measure 15 in particular displays the Aeolian mode. Measures 15 and 16, finally, bring the cadenza, concluding with the major tonic.

There remain, however, certain elements which may seem uncomfortable and ill founded from the modern point of view: the roughness in voice-leading in the middle parts of measure 5 (an inescapable consequence of the technique of consonances of that time), as well as the harmonies in measures 12–13 and 15, which, without any counterinfluence, seem to have flowed from the idea of voice-leading rather than from the concept of the key and therefore, owing to their harmonically ambivalent character, do not support the melody to the extent to which this would have been possible and desirable. Thus we are faced even here, so close to perfection, with a small perfidy of the contrapuntal technique of yore!

It was the evil consequences inherent in this technique which may have called most pressingly for a remedy, although, in general, for the modest purpose of a small *lied* it had its own merits. Once the harmonic element has entered into the life of the work of art, its first appearance, due to the exigencies of voice-leading, inevitably being irrational, it will and must reach, so to speak, knowledge of itself and conquer its own rationality. Now if the overabundance of vertical harmonies, as compared with the paucity of horizontal ones, proved to be the cause of this irrationality, it is natural that artistic genius should feel driven to equilibrate both quantities or, which is the same thing, to create more content in the horizontal direction. Thus we see quite clearly the way in which the artist will have to proceed without having the slightest idea that this very road will carry him ever closer to the solution of that other problem, lurking from the beginning, of how to enlarge the content of a composition.

The task was, above all, to get rid of the overabundance in the vertical direction and to advance, for a change, the horizontal line, which has been the primal element. The melody had to be unfolded and to become ever richer; it was to gain a fresher tempo, uninhibited by any vertical overburdening; it was to learn how to run. All this was achieved by the Italian monody (at the end of the sixteenth century). The creation of much horizontal content and the restriction of vertical tendencies—this is the principle underlying the Italian monody, which becomes technically possible because of a reform of the fundamental bass voice. The individual harmony learns, so to speak, to dictate a vast melodic project and to support and carry it as long as it lasts. Remember the recitatives of a Giulio Caccini (1550–1618) and Jacopo Peri (1561–1633) and, especially, the words of Caccini in the Introduction to his work:

. . . . Did it occur to me to introduce a kind of song, resembling, in a certain way, a harmonious discourse, whereby I demonstrated a certain noble contempt of song, touching, on and off, certain dissonances while leaving the bass voice to rest, except where, in accordance with common usage, I wanted to make use of it with the help of the notes of the middle parts, executed by instruments, in order to express some affect which could be achieved only by them.

Or—as happens in the basso continuo or generale, ascribed to Ludovico Viadana—the bass voice gets emancipated from the stiff technique, noticeable until then, of overstrict dependence on the melody, on the one hand, and, on the other, on a voice-leading which rests almost throughout on the principle of the triad, and it thus acquires an independence, lifting it almost to the rank of a line in its own right, almost co-ordinated, with the melody itself.[10] Thus the bass, too, becomes melody, and its projection undergoes the influence of the harmonic principle no less than the melody: the bass, too, unfolds harmonic concepts; i.e., together with the other voices, it becomes a link in an unrolled harmonic concept.

All roads, then, as they take us away from the pristine strict technique of counterpoint, lead us toward the new goal, the creation of broader content. The idea of the triad comprises a longer series of tones; its own unity bestows on them, despite their length, a unity easy to grasp; boundlessly ever new conceptual material may be accumulated; for the harmonies will always articulate the horizontal line as well into smaller units, and thus any danger of chaos will be obviated. An especially rich source for the creation of content is to be found in repetition, which, however, must be reduced to the principle of imitation and canon, already conquered by the technique of counterpoint. From repetition there arises now—on a considerably higher level—the motif; and thus there remains only one further task, viz., to create a rational relationship among those harmonies which so felicitously gather and articulate the motivic content and to establish them on a rational common foundation. Artistic practice, presentient of Nature herself, recognizes this foundation in the principle of the order of fifths, joined, in addition, by that of the thirds and seconds. Thus there arose the power of the scale-steps, mysteriously ordering, capable, until this day, of rationally creating and articulating large content. What a distance has been covered from that first E-flat major triad in the example from Sweelinck to, e.g., the motif of Beethoven's *Eroica,* derived from that very same triad:

Example 138 (172). Beethoven, *Third Symphony:*

[10. This independence was destroyed later on by the theory of Rameau. Cf. Schenker's critique in §§ 90–92; cf., furthermore, the Introduction to this book.]

§ 89. *The Scale-Step as a Duty in Composition*

The more freely he handles his voice-leading, the more clearly must the artist elaborate this step progression. The significance of the scale-steps entails this duty—a duty, alas! often sorely neglected in our day. There would be no objection to the voice-leading in a number of modern works, and the modern author need not pride himself in so far as his voice-leading is concerned; but if he dare such stormy seas, he would be wiser to provide beacons and lights. In sober but artistic terms, what is lacking is a proper step progression. In some cases this is lacking altogether; in others, the existing scale-steps are too wide, too highstrung, to support with any security the complexities of voice-leading and to cover them.

The paragon of composition founded magnanimously and securely on the scale-steps (even in the fugues), whatever the audacity in voice-leading—the paragon of such composition, it seems to me, is still the work of Johann Sebastian Bach. What planning, what perspicuity, and what endurance! If I confront this work with that even of the greatest of our moderns, the work of Wagner, I must concede that Wagner, too, employs scale-steps and voice-leading with a most beautiful instinct; but how fleeting is this splendor! In most cases it lasts for only a few measures, which form a whole. Whenever he gets ready to produce some larger content, a certain indisposition with regard to the scale-step becomes noticeable, even in the case of this master![11]

[11. Schenker implies that the total of Wagner's composition lacked "middle-ground" and "background." The technique of the leitmotif affected the "foreground" only (cf. note to § 86). Also Schenker says (*Yearbook*, II, 54): "There is a further misunderstanding, which Wagner conjured up: while he responded, with his leitmotif technique, to the demands of an audience accustomed to faith in melody, his stage technique entailed an overemphasis on the musical foreground. . . . Wagner was a musician lacking background perspective! Thereby he burdened his music with an unprecedented weight." *Free Composition*, p. 162: "The technique of 'motivic' repetition in the German music drama, in program music . . . accordingly represents retrogression, a return to the primal position, a decadence." Cf. also note to Example 259.]

CRITIQUE OF CURRENT METHODS OF
TEACHING IN THE LIGHT OF OUR
THEORY OF THE SCALE-STEP

§ 90. *Confusion between Harmony and Counterpoint Resulting from a Misunderstanding of the Scale-Step Concept*

On the basis of what has been said so far, we should now give a critique of the current methods of teaching. Let me quote Example 24 of Richter's *Lehrbuch der Harmonie* (23d ed.; Leipzig, 1902), p. 20:

Example 139 (174):

and let me ask: What is this supposed to mean?

One should feel inclined, first of all, to consider this example as a small piece of strict four-part composition, which would lead us to consider the bass voice as a *cantus firmus.* Such a supposition, however, is shown to be wrong by the progression of the bass voice itself: for a *cantus firmus* whose melodic line is unbalanced to such an extent cannot be imagined.

Thus we come to the conclusion that the author must have had in mind, not a strict four-part composition, but a free composition. This might seem to be indicated also by the fact that the author himself set figures below the bass notes, numbering the scale-steps, which should justify the further conclusion that he wanted us to consider the bass notes merely as symbols of the scale-steps and by no means as a *cantus firmus;* this might seem indicated, finally, by the further fact that the progression of the scale-steps is quite rational, responding to the directions of Nature as we understood them in §§ 14 and 16.

Granted, then, that the bass notes, according to the author's own intention, symbolize the spiritual power of the scale-steps: but what is to be the meaning of the three upper voices? What, in particular, could be the intention of the author in teaching that these voices are to be led here in this particular way and that there is no alternative? Does he want to impart to us a lesson in voice-leading? Why does he do that in a lesson on harmony which ought to be concerned with the psychology of the abstract scale-step, and only with that? Why does he not wait until we come to the theory of counterpoint, which teaches, *ex officio,* voice-leading—obviously without scale-steps, it should be noted, and it could not be otherwise?

If the foregoing example is not pure either with regard to the scale-steps—in this respect, as we pointed out above, the three upper voices are superfluous—or with regard to voice-leading—this would presuppose a *cantus firmus* in the bass—is it not then a *contradictio in adjecto,* a logical misfit, which does not belong either in the theory of harmony or in the theory of counterpoint?

Imagine now that the whole book is based on such nonsense, is teaming with such exercises! The student cannot make head or tail of it, and right he is. What he is yearning to see, the confirmation of theoretical propositions in examples from the works of the great masters, he looks for in vain in this book. It is hard to understand, and yet it is the sad truth that in the textbooks on harmony a real work of art is never mentioned. It seems to me that in other disciplines such books would be unthinkable! They would be rejected as unconvincing. It is funny enough that a theoretician should offer an example which really cannot be accepted as such, because it serves neither the theory of harmony nor that of counterpoint. Even stranger is it, however, if that theoretician flatters himself that he has offered in it a piece of art, which, he thinks, frees him of the obligation of bringing a quotation from living music!

It may be granted—it cannot even be doubted—that the progression of the bass voice in the example quoted earlier could be corroborated by a number of samples from works of art: but what about those unfortunate upper voices? Where are they to be found in works of art? Thus it is not chance but merely a natural consequence of the contradiction inherent in this example that the author could not find a sample from any master-work to fit this example of harmony (i.e., scale-steps), infested as it is with counterpoint (i.e., rules of voice-leading). Now if the teacher himself is suffering from such lack of clarity, what about the unfortunate disciple, with his thirst for knowledge? How can he ever see the light of truth?

I am not moved by any animosity toward Richter. But since it was necessary to show how the scale-step, by virtue of its transcendent power, separated the theory of harmony from that of counterpoint, it was inevitable to pick from the textbooks, which in this respect are all alike, no matter who the author, some example to demonstrate in some detail what happens when the two disciplines are confused because of a lack of artistic (I don't say theoretical) understanding. For the author of our ominous example is sufficiently exonerated by the general tradition, whose force seems so irresistible that even artists like Tchaikovsky and Rimski-Korsakov, certainly without any misgivings, fell into the same error in their textbooks on harmony.[1]

§ 91. *Pedagogical Failure of Our Time as a Consequence of This Confusion*

And these are those famous chapters on the so-called "progression" in triads and seventh-chords, with which the disciple of art is maltreated in conservatories and other institutions for periods of one or two years!

If the teacher is unable to explain his own propositions—e.g., what is the difference between strict composition and free composition; what is the original and inalienable meaning of this or that rule of voice-leading in strict composition; and what would be the aspect of a prolongation or extension of such rule in free composition, etc.— and if the teacher finally fails to illustrate and confirm such rules with examples from works of art,[2] the student, in his blessed state of

[1. Cf. Schenker, *Yearbook*, Vol. III, essay on "Rameau oder Beethoven?" See, furthermore, Introduction to this book and § 181, second-to-last paragraph.]

2. My teacher, a composer of high renown, used to say on such occasions: "Segn's, mein' Herrn, dass ist die Regl, i schreib' natirli not a so"—which, in Austrian dialect, means: "Look, gentlemen, this is the rule. Of course, I don't compose that way." What marvelous snarls of contradictions! One believes in rules which should be laughed at; one pokes fun at them rather than ridicule one's own belief in them! And if there are rules which lack any reasonable

youth, may be careless enough to overlook for the time being all those gaps; he may be content not to understand the meaning of the proffered doctrine while silently hoping for a time to come when he might meet art in theory. Vain hope! The teacher closes his classes in harmony; he closes his classes in counterpoint, finishes them off in his own way; but not even the first step toward art has been taken. It is unbelievable, alas! what hecatombs of young people, full of talent and industry, fell victims to that confusion between harmony and counterpoint! I do not mean here those professional musicians, whether they blow the oboe or stroke the fiddle, whether they sing or play the piano, conducted or conducting themselves, who finally put themselves beyond all theory (I am the last one to grudge them such an attitude under the circumstances). Still closer to my heart are those numerous amateurs—good fellows, really good fellows—who, moved by sheer enthusiasm, would sacrifice to art their scarce leisure hours, to gain insight, if possible, into the inner workings of a composition. Shortly, alas! such people will take leave of textbook or teacher, driven off by a disillusion which is as bitter as it is incurable.

Owing to these people's favorable social position, their specific musical talent, their intellectual power (the importance of which is not to be underrated in art), they should have become the best possible media for the transmission of artistic achievement. Yet the disillusion they had to undergo in some cases so disgruntled and disoriented them that all too often they turned their backs on art and artists when, under other circumstances, they would have embraced their ideal joyfully.

§ 92. *Theory of Chord Progression Justified in the Epoch*
of the General Bass

To illustrate still further that mistaken approach of our current methods of teaching, I should like to beg permission to return to the

sense—whence they ought to be considered nonexistent—and if, for this very reason, a relationship, let alone a contrast, between that alleged rule, on the one hand, and art, on the other, is out of the question, how odd is it to behold this or that individual assuming the pose of a hero who allegedly transgresses the rule! Can there be heroism more amusing, more lacking in substance? If they only knew how whatever they write, even in their most audacious moments, is deeply rooted in rules and norms, albeit quite different ones!

past epoch of the general bass and to show by an example that the theory of chord progression was at that time not only justified but necessary. I pick my example from Johann Sebastian Bach's *Generalbassbüchlein* (Example 6), which Philipp Spitta fully reproduces in the Appendix to his Bach biography:

Example 140 (175):

What do we see in this example? A bass line, showing rich rhythmical articulation. Its development could constitute part of a real live composition; In other words, we have in this bass line more than mere scale-steps such as in the example quoted from Richter. The bass notes are equipped with figures, indicating intervals. And what is the meaning of the upper parts? These develop partly in accordance with strict contrapuntal rules, partly in free style. All considered, bass line and voice-leading present the aspect of a free composition, a piece that could almost be considered real art. To attain the full reality of a work of art, we should have—and this is all that is missing here—a living, warm, vocal or instrumental melody; that the soprano in this Bach example is no such melody need not be demonstrated any further.

If Bach, generally and in particular by the conduct of the bass line, feigns the liberty of a real piece of art, whereas the soprano part lacks the character of a true melody such as we would expect in a real composition, this still does not imply any contradiction: We have but to realize the true purpose of the upper parts. They are nothing but so-called "fillers." As fillers—and only as such—they have as much reality as the bass line. The whole example, accordingly, may well be considered a compositional possibility. There are innumerable melodies for which this bass line, with its filler parts, would form a suitable accompaniment!

At that time there seems to have been some kind of tacit agreement between the creative artist and his performers, which eased the task of the former. Rarely was the composer obliged to complete more than the melody and the bass, while he could leave to the performer the task of filling in the accompanying voices. It goes without saying that the latter needed particular training for this purpose. This training in accompaniment was called the "study of the general bass." Thus all doctrine and precepts, together with the examples, are directed toward the *practical* purpose of *real* accompaniment, such as was demanded by the works of art. This is indicated even by the title of Bach's *Generalbassbüchlein* from which we quoted above: "Precepts and Principles for the Four-Part Performance of a General Bass or Accompaniment. By Johann Sebastian Bach of Leipzig. For His Disciples in Music." The word "performance" is to be taken in its literal and practical sense. This results, incidentally, quite clearly from the definition given in chapter ii of this little opus:

The General Bass is the most perfect fundament of music. It is to be played with both hands in such fashion that the left hand plays the prescribed notes while the right hand supplements consonances and dissonances so as to provide a euphonous harmony.—Where this is not done with care, there is no true music.

Fundamentally, this theory of the general bass, which is directed unswervingly toward the practical purpose of accompaniment, constitutes the most important part, if not the totality, of all theory of that time; for, as is well known, the newer harmonic theories of Rameau and the contrapuntal theories of Fux originated at the time of Bach, without, however, exercising any sizable influence on the theory of the general bass, which, as long as the purpose it served remained unchanged, retained its *raison d'être*. This gives us a spontaneous explanation for the physiognomy of the Bach example and the liberty and variety of its bass and upper voices, which display the characteristics of a real composition.[3]

The practical purpose, which we have just shown in the case of the general bass example from Bach, does not exist in the case of the Richter example. The two examples differ with regard to the character of the bass line: in the latter case, we are faced with scale-steps; in the former, with a true bass line. It is impossible that every note of a true bass line should be a scale-step and that the progression of the bass notes should be identical with the progression of the scale-steps. The Richter example, which, as we have seen earlier, cannot be considered either as contrapuntal or as harmonic, is thus, finally, not even an example of a general bass. Such an example, incidentally, would not serve any purpose today, because we have formed the habit long since of executing our compositions thoroughly and completely, taking care even to cross the *t*'s and dot the *i*'s.

3. I personally do not believe, however, that accompaniments in the works of art of that period called in all cases for so much restraint as the practical examples, offered by the theory of the time, might make us believe. The situation rather is this: that the theory of the general bass, like any theory directed toward a practical purpose, took account, to begin with, only of average talent. Since in the real life of art, genius is not always rampant, such an attitude was inevitable if an even halfway satisfactory minimum of style was to be attained by the accompanists. Unless this could be achieved, hardly any work of art of that epoch could have reached actual performance. I do not doubt, however, that for a more richly endowed artist it was perfectly legitimate to elaborate his accompaniments somewhat more freely, i.e., to treat his *obbligatos* with both thematic and motivic inventiveness.

As far as we and our desire, manifested so frequently today, to revive works of the older masters are concerned, we must conclude from what has been stated above that an accompaniment in the restrained style of the quoted examples is not erroneous but that, on the other hand, the performer who, trusting his own power and dexterity, is able to raise the quality of his accompaniment to a higher motivic level, does not in any way, by so doing—provided that he masters his task—violate the intentions of the older authors.

This concise remark disposes, I think, at least to a large extent, of the problem of how to treat the *basso continuo*—a problem which is so much discussed today.

Theory of Triads

CHAPTER I

CLASSIFICATION OF TRIADS

§ 93. *Classification According to the Fifth*

We have already discussed the construction of the triad in § 13. Furthermore, we saw in § 18 which triads belong in our system and how they originated. It remains to explain the principles according to which they are to be classified. Let us take, to begin with, the major system. If we consider the fifth in each case, there are two groups of triads:

Example 141 (178):

Group *a* contains triads with perfect fifths; group *b* contains only one triad, with a diminished fifth.

§ 94. *Classification According to the Third*

The first group, *a*, may be further subdivided according to the third it contains. The third is major in the triads on the I, IV, and V steps, whereas it is minor on the II, III, and VI steps.

§ 95. *The Three Types of Triad in the Diatonic Scale*

If both criteria are combined, the result is three kinds of triad:

A: with perfect fifth and major third: the so-called "major triads"
B: with perfect fifth and minor third: the so-called "minor triads"
C: with diminished fifth and minor third: the so-called "diminished triads"

Written in notes, these types look as follows:

Example 142 (179):

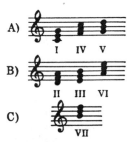

It need hardly be added that the Aeolian (minor) system does not contain any additional triads. It is only with regard to their meaning as scale-steps that there is a shift (cf. also § 45). The triads in the minor system, accordingly, present themselves as follows:

Example 143 (180):

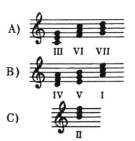

§ 96. *The Augmented Triad as a Result of Combining Major and Minor*

If major and minor are combined, which combination, as is well known, introduces the augmented fifth, with the twofold meaning of $\frac{\flat 3}{\natural 7}$ and $\frac{\flat 6}{\natural 3}$, we obtain a triad with augmented fifth and major triad, called, therefore, "augmented triad."[1]

[1. Later on, Schenker relegated the augmented triad, like all other dissonant chords (seventh-chords, cf. §§ 99 ff.) to the sphere of voice-leading.]

CHAPTER II

THE MODULATORY MEANING OF TRIADS

§ 97. *The Modulatory Meaning of Triads*

If we now investigate the modulatory meaning of these triads from the angle applied in § 64 to the intervals, we shall see that, in both the major and the minor systems:

A: the diminished triad occurs on only one scale-step
B: the augmented triad occurs on two scale-steps
C: the major as well as the minor triad occurs on three scale-steps

Accordingly:

The diminished triad is univalent
The augmented triad is bivalent
The major triad is trivalent

and the minor triad, likewise, is trivalent.

From this it follows that, e.g.:

Example 144 (181):

occurs only on the VII scale-step in major, thus referring us to the A major key; while in minor the same triad appears on the II step, thus indicating F-sharp minor.

Likewise it follows that:

Example 145 (182):

occurs on the III as well as on the VI scale-step and thus would indicate the keys of B-flat $\frac{major}{minor}$ and F $\frac{major}{minor}$, resulting from a combination of major and minor.

Likewise it follows that:

Example 146 (183):

184

may appear, in major, on the I, IV, and V scale-steps, which refers us to E-flat major, B-flat major, and A-flat major; whereas in minor this triad has the meaning of III, VI, VII, in C minor, G minor, and F minor, respectively.

It follows, further, that:

Example 147 (184):

may appear, in major, on the II, III, and VI scale-steps, referring us to D-flat major, C-flat major, and G-flat major, respectively; in minor, on the other hand, it would occur on I, IV, V, in E-flat minor, B-flat minor, and A-flat minor, etc.

For beginners it is particularly instructive to form all possible triads on the same root tone and then to explore their modulatory meanings. On G., e.g., we obtain the constructs shown in Table 2.

TABLE 2

	A	B	C	D
G major I	F major II	A♭ major VII	E $\frac{\text{major}}{\text{minor}}$ III
D major IV	E♭ major III	F minor II	
C major V	B major VI		B $\frac{\text{major}}{\text{minor}}$ VI
E minor III	G minor I		
B minor VI	D minor IV		
A minor VII	C minor V		

In this table, which exhausts all possibilities offered by both diatonic systems and their combinations, the triads are grouped in the classes *A–D*, and perhaps this method should be recommended as the most practical also for the beginner.

§ 98. *The Sixth-Chord and the Fourth-Sixth-Chord*

The principle of "inversion," which we first applied to intervals (§ 72), can naturally be extended to the triads, since they are made of intervals. If the root tone of the following triad:

Example 148 (185):

is transposed from the bass to the soprano, thus yielding to the third the place of the bass, we obtain I, the so-called "sixth-chord":

Example 149 (186):

This chord owes its name to the simple fact that, first of all, we look for the new position of the root tone which has escaped upward: and we recover it as a sixth. The inversion of the third could not have yielded any other result. As the fifth, G, belongs implicitly to the root tone, which we have now located in the sixth, it would be supererogatory to present this tone, in its new position, explicitly as a third and to designate the chord, somewhat clumsily, as "third-sixth-chord." The customary abbreviation of this designation thus rests on a convincing reason.

But if the fifth of the triad takes the place of the bass, root tone and third having been displaced by an octave, we obtain the second inversion of the triad, i.e., II, the so-called "fourth-sixth-chord":

Example 150 (187):

Also in this case it is the original root tone, C, changed by the inversion into a fourth, which concerns us first of all. According to what has been said above, it might have been more expedient to call this chord simply "fourth-chord," since no tone but E could belong, as a third, to the evanescent root tone C. However, prudence counsels us to specify also the sixth in designating this chord, as the fourth, forming the lower interval, as in this case, may give rise to misunderstandings, a point to which we shall come back in the discussion of counterpoint.[1]

Inversion, however, does not alter the identity of the triad, so that its modulatory meaning is in no way affected. In other words, the triad in its inversions retains its univalence, bivalence, or trivalence.

[1. In so far as the fourth-sixth-chord is not merely an inversion of a triad but a conformation of passing notes or a suspension, cf. Schenker's note to § 78, where he derives this phenomenon historically. Furthermore, Schenker discusses the fourth-sixth-chord in the frame of the cadence in §§ 124 and 127.]

Theory of Seventh-Chords

CHAPTER I

NATURE OF THE SEVENTH-CHORD

§ 99. *The Origin of the Seventh-Chord*

After what has been fully stated in § 11, I need not repeat here that the seventh-chord outpasses the directions given by Nature and therefore must be considered entirely as a product of art. The artist obviously found it challenging to obfuscate temporarily the pure, natural effect of the triad, to generate thereby a certain tension, and to render the more effective the return of the pure triad, confirming, as it were, Nature as the authoritatively recognized godmother of the triad.[1]

The artist achieves this tension simply by combining two triads, selecting the third or the first triad as root tone of the second. Thus:

Example 151 (188):

[1. As Schenker had not yet penetrated (1906!) to the full understanding of the dissonance as a phenomenon of passing notes and hence to the rejection of the seventh-chord as a harmonic unit, his intuition, which dictated several of the formulations in this paragraph, is all the more admirable. He calls the seventh-chord a mere "product of art" and then continues: "to *obfuscate temporarily* the pure natural effect and to generate thereby a certain *tension*." A few years later (*Counterpoint*, I, 366), he writes more explicitly: "Thus we obtain the free suspension, and perhaps it would be most opportune to explain the origin of the seventh-chord, fundamentally, as elision of a suspension or, respectively, as a consonance preceding a conformation of passing-notes." Cf., furthermore, the *general bass* example from Bach as quoted in the Introduction.

If Schenker had later revised his *Harmony*, he would not have insisted on explaining the seventh-chord, as he did here, as a combination of two triads and on emphasizing conventionally the "structure of rising thirds." He would rather have omitted the chapter on the seventh-chords or modified it essentially. Although this seems to be evident, this editor thought it nevertheless advisable to include the chapter here, at least in part, in its original form, if only to throw some light on the course of Schenker's further development.]

added up to:

Example 152 (189):

Now this sum total is called "seventh-chord" and is characterized by its structure, rising in thirds above the root tone.

Every seventh-chord basically represents a conflict between two triads, from which conflict, however, only one triad can emerge as victor and, eventually, as peacemaker. In so far as the seventh-chord has to be considered a scale-step, it goes without saying that it is the root tone of the lower triad, not that of the upper one, which determines the scale-step. The lower root tone, then, is decisive for the entire seventh-chord.

We shall now apply to the seventh-chord the criteria applied previously to the triad.

§§ 100–106. [Classification of the seventh-chord, its inversions and modulatory meaning.]

The So-called Dominant Ninth-Chord
and Other Higher Chords

CHAPTER I

THE SO-CALLED DOMINANT NINTH-CHORD

§ 107. *Anomalies Resulting from the Customary Conception*
of the Dominant Ninth-Chord

Most textbooks at our disposal teach that the ninth-chord is another independent chord formation, basing this theory on a merely mechanical application of the principle of constructing by thirds. Strangely enough, however, those textbooks in general deal with only one such ninth-chord, viz., that on the V scale-step:

Example 153 (214):

They reject the ninth-chords on the other scale-steps as not customary and, so they say, more easily understandable as a suspension.

A second anomaly resides in the fact that this allegedly autonomous ninth-chord is never accorded the treatment of inversion, which all other independent chords have to undergo.

It is hard to understand, then, why this particular and singular chord formation had to be thought up in the first place.[1]

§ 108. *The Kinship of All Univalent Chords as the*
Root of This Misunderstanding

The truth of the matter is as follows:

If we pick from the diatonic scale the univalent formations—

[1. In rejecting the ninth-chord, Schenker has taken here the step which he did not dare to take with regard to the seventh-chord. Cf. also §§ 112 and 113.]

whether triads or seventh-chord—and list them in one series as follows:

Example 154 (215):

we shall see that one interval, viz., the diminished fifth, has forced its own univalent character also on the dominant seventh-chord, V^7, and the seventh-chord on the VII scale-step, VII^7. This fact forms the basis of a peculiar psychological kinship among these three phenomena—a kinship which the composer often likes to exploit practically by substituting one for the other, without any intention, however, of changing the meaning of the step progression.

All three phenomena lie within the span of a ninth:

Example 155 (216):

(1) the diminished triad on the VII step; (2) the dominant seventh-chord on the V step; and (3) the seventh-chord on the VII step and may substitute for one another with the same effect of univalence.

Now it is the span of this ninth, within which the mutual substitution of those (related) univalent chords takes place, that engenders this deceptive effect; and it has therefore occurred to some to treat this phenomenon as a particular chord formation, viz., the ninth-chord. The fact that those related univalent chords appear only on the dominant explains, at the same time, the anomaly we mentioned earlier: that the ninth-chord is assumed to exist only on this one scale-step.

The diminished seventh-chord, which, as we saw, results from a combination of major and minor and is therefore the most univalent phenomenon of all, is probably no less inclined to share the advantages and disadvantages of this kinship with the other univalent chords than is the diatonic seventh-chord on the VII step. It would be superfluous to expand this in greater detail.

Example 156 (217):

1. VII³ in C major.
2. Dominant seventh-chord V⁷ in C major.
3. Diminished seventh-chord on the VII step in C $\frac{major}{minor}$.

§ 109. *Possibility of Obtaining from This Kinship a
More Suitable Scale-Step*

Thus we reject the conventional conception as erroneous. We explain the so-called "dominant" ninth-chord not as a real, hence not as an independent, chord formation but as a mere reflex of a kinship, sensed unconsciously, among all the univalent chords rising on the fifth (and only on the fifth!) scale-step. It remains to point out where mutual substitution takes place in practice and where it cannot. The conditions under which substitution can take place may be specified as follows:

Only where the compositional momentum requires that we should hear and recognize a scale-step (cf. § 79) can such a substitution be made effective. Thus the need for a scale-step is the first prerequisite for a substitution to take place. Now, once this precondition is fulfilled, it may happen that in those very places where, for reasons of voice-leading, only the VII⁵ or VII⁷ appear, yet our immanent feeling for the logic of step progression requires us to hear the V⁷ chord. In those cases, such a substitution can be effected. For, with the help of the root tone of that latter chord—this being the dominant fifth of our diatonic scale—it is easier for us to find our bearings and get along in the vicinity of the tonic. Pressed by our feeling for the scale-steps, we naturally prefer the root tone of the near-by V step to that of the remoter VII, intent as we are on explaining the development of the contents in terms of step progression.

The possibility of reducing a diminished seventh-chord to the underlying V⁷ chord offers in most cases at the same time a further possibility: where, according to its real modulatory meaning, the diminished seventh-chord should refer us to a quite remote key, we may insist on our main key; for in attaining the V we may adopt such processes of chromatization (cf. §§ 136 ff.) as may serve this tendency. Some examples may illustrate what has been said so far.

Example 157 (218). R. Wagner, *Tristan and Isolde:*

The step progression in this example is as follows: I in the first two measures; IV in measures 3 and 4; V in measures 5 ff. (cf. §§ 136 ff.) —this, if we disregard the pedal point on C, which is continued through all these measures and must not deter us from interpreting the overlying step progression (cf. § 169) in the sense I have just ascribed to it. Actually, all we see is a VII⁷ in F $\frac{major}{minor}$ in measures 1 and 2; likewise, nothing but a VII⁷ in B-flat $\frac{major}{minor}$ in measures 3 and 4; and, finally, nothing but a VII⁷ in C $\frac{major}{minor}$ in measures 5 and following. In reality, the true root tones are E, A, and B, and their harmonies are the following:

Example 158 (219):

But, because of the kinship between the diminished seventh-chord on VII and the dominant seventh-chord, our instinct supplements, beyond or behind these sounds, the root tones C, F, and B-flat, which, in each case, lie a major third below:

Example 159 (220):

as if we were dealing here with a sequent V⁷ on C, V⁷ on F, and V⁷ on G. We do this merely because these root tones combine in the same key, viz., the C major or minor diatonic system, where they represent the most closely related fifths, whose absence would disturb our orientation in the diatonic system as such and detract from the quality of the musical form. At any rate, the root tones C, F, and G as I, IV, and V steps in this context are infinitely closer and more precise for our ear than the tones E, A, and B, which are set here in reality but which are root tones only apparently. Likewise, the key C $\frac{major}{minor}$ is more welcome to our ear than the three different keys represented by the diminished harmonies. Here is another example:

Example 160 (221). Chopin, Scherzo, op. 31:

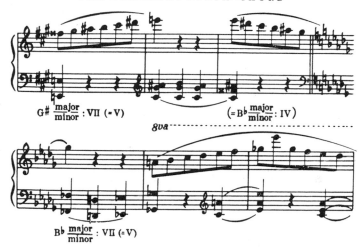

Here, too, we penetrate beyond the harmonies as they appear.

Example 161 (222):

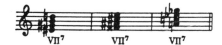

(which, in reality, are nothing but diminished seventh-chords in F-sharp $\frac{major}{minor}$, G-sharp $\frac{major}{minor}$, and B-flat $\frac{major}{minor}$) to the underlying root tones C-sharp, D-sharp, and F, as if they were the secret carriers of the always univalent meaning of the dominant seventh-chord in F-sharp $\frac{major}{minor}$, G-sharp $\frac{major}{minor}$, and B-flat $\frac{major}{minor}$. It would be more correct, accordingly, to hear this same sequence of harmonies as follows:

Example 162 (223):

whereby it is perfectly legitimate to consider the sequence of the root tones C-sharp and D-sharp, having transmuted the meaning of the C-sharp into that of the IV step of the diatonic system of G-sharp $\frac{major}{minor}$, to be a sequence IV–V in this very key; likewise, the sequence

D-sharp (to be taken, for this purpose, as an enharmonic E-flat) and F, to be a sequence IV–V in B-flat $\frac{major}{minor}$.

The opening of the development part of the last movement of Mozart's *G Minor Symphony*, e.g.,

Example 163 (224):

presents itself as a chain of diminished seventh-chords. All we have to do is to interpret them, by virtue of their univalence, as dominant seventh-chords, and suddenly we can understand the step progression by fifths as well as the modulation effected thereby. Literally understood, the step and key progression would present itself at first appearance as follows:[2]

Example 164 (225):

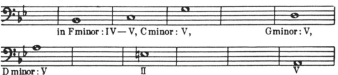

Or, if we prefer to include the tonic as mediating the modulation:

[2. With regard to the "keys" indicated by Schenker in Examples 160–65, cf. notes to §§ 155 and 161.]

Example 165 (226):

110. *Rejection of the Ninth-Chord on Account of*
Its Passing Character

This process of substitution, which helps us to gain a scale-step, can obviously be dispensed with where no scale-step is called for.

A pedal point, for example, or the consideration of an auxiliary note may save us the trouble of reducing a phenomenon to a scale-step, even where such reduction would be quite justifiable on account of the univalence of the chord in question. Despite the latent possibility of explaining such univalent harmonies as scale-steps, they are, in such cases, to be interpreted as passing notes.[3]

Here again are some examples:

Example 166 (227). Wagner, *Faust,* Overture, measures 15–18:

(Tympani)

[3. This paragraph is very important for Schenker's later development. Although he speaks here of a "pedal point," he seems to anticipate the idea of prolongation. Cf. § 79.]

Any attempt to deduce from all those diminished seventh-chords the corresponding V⁷ chords would be futile. It is advisable rather to accept the trill, performed by the kettle drum on *A*, as the dominant in D minor and to consider the line of highest notes, extending above it, in its entirety as a train of passing notes, each of which is weighed down by a diminished seventh-chord. The sequence of passing seventh-chords thus presents itself simply as follows:

Example 167 (228):

The highest notes of these passing harmonies, incidentally, are executed not only by the bassoons and violas but also by the violins, moving in most inspired and expressive figurations one octave higher up, the first and second violins alternating.

The author prepares us for the coming of this sequence, based on the principle of passing notes, by writing immediately before (score, p. 1, measures 3 and 4):

Example 168 (229):

Here, at the fourth beat, while the bass note G-sharp is held over between two *B*'s, forming a third, the auxiliary note *C* takes on a chord of its own, whose effect, however, is as passing as that of the auxiliary note to which it is attached. In the relation between that chord, attached to the auxiliary note, and the next diminished seventh-chord, the effect of the passing note is the one that prevails, despite the fact that the notation, as set for the figurating viola, might suggest a sequence V–I (or II–V):

Example 169 (230):

Example 170 (231):

albeit with the fifth, *A*, of the first harmony undergoing an alteration (cf. §§ 146 ff.) and a chromatic alteration affecting the root tone, *G*, of the second harmony.

Likewise, we see how the holding-over of the bass note, *C-sharp*, in measure 1 of our example (cf. Examples 166 and 167), continuing, so to speak, a trend initiated in measure 3 of the overture, gives the character of a passing harmony to the chord on the second beat, although this diminished chord could be interpreted as a V^7; the second beat in the following measure is subject to similar considerations. It is only in measures 3 and 4 that one diminished seventh-chord after another rushes in, and the former trend and its effect of passing-notes are abandoned. A way of notation, incidentally, could be found to suggest, from chord to chord, an interpretation in the sense of scale-steps and keys. This would be in keeping with what has been said above (cf. Examples 169 and 170). The principle of passing notes, however, is far more determinative in this case, and for its sake we are ready to renounce individual root tones and individual scale-steps; for the broad rhythm of the scale-steps (cf. § 79) is clearly initiated in the exposition of this work. Here is a second example:

Example 171 (232). Beethoven, Piano Sonata, op. 90:

The domination of the fifth scale-step, conceived as a unifying regulator, is so unchallengeable that all individual phenomena, among which are several diminished seventh-chords, assume the character of mere passing notes. In this context see also some of the examples quoted in § 79, especially those from Wagner and Chopin.

§ 111. *Rejection of the Ninth-Chord on the Ground of Chromatization*

I should like to emphasize again that the univalent chords possess inherently the power and possibility of suggesting to us a V step but that, on the other hand, we are not entitled, let alone obliged, to urge such an interpretation in all cases. We are obliged rather under all circumstances to mind the inner coherence of a composition and to see from the context whether the univalent chord—which otherwise so easily suggests a dominant—should not be heard and interpreted differently. The preceding paragraph has already indicated this possibility. I shall add here another example:

Example 172 (233). J. S. Bach, Italian Concerto, measures 26–30:

I   V   —   ♮IV   V — I — II V   I

The rhythm of the step progression demands here, for formal considerations, the assumption of a kind of deceptive cadence (V–IV; cf. § 121), in spite of the fact that the IV step, as will be seen, is affected by a *chroma* and constitutes a diminished triad. What is the meaning of such a *chroma* I shall have occasion to show later on (§ 162, on tonicalization). In no case, however, would it be permissible to take the diminished triad merely as such, in its original significance, and to consider it as anything but a chromatic alteration of the IV step, demanded by the false close.[4]

In this connection we should mention, finally, that the VII step (cf. § 16) is at the same time the fifth fifth, in rising order, in the diatonic system; but if it is to assert itself as such, it must be confirmed in the composition by the full inversion VII–III–VI–II–V–I or an abbreviation

[4. At a later stage of his development Schenker would not have stressed the bass notes in indicating the scale-steps, but he would have seen a movement of passing notes from *C* to *F*.]

of this process. Otherwsie, and especially if it is followed immediately by the I step, we are certainly dealing with a substitution (by virtue of their kinship) of the VII for the V.

CHAPTER II

THE REMAINING NINTH-CHORDS AND
HIGHER CHORDS

§ 112. *The Lack of Ninth-Chords on the Remaining Scale-Steps*

It goes without saying that I reject the ninth-chords on the remaining scale-steps—in this I agree with conventional theory—and that I feel the more justified in this rejection, because those chords can be explained much more plausibly otherwise. For either all those other chords which apparently are ninth-chords are, in reality, superadditions of two scale-steps above a pedal point, or they originate in a suspension, and, rather than form an individual chord, they emphasize or prove the organ point or suspension. For example:

Example 173 (234). Wagner, *Rheingold,* Scene 4:

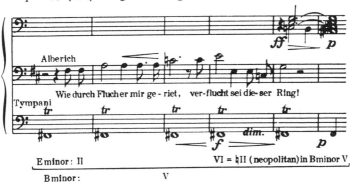

At a first and superficial glance it might seem as though the first five measures of our example already presented an independent seventh-ninth-chord: F-sharp, *A, C, E, G,* and, oddly enough, on a II step—here the II step in E minor. It might be preferable to dissolve this alleged ⅞ chord on II and to consider it as a pedal point of the II step in E minor, above which a progression II–VI takes place. This problem, on the other hand, becomes quite pointless if one considers that the further content of measures 5 and 6 shows clearly a V step in B minor. This key, incidentally, had also prevailed previously (in the measures preceding our example). Thus, in the best of cases, we have here again a so-called "dominant" seventh-ninth-chord in B minor; in this case, however, it would be more correct to interpret it as a pedal point of the V step (cf. the previous chapter), maybe with a modulation to E minor and back; or, finally, as a suspension (*A* and *C* before *A*-sharp and *C*-sharp), unfolded in the singing part. This is indicated in the following figure:

Example 174 (235):

V

However this may be, the ninth-chord is never self-sufficient. It is occasioned by other forces, such as univalence, pedal point, or suspension. Accordingly, the ninth-chord lacks individuality as it is manifested by the triad or the seventh-chord.[1] Therefore, it is to be rejected as an original formation. It must be dissolved in each case into the elements from which it originated. Such a conception, such a way of hearing a phenomenon in its causation, is infinitely more artistic than a merely theoretical grasping of intervals which have no common causation.

§ 113. *Rejection of the Ninth as an Interval*

For the sake of completeness we should mention here a corollary of our rejection of the ninth-chord as a self-sufficient formation. If—as explained in § 55 ff.—"harmonizability" is a precondition of the interval, the rejection of the ninth-chord as harmony entails the rejection of the ninth as a true interval. It becomes clear now why in my theory of intervals (§ 58) I have avoided mentioning the ninth.

On the other hand, we see how the principle according to which so much in music is determined by the number five fails us with regard to the higher chords.[2] It is only on the ground of the V scale-step that the kinship among univalent chords (cf. § 108) induces a ninth-chord, but even this is a deception. Thus Rameau was right when he admitted the ninth-chord only as an *accord par supposition*.

[1. Cf. note to § 99.]

[2. Concerning the "number five" see Introduction.]

§ 114. *Rejection of Remaining Higher Chords*

The inescapable consequence of the rejection of the ninth-chord is that the higher formations of the so-called "eleventh-chord," extending allegedly from the root tone to the eleventh,

Example 175 (236):

and of the so-called "thirteenth-chord":

Example 176 (237):

have even less of a *raison d'être* than has the ninth-chord. In fact, such phenomena are again based on a pedal point, in most cases in conjunction with the dominant V; and it is thus in all cases the power of the pedal point, not the sum of the intervals heaped above it, that creates a unity. For example:

Example 177 (238). Wagner, *Rheingold, Scene 2:*

On the pedal point of the dominant in B-flat minor—note well, again on the scale-step of univalent chords—we find here, first, a seventh-chord on the II diatonic scale-step: C, E-flat, G-flat, B-flat, in measures 1 and 2; then the diminished seventh-chord of VII (measures 3–6), of IV (measures 7–8), of II (measures 9 and 10), and of VII (measures 11–14). To this progression we should compare the phases of the melody itself:

Example 178 (239):

Considering the horizontal harmonies,[3] would not this melody

[3. This expression, again, anticipates Schenker's later concept of unfolding (*Auskomponierung*).]

offer the sight, first, of the seventh-chord on IV in B-flat minor (measures 1–5) and, subsequently, of the diminished seventh-chord on VII (= V), if it were not for the fact that with the *A* in measure 5 the effect of the VII scale-step began to make itself felt?

And—more important yet—does not Wagner, in measure 7 (Example 177), where the seventh-chord of IV gets built up, avoid the note *C*, which would have signified the root tone of II?

This column of chords and this melodic line may be articulated as one may desire (i.e., even in a way different from the one proposed here); the result will always remain the same: at any given moment we get to hear only a seventh-chord, not a ninth- or an eleventh-chord. To include here the note of the pedal point, viz., the *F*, in the addition would mean to negate one's own musical instinct and to deliver it up to a theoretical obsession. Who would ever think in any other situation of adding the note of the pedal point to the several scale-steps and other phenomena of passing notes which devolve upon it? For the pedal point is the most vehement and drastic expression of the scale-step, which may wait long, very long indeed, for the fulfilment of its transcendent content—until the chain of manifold harmonic links has unrolled itself above it, often in a tempestuous manner.

Thus we see that our urge to hear a complex phenomenon as simply as possible induces us to hear a pedal point rather than an eleventh-chord or thirteenth-chord; this same urge often leads us to yet another assumption, viz., that of a suspension (§ 165), which, again, is much simpler than those higher chords. In the example from Wagner quoted above, such a suspension (for the full compositional execution of which we shall substitute here merely the abstract plan) would normally have to take the following course:

Example 179 (240):

It is easy to see that the root tone is not in any way affected if its fifth and third, *C* and *A* in our example, are suspended in the sixth and fourth or if these latter notes, *D*-flat and *B*-flat, make their retarding effect felt in so far as they constitute, e.g., the seventh-chord on *E*-flat (IV scale-step: *E*-flat, *G*-flat, *B*-flat, *D*-flat) or, respectively, on *C* (II scale-step: *C*–*E*-flat, *G*-flat, *B*-flat); for as long as the root tone *F* lacks the tones *C* and *A*, which belong to its harmony, the effect of *D*-flat and *B*-flat will always be that of a suspension, no matter how they be introduced.

I think I have proved, at any rate, that such a higher chord is unthinkable as an independent formation, as in most cases the pedal point, in conjunction with various seventh-chords (scale-steps) or even a suspension, will assert itself in the foreground of our consciousness.

PART II

PRACTICAL
APPLICATION

SECTION I

On the Psychology of Contents and of Step Progression

CHAPTER I

SCALE-STEPS AND CONTENTS

§ 115. *The Motif as Interpreter of the Harmonic Concept*

In practical art the main problem, in general, is how to realize the concept of harmony (of a triad or seventh-chord) in a live content. In Chopin's Prelude, op. 28, No. 6, thus, it is the motif:

Example 180 (244):

that gives life to the abstract concept of the triad, *B, D, F*-sharp; whereas

Example 181 (245):

by itself would have the effect of an assertion merely sketched for the time being.[1]

§ 116. *Harmonic Concepts Must Be Unfolded*

To the extent that the harmonic concept uses as its interpreter the motif, which, as we saw earlier, constitutes the primal part of content—to this extent harmony and content become one. From this point on, it is only a certain member of the total organism of content that makes us aware of the presence of a triad (or seventh-chord); and, vice versa, the laws governing the harmonic developments exercise an influence on the rise of content. Thus each harmony is not merely asserted but unfolded and demonstrated in this unfolding;[2] as content and harmony join each other, the feeling for the scale-step awakes in us.[3]

§ 117. *The Origin of Content from Harmony*

If we follow the phases of this process, two things become clear: Gradually we understand the form of a composition, and, vice versa, it is this form that reveals and stresses the psychology of the step progression.

Let us take, for example, the four opening measures of Mozart's Piano Sonata in C major (Köch. V, No. 330):

Example 182 (246):

[1. Here, as in the following §§ 116–17, the concept of unfolding is anticipated again, in § 116 even in the caption. Schenker shows that the motif does not represent a series of tones in general (§ 4) but that it unfolds the concept of a certain triad.]

2. The mutual organic influence between musical content and harmony cannot be emphasized enough, especially in times like ours, when composers often heap chords upon chords, without unfolding them in motivic substance and thereby clarifying the step progression.

[3. The mere substitution of the concepts "voice-leading," "scale-steps," and "tonality" for the words "contents," "harmony," and "scale-step" will reveal the development of Schenker's theory! (Cf. note to Example 89 as well as *Free Composition*, § 18.)]

Or, again, the first four measures of Chopin's Prelude, which we quoted in § 115:

Example 183 (247):

In both cases we see triads, unfolded as such in a rather satisfactory way (in Mozart we may find, if we so wish, even a modest pedal point).[4] But since throughout these four measures it is only one single triad that is asserted, it is impossible for us to find any satisfaction, particularly considering that the triads C, E, G (in Mozart) and B, D, F-sharp (in Chopin), by virtue of their trivalence or six-valence, may belong in three or six different keys. Thus harmony by itself calls for a further clarification, which, in turn, creates in us the need and expectation of a continuation—in us, and, naturally, in the composer as well. Hence we find, in the places from which we quoted, the complements, which in Mozart read:

Example 184 (248):

[4. The "pedal point" symbolizes the scale-step.]

and in Chopin:

Example 185 (249):

VI   II(♯3)   V   I   IV   V

In the former example, the IV and V scale-steps are unfolded, each with a new motivic content; until the tonic, following the dominant, finally brings us a certain satisfaction, harmonic as well as conceptual, such as could not have been reached before.

In the Chopin example we find a different kind of continuation, leading to a different conclusion. It is true that the point of departure is sufficiently well established by the step progression VI, II, V, I, IV, V, and it becomes quite obvious that we are in B minor; however, unlike the Mozart example, this step progression does not end with the tonic but with the dominant. But this dominant, too, conveys to us a sufficiently clear demarcation of the content.

CHAPTER II

ON DIFFERENT KINDS OF CONCLUSIONS

§ 118. *Antecedent and Consequent*

The satisfaction we obtained in the two instances quoted in chapter i cannot be considered as final, however; it is only a preliminary, relative kind of satisfaction, inasmuch as, for the time being at least, we lack the conceptual association which would be introduced by a repetition (cf. § 5) and which is indispensable if the content so far expressed is to be further clarified. In both examples we find, accordingly, a further continuation. In Mozart:

Example 186 (250):

with the step progression IV–I–V–I. In Chopin:

Example 187 (251):

with the step progression I–VI–II–V–I–VII(= V)–IV–V, and VI, etc.

Thus two separate parts are created, the first of which, as stated earlier, gives a satisfaction of a preliminary, relative kind, while the second—at least, in the example from Mozart—brings the final and absolute satifaction of a concluded thought. The complete and closed thematic complex is called *period;* its separate parts are called *antecedent* and *consequent.*[1]

§ 119. *The Full Close*

We still have to pay some closer attention to the feeling of satisfaction reached in the different phases of the examples quoted.

First, let us have a look at the consequent in the Mozart example. In this case our satisfaction is most complete and absolute. Why? Obviously, there are two reasons, intertwined and conditioning each other, the one formal, the other harmonic. In so far as this consequent has offered the repetition demanded by our need for association, our formal requirements have been fully met, so that no uncertainty, no doubt, remains in our mind, in so far as we restrict our observations to this one thought. The harmonic element, on the other hand, which is represented here by the step progression IV–V–I, is led by the form itself to arouse in us a feeling of complete satisfaction (§ 117).

[1. According to Schenker's theory of the *Ursatz*, the soprano (melody), too, plays a role in the construction of *antecedent* and *consequent* (see Example 5 in the Introduction). Some notion of this kind is already implicit in the following paragraph, where Schenker says that the full close remains imperfect because the melody merely brings the third of the triad at the moment at which the tonic returns. The same is true for Example 189, where Schenker does not hear a final conclusion, despite the *fermata*, because the voice-leading in the background has not yet reached any conclusion, as shown in the elaboration of this example in Appendix I (A9). Cf. *Yearbook*, I, 199, "Am Meer" by Schubert, where Schenker defends Schubert's declamation against Halm.]

Such step progression, IV–V–I, may occur anywhere—at the beginning, in the middle, or at the end of a musical thought. The particular significance of the IV step in such a process has been discussed in some detail in § 17, dealing with inversion. If we consider such a step progression, I–IV–V–I, from the harmonic angle alone and disregard any question of form, we find that it emphasizes, first of all, the tonic and, second, the key of the tonic. If we now consider that, in addition, the return to the tonic coincides with the formal conclusion—as it does in this consequent—and that it thus signifies a return to the harmonic point of departure, we see that the motion has reached its goal: form as well as harmony have closed their circle; and for this reason we call such a conclusion a *full close,* a *perfect cadence.*

The conclusion of the *antecedent* in the same example offers an inferior degree of satisfaction. It is true that the step progression is identical with that of the consequent; but in so far as the melody, with the reappearance of the tonic, brings merely the third instead of the root tone itself, the full close here is imperfect.

No less imperfect would be a full close which would bring the fifth of the tonic instead of the root tone. For example:

Example 188 (252). Beethoven, Piano Sonata, op. 57, Last Movement:

One might feel tempted to think that the perfect full close should be used only at the conclusion of the consequent, while the antecedent should always be concluded by an imperfect full close. This may hold true for most cases; such a connection between form and cadence, however, is not absolutely obligatory, and a perfect full close may occur also at the conclusion of an antecedent. For example:

Example 189 (253). Haydn, Piano Sonata, E Minor, No. 34 (see Appendix I, Example A9):

in which example the perfect full close (despite even the *fermata*) is not strong enough to obliterate our desire for a mental association, i.e., in this case, for a consequent. Thus we see that basically the cadence rests on the harmonic principle of step progression. When form enters as a codetermining factor, the cadence reaches a point of satisfaction as soon as a resting point, however minimal, is formally reached.

§ 120. *The Half-Close*

The conclusion of the antecedent in the example from Chopin quoted in § 117 offers us still another kind of satisfaction. In the first three measures of the continuation we see a step progression which, considered in itself, could signify a full close, viz., (I)–VI–V–I. But since the return of the tonic does not coincide with a formal conclusion[2]—which coincidence, as we have seen, is a *sine qua non* of the cadence—we do not yet have the effect of a cadence. The content rather proceeds beyond the tonic, brings the IV and V scale-steps, whereupon the dominant V finally coincides with the formal conclusion.

Our example thus shows that the step progression I–IV–V, too, may indicate a formal conclusion, although the order of the scale-steps is the reverse of the order of the full close.

If one considers that the dominant is the first fifth (above the tonic), it follows from the very fact of its secondary nature that it can never symbolize the return to the point of departure, as does the tonic. In order to make a distinction between these two kinds of conclusions, the latter is called a *half-close*.

If it is never conceded to the dominant to play the role of the tonic, the dominant has another precious quality, viz., to indicate that the tonic is yet to come. Under certain circumstances, the dominant is thus perfectly able to demarcate a part of the content, if not with the weight of a full stop—to use a metaphor from language and grammar—at least with that of a subordinate division, such as a comma, semicolon, colon, or question mark.

But if the dominant is to have the effect of a half-close, it must be clearly unfolded as a dominant. This, however, cannot be achieved except if it be preceded by the tonic which, so to speak, creates and explains it. In the step progression I–IV–V the tonic thus has two effects: on the one hand, it signifies development; on the other hand, by this very fact it enables the dominant to create the effect of a half-close.

It need not be stressed that the order I, IV, and V may well be replaced by the order IV, I, V.

This characteristic of the dominant as a function of form explains why composers use it sometimes even at the end, the very end, of a composition, when the intention is to dissolve the whole structure, as it were, in a question. Compare, in this respect, e.g.,

[2. Later, Schenker would have identified the conclusion of the form and the conclusion of voice-leading.]

Example 190 (284).[3] Schumann, "Dichterliebe," op. 48, No. 1:

VI — II — V — — IV — II — V⁷ —

An especially ingenious connection in one point of both kinds of conclusions (viz., the half-close and the full close) at the end of an antecedent, is the following:

Example 192 (255). Schumann, "Dichterliebe," op. 48, No. 2:

3. A similar effect as reached here by Schumann with the half-close at the end of the composition was undoubtedly aimed at by Richard Strauss, in the conclusion of "Thus Spake Zarathustra." He tried to achieve it by vacillating between two keys, viz., B major and C major. The effect, however, though it might have been reached under certain circumstances, was flouted because, after the preceding, broadly displayed B $\frac{major}{minor}$, including, still eight measures before the end, the following phrase:

Example 191 (256):

the last C's of the violoncellos and double basses could not possibly suffice (just to please the author) to prove the coexistence of C $\frac{major}{minor}$, as, in reality, these C's represent the II Phrygian scale-step of B $\frac{major}{minor}$. Despite the author's intention, the net result is thus, beyond the shadow of a doubt, a B $\frac{major}{minor}$.

blü - hen - de Blu - men her - vor, und

The vocal part first brings the half-close, whereupon the piano follows immediately with the full close. The author most appropriately indicates the distinction between both kinds of closes by the position of the legato slur in the piano part. It is true that basically this example represents a perfect full close; by interrupting at the dominant, however, the vocal part succeeds, at least for the duration of the *fermata,* in most convincingly simulating the effect of a half-close.

§ 121. *The Deceptive Cadence*[4]

Yet another closing effect is achieved by the consequent in the Chopin example quoted in § 118. Here the author gets ready to conclude his thought, as results obviously from the step progression V–I–V–VI and V, in measures 7–9 of this example. At the last moment, however, instead of using the I step, which would have brought the closing effect, he introduces a VI, viz., G, which, here in the minor mode, lies half a tone above V. This, for the time being, defers the closing effect. Apparently, the effect of the tonic, *B,* is omitted, since it has been replaced by the VI; but if we hear and feel

[4. Later, Schenker explained the deceptive cadence also from the point of view of voice-leading. This, however, does not in any way encroach on the psychological explanation offered here (cf. *Free Composition* § 191, Fig. 71).

V - VI   V — I   (V VI II VI)

It should be noted that there is a premonition of his later view in the explanation of Example 194. Schenker writes there: "At the same time II×$^{7}_{3}$ is already in a process of development." We only need to substitute "unfolding" for "development."]

how the expected *B* arrives not as a root tone but as a third, im-prisoned, so to speak, by another root tone (viz., that of VI, *G*), we will understand that we are dealing here with a type of closing effect which is fittingly called a "deceptive cadence." The author now is faced with the task—to continue our metaphor—of delivering the tonic from its imprisonment, i.e., to express it now in terms of scale-steps; he must find the way from VI, which is heard as the third fifth (in rising order), back to the tonic, descending through the second and first fifths. The continuation reads, accordingly:

Example 193 (257):

The following is another example of the same kind of deceptive cadence, V–VI:

Example 194 (258). J. S. Bach, *Well-tempered Clavier*, I, Prelude, C-Sharp Minor:

But if we look at the following example:

Example 195 (259). Haydn, Piano Sonata, E Major, No. 22:

we find here similarly the effect of a deceptive cadence, just as in examples 187 and 194, with the one difference that the tonic, B, which is expected at the third beat of measure 3, gets captured by the IV step, with the root tone E, a captivity from which it is freed in the course of the succeeding last two measures. Incidentally, one should take time to admire the sensitiveness and inspiration which could reach the effect that this modest thirty-second note, *E*, gets to symbolize a scale-step which lasts for no less than four quarter-notes! a proportion of a thirty-second note to a whole note, i.e., $1:32$!

The two deceptive cadences we just examined are best described by the following formulas:

1. V–VI (=I as third).
2. V–IV (=I as fifth).

These are the only two possible forms of a deceptive cadence with the tonic itself as basis, i.e., in accordance with the expectation aroused by the perfect full close.

§ 122. *The Plagal Cadence*

With these three kinds of cadences (full close, half-close, and deceptive cadence) we have practically exhausted the main possibilities. One could think, however, of a good many modifications to which the artist could resort. The so-called "plagal cadence" thus occupies a peculiar position between the full close and the half-close. In general, it is considered as a form of the half-close. I would rather consider it as a peculiar variation of the full close, with the only difference that the subdominant and the dominant change places. While in the full close the sequence is IV–V–I, we see here V–IV–I (cf. Example 130; cf. also Brahms, conclusion of the last movement of *Symphony No. I*, and conclusion of the Andante of *Symphony No. III*, etc.).

In general, the character of the full close is defined merely by V–I; that of the plagal cadence by IV–I. However, I should warn the student not to forget the IV in the former case and the V in the latter. Both form an essential part of the character of these cadences, except where the quickly passing or modulatory character of a passage permits, or even requires, a deviation from such particularization, as often happens in the development or modulatory part of a composition.

§ 123. *Other Cadences*

The half-close, too, allows for various modifications; for, besides the dominant, there are other scale-steps which can be used as temporary conclusion. For example:

Example 196 (260). Beethoven, Piano Sonata, op. 109:

Example 197 (261). Schubert, Piano Sonata, A major, op. posth.:

It is true that in this case, too, the antecedent ends with the dominant, but not with the dominant of the original key, C major, but with that of E minor, to which the antecedent has modulated. The antedecent thus presents a combination between a modulation and the regular use of the dominant. The modulation[5] begins in measure 3, where the IV step of E minor is developed. That this harmony, A, C, E, which could as well belong to C major as the VI step, already forms part of E minor, as the IV step, is clearly shown by the use of the diatonic F-sharp in the melody of the soprano in measure 4. It is true that Schubert resorted to the most refined means to make plausible this fantastic development from a I step in C major to the V of E minor, in the course of barely five (note well, five!) measures. Note especially the holding of the bass note C through four measures, followed by a descent by a half-tone. The bass voice does not make any big steps; modulation takes place, not in a strong, imposing manner; ghostly and silent, it slips by. Consider the power of genius which could create a consequent to such an antecedent, a consequent which likewise occupies no more than five measures! What joy in synthesis, what rounding-out! How many other artists would simply renounce the consequent in such a case, owing to a lack of power to synthesize—supposing even that they were able to conceive a similarly fantastic antecedent!

Finally, also, the deceptive cadence allows for various modifications; for, in a broad sense, any step progression, not merely V–IV or V–VI, may be heard as a deceptive cadence, provided that it pre-

[5. In the context of his theory of tonality—which he considered as the unifying factor in a piece of art—Schenker treated modulation merely as a "foreground" phenomenon. Accordingly, he would have seen here an unfolded auxiliary note B rather than a "key" (cf. § 171).]

vents the fulfilment of an expected full close. For example:

Example 198 (263). Beethoven, *Symphony VI:*

Andante molto moto

Here the sequence V–III$^{\sharp 3}$ in F major has somehow the effect of a deceptive cadence. Or

Example 199 (264). Beethoven, Piano Sonata, op. 57:

Compare, in this respect also, the last measures of Example 125. Note, finally, the following interesting conclusion (J. S. **Bach**, Partita III, Sarabande):

Example 200 (265):

§ 124. *Some Modifications of the Cadences*

We still have to consider certain modifications which may occur in regular cadences without changing their character. We have already described the function of the IV step in the cadence. This function is not disturbed if the II is substituted for the IV. Such substitution[6] is based on the following consideration: If a cadence demands the playing-up of the subdominant with regard to the tonic, the most obvious thing to do is to use the subdominant as root tone, i.e., as IV step. But the demand for the subdominant is satisfied even when it appears only as third, i.e., within the triad of the II step. The formula for the full close thus modified reads accordingly:

II–V–I;

for the half-close, in so far as it takes advantage of this substitution:

I–II–V.

The aspect of the cadence, II–V–I, might suggest that we are dealing here with a regular inversion, from the second fifth (above the tonic) to the first to the tonic. The process of substitution (II for IV) thus transforms the force inherent in the subdominant in the formula IV–V–I—a force tending toward the tonic (cf. § 127)—into a force of pure inversion.

One may ask why this substitution for the IV step can be made only by the II and not by the VII step as well, since the VII, no less than the II, contains the root tone of the subdominant, albeit as a diminished fifth rather than as a third. This question is easily disposed of if we remember that the diminished triad of the VII step, as we

[6. Cf. *Free Composition*, p. 186: "It is not always easy to discern whether we are dealing with a IV or a II step." Cf. also Examples 224 and 230.]

saw in § 108, is psychologically akin, by virtue of its univalence, to the V^7 chord; accordingly, it would take us straight to the dominant, where we would need a subdominant instead. In other words, the cadence VII–V–I could not mean anything but V–V–I; it would lack the desired and obligatory IV step.

In cadences in general, but particularly in the full close, the dominant often appears in the company of an apparent six-four chord, thus:

$$\text{IV (or II)–V}^{6\ 5}_{4\ 3}\text{–I.}$$

Compare, in this respect, Examples 6, 11 (measure 5), 13, 25, 73, 78, etc.

Again and again one speaks in such cases, merely on account of this six-four phenomenon, of a real tonic triad, i.e., of a I scale-step. For psychological reasons I consider such a conception as lacking in artistry. From a theoretical point of view, if the six-four chord is to be considered as an inversion of the triad of the tonic, the cadence would take the following aspect:

$$\text{IV–I–V–I.}$$

Obviously, it would make no sense to suppose that the artist would intentionally spoil the effect of the concluding tonic by introducing another tonic just before and, to boot, between the IV and V steps. It is true that under certain circumstances such an intention could seem acceptable to an artist; but he certainly would express it differently from what happens in those cases where such an intention is usually imputed to him.

We must renounce here the six-four chord as a I step and consider it merely as a suspension—cf. §§ 165 ff.—on the V step. From such an interpretation we should not be deterred even if the suspension lasts for a long time; for, as I have emphasized repeatedly, duration is no criterion for the determination of a musical concept. Note, for example, the broadness of the suspension in the following example (measures 3–8) from Mendelssohn's String Quartet, op. 44, No. 1, Andante:

Example 201 (265):

A beautiful, poetic, almost visionary, conclusion is shown in Bach's Gigue, Partita I. If one so wishes, one may suppose here an ellipsis of the suspension's resolution in the second half of measure 15, merely for the sake of the bass voice, which seems to indicate, with the B, a chromatically changed IV step, and with the C, the V step (cf. Example 195, measure 3).

Similar ellipses may be found in Example 9 (measure 8) and in Beethoven's *Symphony No. IX*, first movement, measures 33–35, with a particularly drastic effect and elevated character!

An incredible audacity is manifested in the following passage:

Example 202 (267). Mozart, Piano Sonata, A Minor, K. 310:

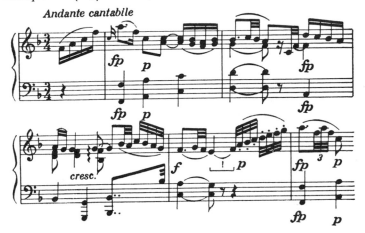

where the half-close of the andecedent (measure 4 of the example) is both softened and burdened in a most peculiar way by the quite inconspicuous legato slur from the second to the third beat of the soprano, taking the place of the eighth-rest ("suspir") which would have been expected here.

CHAPTER III

VARIOUS KINDS OF STEP PROGRESSION

§ 125. *Step Progression by Fifths*

If we consider step progression as it is practically applied in works of art, we find that it moves now in fifths, now in thirds or seconds. Therefore, we are also justified in speaking theoretically of step progression by fifths, thirds, and seconds.

As concerns progression by fifths, we need not deal with it here more explicitly, since its psychology—as we have shown in the theoretical part (Part I)—results clearly from the principles of development and inversion. In this sense, step progression by fifths could be called *natural,* in contrast to step progression by seconds, which, as we shall see in § 127, must be considered *artificial.*[1]

Example 203 (268). J. S. Bach, Partita III, Violin Solo, Prelude, Measures 50–59:

[1. In characterizing step progression by seconds as "artificial," Schenker anticipates his later theory, according to which this kind of step progression is relegated to the field of voice-leading. See *Free Composition,* § 56: ". . . Progression by seconds, which is to be considered as the real bearer of the contrapuntal-melodic component." Cf. also note to § 127.]

This example offers an uninterrupted series of descending fifths.[2]
Cf. also Examples 38, 119, etc.

Example 204 (269). J. S. Bach, Organ Prelude, E Minor:

Here we find an upward step progression by fifths: VI–III, V–II,
IV–I, while the following example shows a progression by fifths,
rising to the root tone, *E*, and descending from there on:

[2. In addition to this explanation, which rests on a purely harmonic basis, Schenker has
given another one, from the point of view of voice-leading: viz., that the ultimate cause of this
motion is in the need to avoid parallel fifths and octaves. Cf. Schenker's analysis of Example
203 in *Yearbook*, I, 75, where the measures in question appear as follows:

With regard to interpolated fifths, cf. *Free Composition*, §§ 282–83.]

Example 205 (270). Scarlatti, Sonata, D Minor:

§ 126. Step Progression by Thirds

Progression by thirds may be considered no less natural than progression by fifths. For, just as the latter is based on the principle of the third partial, so the former rests on the principle of the third, i.e., of the fifth partial.[3]

Development and inversion can be applied to progression by thirds as well as to progression by fifths; so that progression by thirds can take two forms: (a) rising, or (b) descending.

If progression by thirds is thus justified by Nature, we must nevertheless remember what has already been said in § 12, viz., that the fifth takes precedence over the third, and we should keep in mind all the consequences of this fact. A more powerful development will always be expressed by an upward progression by fifths, not by thirds: likewise, a downward progression by fifths will have a stronger and richer effect than a downward progression by thirds. In this sense, the fifth remains to our ear, also in the practical application of step progression, the unit as defined in the paragraph just quoted (§ 12).

The psychological effect of the progression by thirds is quite often that it makes progression by fifths (upward or downward) appear as though it were divided into two phases. It does not matter, obviously, whether in such cases both phases are exploited together or only one. Thus upward progression by thirds consists in the fact that the tone, which just now was the fifth of the root tone, becomes a third before it elevates itself to the rank of a root tone. Conversely, downward progression by thirds consists in the fact that the tone which just now was a root tone undergoes the less important fall to the third, before humbling itself to the place of a fifth.

[3. Later, Schenker dropped this derivation of progression by thirds from the series of partials and its justification by Nature. The explanation which is offered here as secondary (that it is a phenomenon of passing character, dividing progression by fifths, into two phases—for instance, F between A and D in Example 206) later became the determinative one (Free Composition, § 55). But here, in his Harmony, Schenker already gives examples of progression by thirds within a wider form: § 131 (Beethoven, op. 106, and Brahms, op. 34). In Free Composition, § 279, last paragraph (Examples 113, 36, and 137, 2), Schenker mentions another function of progression by thirds, viz., the support it affords to an auxiliary note by providing it with an independent chord.]

Example 206 (271). Mozart, Piano Sonata, A Minor, K. 310:

C:IV- II   II - V - I - VI - II - - (♯3)   V

§ 127. *Step Progression by Seconds*

In § 125 I characterized progression by seconds as artificial,[4] in contrast to the natural progression by fifths and thirds. The reason for this distinction is that in the series of the first five partials (cf. §§ 10–12) the second has no place. Progression by seconds must thus be considered as a secondary derivation from progression by fifths and thirds. This derivation also accounts for the fact that each progression by seconds—whether upward or downward—can be interpreted psychologically in two ways. The result varies according to whether the natural step progression from which the progression by a second derives is a development or an inversion.

a) An upward progression by a second, e.g., I–II, thus falls into the phases shown in Table 3.

b) Downward progression by a second, II–I, similarly divides, as shown in Table 4.

In those cases where we are faced with a progression of $1\frac{1}{2}$ fifths,

[4. Here again progression by seconds is called "merely artificial." Cf. note to § 125. In § 131, Schenker mentions a modulation from B major to C-sharp minor in Schubert's "Ländler," op. 67, No. 14—i.e., a step progression by seconds as a factor codetermining the form of the composition. He disregards the fact that in the second part the C-sharp moves on to D, which, in turn, is nothing but a stopover on the III on the way to the dominant.]

i.e., in Table 3, part 2, and Table 4, part 1, the order may be reversed under certain circumstances, i.e., fifths and thirds may exchange places.

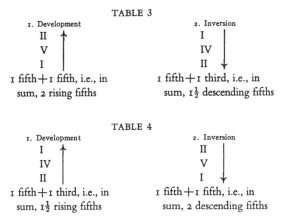

TABLE 3

1. Development	2. Inversion
II ↑	I
V	IV
I	II ↓

1 fifth + 1 fifth, i.e., in sum, 2 rising fifths — 1 fifth + 1 third, i.e., in sum, 1½ descending fifths

TABLE 4

1. Development	2. Inversion
I ↑	II
IV	V
II	I ↓

1 fifth + 1 third, i.e., in sum, 1½ rising fifths — 1 fifth + 1 fifth, i.e., in sum, 2 descending fifths

Thus in Table 3, part 2, I–II may be heard as an inversion:

I
VI   descending,
II ↓

and in Table 4, part 1, II–I, as a development

I ↑
IV   rising.
II

The chromatization of a progression by seconds (cf. § 142) quite frequently demands that we assume first the inversion of the third, then that of the fifth.

As these tables show, there are always at least two possible interpretations of a progression by seconds. In practice, however, we shall have to adopt always the one which fits best into the particular context. In the case of a perfect cadence (IV–V–I), e.g., I hear the one upward progression by a second (IV–V) not as an inversion,

IV
VII   descending,
V ↓

237

but as a development,

$$\left.\begin{array}{l} \text{V} \\ \text{I} \\ \text{IV} \end{array}\right\} \uparrow \quad \text{rising,}$$

though both interpretations would be possible. This interpretation
is confirmed by the six-four suspension[5] which is almost regularly applied to the V step and which, so to speak, contains a vestige of the
missing I step, without entitling us, on the other hand, to assume here,
for the sake of this vestige, the existence of a real I step. As we have
already stressed in § 124, we must consider this phenomenon merely
as a suspension. This example thus shows us an upward progression
by a second interpreted as upward development.

In the following example, on the contrary,

Example 207 (272). Beethoven, Piano Sonata, op. 2, No. 2:

which shows a step progression I–II–V–I, the upward progression
by a second, I–II, should be heard as an inversion (descending), I
(–IV)–II–V–I, rather than as a development (rising), I (–V)–II–V–I;
for the assumption of a IV step, in the first interpretation, reinforces
the meaning of the step progression as outlined here, while in the
second hypothesis the V step would weaken the effect of the immediately following dominant.

[5. Cf. note to § 98.]

How an upward progression by a second may have to be interpreted in the sense of an inversion (descending) is shown by the deceptive cadence in the example from Chopin quoted in § 118. There the inversion appears immediately as the decisive factor, and the sequence V–VI must be heard as

$$\left.\begin{array}{l} V \\ I \\ VI \end{array}\right\downarrow \quad \text{descending;}$$

for the arbitrary assumption of a development upward,

$$\left.\begin{array}{l} VI \\ II \\ V \end{array}\right\uparrow \quad \text{rising,}$$

would psychologically contradict the idea of the deceptive cadence.

Our other example of a deceptive cadence, that from Haydn quoted in § 121, shows a downward progression by a second, V–IV. In the sense of the deceptive cadence, this example, too, can be interpreted only as an inversion, descending from V–I–IV; while, on the other hand, the descending sequence, II$^{\sharp}_{\sharp 3}$–I in Schubert's String Quartet, A minor, first movement, measures 15–16, must be heard as a development (rising), II–IV–I.

§ 128. *Summary of All Step Progressions*

Summing up, we must distinguish between the following kinds of step progression:

A. Progression by Fifths

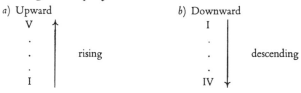

B. Progression by Thirds

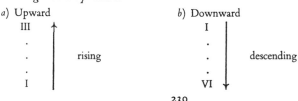

C. Progression by Seconds (*Whole or Half*)

a) Upward

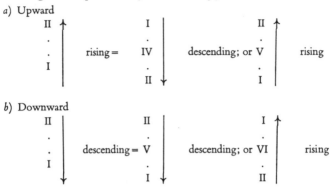

b) Downward

It goes without saying that, in practical application, step progressions do not follow one another uniformly, one like the other, but are always used in combinations, which enhance the variety of the effects.

CHAPTER IV

ON FORM ON A LARGER SCALE

§ 129. *The Rise of Groups of Ideas*

The following example from Beethoven's String Quartet, op. 95, will reveal to us the connection between harmony and form on a higher level:

Example 208 (273):

The key is already established clearly in measures 1 and 2, especially after the preceding D-flat major in the modulatory development; from the harmonic point of view, we find the I and V steps predominating; but motif, as well as harmony, calls for a continuation—the motif needs its repetition; the harmony, an enlargement of its sphere by drawing in other diatonic scale-steps. Thus we move into measures 3 and 4. But since these measures, too, lack certain decisive scale-steps, we still do not feel satisfied: we feel bound to hear the total of those four measures as the antecedent, leaving us in the expectation of a consequent. But not even the consequent brings us total satisfaction, as measures 5 and 6, for the time being, bring nothing but a further (the third) repetition of the motif, again within the I and V scale-steps, while the cadence, initiated in the following measures 7–10, instead of leading us, as in a full close, toward the tonic, merely leads to the dominant, as in a half-close; thus harmonic exigencies again make it necessary to continue the development of the content, as if the consequent were no final fulfilment of the antecedent but both together a kind of antecedent of a higher order. This is followed by measures 11–14. But, despite the fact that they bring an independent motif, they do not afford any final satisfaction. For they are composed on one single scale-step, viz., the V: with the harmonic development approaching its goal only step by step, the augmentation of the content up until now remains quite deficient; again, it is the harmonic factor which makes a further augmentation of the contents obligatory. Greater liveliness is aroused only in measures 15–19, which show a considerable abundance of new motivic content and scale-steps (VI–II–V) and, finally, in measure 20, lead us to the longed-for tonic.

Incidentally, the D major resulting from the chromatic changes in measures 15 and 16 may still be considered, if so desired, as part of the main diatonic key (D-flat minor, in this case), of which they would form the VI and II (Phrygian) scale-steps:

Example 209 (274):

VI   II

Cf. in this connection, Beethoven, *Symphony No. VII,* fourth movement, measures 79–80 and 91–96; scale-steps *A* and *D,* i.e., VI and ᵇII, in C-sharp minor.

What follows in measures 20–23 is a pedal point on the tonic, D-flat, on which we find a motif taken from the preceding main idea (measures 13–14 of the movement). As it is quoted here, it alternates between the I and the V scale-steps. The formula for this passage reads:

$$\frac{\text{I–V}:\text{I–V}}{\text{I}},$$

if one chooses to consider just measures 20 and 21 as statement, to be answered by measures 22–23. Here, finally, on this pedal point it sounds as if the whole tension, accumulated in the statement during measures 1–19, were released in the long-expected consequent.

He who already hears the concluding idea on this pedal point must marvel even more at such an organic connection between a so-called "subsidiary" section and the closing section—a connection which formally makes of the subsidiary section the introductory antecedent of the closing section.

However one may look at this situation, this much is clear, that Beethoven, instead of basing his conception on one single theme, has offered here a major group of several variegated motifs and elements, which nevertheless yield the effect of a closed conceptual unit. He reached this effect by using few, relatively very few, scale-steps for each single element while attempting to make the most, motivically, of each given scale-step.

This technique—more content, less harmonic dispersion—thus allows for a variety of characterization. It exhausts the contents of each scale-step by interpreting it conceptually[1] (cf. § 76, note to § 88; and §§ 115-16). By never wasting any harmony, it spares each one for whatever effect it may yet yield. The scale-steps and the themes motivated by them are assured, in any case, their desired effect, and there arises the image of organic unity which is so essential to a cyclic movement.

§ 130. *The Technique of Cyclic Composition*

The technique just described satisfies the exigencies of cyclic composition so completely that it may be considered a *sine qua non* of this form, a basic element of the cyclic style as such. As long as we consider as "cyclic" only those compositions which organically join a splendid plurality of ideas—not, as has often been held, such compositions as offer merely three themes, carefully counted and mechanically juxtaposed, i.e., the so-called "main" section or strain I, "subsidiary" section or strain II, and "closing" section—the underlying technical principle will have to be: Spare your harmonies and develop out of them as much thematic content as possible.

The composition, first of each single theme and later of groups of several variegated ideas—no matter whether the first, second, or third thematic complex—on one single scale-step is thus the decisive criterion of cyclic composition. We see our classical masters deviate but rarely from this principle and only in those cases where they are about to replace its effect with other particular harmonic or melodic constructions or where we are dealing, for example, with a mere modification of the variation form.

I need not stress the invaluable advantages, hard to reach by any other technique of composition, which this principle of composition offers in general and for the "development" part in particular. The whole capital has already been invested in the construction of the themes, so that the interests accrue to the author without any further toil. Each single component part merely gets loosened from its original setting, and, one by one, each is elaborated the more efficiently, i.e., it manifests its own latent, original, and independent nature.

[1. Here again Schenker hints at the concept of *Auskomponierung* or "unfolding."]

§ 131. *On the Analogy of Step Progression in the
Larger Form Complex*[2]

The psychological nature of step progression, which we have described so far in the context of form in the narrower sense, manifests itself in a marvelous, mysterious way also in the context of form in a wider sense—on the way from thematic complex to thematic complex, from group to group. In the form of established keys we have the same step progression, albeit at a superior level.[3] For the sake of the construction of content in a larger sense, the natural element of step progression is elevated correspondingly.

On this superior level, compare, for example, the plan of the "development" part of the first movement of Beethoven's Piano Concerto No. V, in E-flat major, op. 73, where the composition modulates from E-flat major to the key of the dominant, B-flat. Combining major and minor, the piano part brings, instead of E-flat major, an E-flat minor; this is the I scale-step in this key. After 6 measures we have arrived at G-flat major, i.e., there has been an upward step progression by a third. The step progression continues by a fifth, leading us to C-flat, so that we find in this step progression up to this point, a triad, E-flat, G-flat, and C-flat:

Example 210 (275):

so to speak, as an emphatic confirmation of Nature!

That on the scale-step C-flat it is, for the time being, C-flat minor that comes up, by virue of a combination between major and minor, rather than C-flat major—for to have written simply B minor instead of C-flat minor merely indicates Beethoven's desire to simplify —and that the fifth, G-flat, which erupts from this C-flat is used, besides, as ♭VI in B $\frac{major}{minor}$ for the purpose of modulating to B major, does not change the situation as we have interpreted it.

More than that: the principle of the fifth and of the third not only affects the form in so far as the extension of an individual idea or even

[2. Cf. *Yearbook*, II, "On the Organic of the Sonata Form," 43 ff. With regard to Examples 213 and 214, cf. note to § 126.]

[3. Does not this clearly anticipate the concept of "layers" (*Schichten*)? Cf. Introduction.]

a group of ideas is concerned, but affects the form in so far as form is the sum total of all ideas brought to interplay, i.e., the form of the whole. We see how in most cyclic compositions the content is developed from the starting point of the main key to that of the dominant: the complex of the subsidiary section and that of the closing section, i.e., the second and third thematic complexes, are usually set in the key of the dominant. On the other hand, the recapitulation brings an inversion from the dominant back to the tonic. Most compositions in the major mode take this turn.

Compositions in the minor mode, more often than those in the major, show a deviation from this natural law of development.[4] According to what has been said above, the thematic complexes following the main group should all appear on the minor dominant key. The result would be a composition continuing throughout in the minor mode. But while in a narrower frame a continuous minor mode may not get tiresome under certain circumstances, it proves altogether impossible to continue it in a larger frame, i.e., to insist on this mode in the key of the tonic (first thematic group) as well well as on the dominant (second and third groups), especially in view of the recapitulation, which unites all these groups on the basis of the same key and would keep us imprisoned by this minor mode forever. The sensitivity of the artist justly rebels against yielding, in such cases, to the natural law of the dominant. If we remember, however, that the minor system, as shown in chapter ii of Part I, is not really a natural system but is subjected to the laws of nature by the artist arbitrarily and in imitation of the major system, we cannot even say that the artist violates Nature if, in a larger composition in the minor mode, he prefers to resort to the major of either the third above or the third below—according to whether he is dealing with development (upward) or inversion (downward)—rather than use the minor of the dominant. To understand the artist in this respect, it may suffice to imagine how we would react if the first movement of Beethoven's *Symphony No. IX* in its further development got us into A minor rather than B-flat major! The danger of such an overabundance of the minor mode reveals the more clearly the artificial

[4. Cf. notes to §§ 20 and 50.]

character of the minor system and the revengefulness of Nature, which favors only the major system.

Art would not be free art, however, if it insisted always and under all circumstances on a development of a composition in major toward the fifth and of a composition in minor toward the third. Both in the progression of steps, as they complete a single thematic complex, and in the succession of keys, as they produce the total of the content, we therefore find deviations from the development toward the fifth or the third.

For example, the first movement of Beethoven's Piano Sonata, op. 106, descends from the tonic, B-flat, to the key of the VI scale-step, G (i.e., $G^{\text{major}}_{\text{minor}}$), which is the third below the tonic of B-flat:

Example 211 (276):

Brahms, in the Piano Quintet, op. 34, follows the main key, F minor, with a D-flat major rather than with an A-flat major, as would have been expected. This D-flat major appears first, by virtue of the combination between major and minor, as a D-flat minor (written as C-sharp minor):

Example 212 (277):

It should be noted, however—and this is most important—how Beethoven in the work just quoted emphasizes E-flat major, i.e., the key of the subdominant, in the development part, whereby the sequence B-flat major, G major, and E-flat major so mysteriously comes into its own.

Example 213 (278):

The example from Brahms offers a similar spectacle: in the development part Brahms brings B-flat minor, and the sum total of the keys thus yields F, D-flat, and B-flat.

Example 214 (279):

Besides progression by fifths and thirds, progression by seconds, too, may affect the form of a composition. Although such progression seems to deviate strongly from the natural, its form-determining effect must be considered not as exceptional but rather as a simple modification of the principle of progression by fifths and thirds, as has already been explained with regard to the scale-steps themselves. A strange example for such a progression by seconds is offered by the first movement of Mendelssohn's String Quintet in A major, op. 18. The second thematic complex here is set in E major, this being the dominant of A major; the last thematic complex, however, takes to the II step, F-sharp, of E major (and this on the occasion of a mere deceptive cadence!) and really sticks to F-sharp minor, a key which is one second higher than E major, up to the conclusion of the first part.

No less interesting is, for example, the first part of the "Kleiner Walzer," No. 14, from Schubert's "Wiener Damenländler," op. 67, which modulates from B major to C-sharp minor.[5]

In general, however, key-changes through step progression by seconds are far more frequent in modulatory and development parts. For this the reader may find his own examples.

§ 132. *Regularity of Step Progression in Larger Form Enhances Impression of Plasticity*

By such dispositions and correlations of the keys the form of our masterpieces becomes to us the more plastic. I am almost afraid that it is just this structural definiteness that the layman mistakes for mere formalism. Without comprehending what is really ingenious, he lets

[5. Cf. note to § 127.]

himself be seduced by this plasticity to renounce any further distinction between the works as such: Whatever is plastic, for him, seems to have the same form. With gleefulness and often not without a certain reproachfulness, he speaks of a so-called "classical form" as if it were something stabilized; he speaks of a "sonata form," a "symphonic form," etc., as if, e.g., all sonatas were the same merely because their harmonic development often moves from the tonic to the dominant, etc. Instead of recognizing in this a feature of Nature, which cannot be rejected by any genius but can at most be replaced at certain times by modifying surrogates; instead of understanding that Nature must penetrate all forms of music—be they sonatas or waltzes, symphonies or potpourris—the layman will mistake the command of Nature for a quality of form! Before arousing himself to hurl the insult of formalism in the face of the masters, would he not be well advised to study more closely the really distinguishing qualities of form in cyclic composition, apart from such common qualities?

On the Psychology of Chromatic Alteration

CHAPTER I

SCALE-STEPS AND VALUATION THEORY

§ 133. *The Natural Urge toward the Value of the Tonic*
When we listen to the opening measures of Beethoven's Piano Sonata, op. 90:

Example 215 (280):

our instinct suggests unfailingly that we are probably dealing here with a tonic in E minor. Why should that be so, if we know (cf. § 97, Table 2) that the E minor triad may have five additional, different meanings?

Likewise we take, for example, the beginning of Chopin's Prelude No. 2:

Example 216 (281):

to be the tonic in E minor; or the first measure of Schumann's Andantino (Piano Sonata, G minor, op. 22):

Example 217 (282):

to be the tonic of C major; for the same reason we assume a C minor tonic in the first measure of the sonata by P. E. Bach, quoted in § 16. Our assumption, however, will not be confirmed equally in each of these cases. In the Beethoven sonata, the E minor triad reveals itself soon enough to be a VI step in G major;[1] the same happens in the Chopin example, while in the Bach example the C minor step turns out to be the V in F major, and only Schumann confirms the tonic interpretation in the following development. Should we conclude from these various possibilities that our assumption was erroneous to begin with? Or is our instinct rooted nevertheless in a natural cause?

It is the latter alternative that is correct. Our inclination to ascribe to any major or minor triad, first of all, the meaning of a tonic fully corresponds to the egotistic drive of the tone itself, which, as we recommended earlier in the theoretical part (Part I), has to be evaluated from a biological point of view. This much is obvious: that the significance of the tonic exceeds that of the other scale-steps; and these lose in value the farther they go from the tonic. Thus a scale-step does not aspire to the place of a VI or II in the system, but, on the contrary, it prefers to be a V at least, if not a I, a real tonic, for the simple reason that these two scale-steps, because of their vicinity and undoubtedly greater precision, have a higher value.

[1. Obviously, Schenker made a mistake here. As a matter of fact, the sonata is in E minor, and the G can be understood only as the result of a progression by a third, dividing into two the ascent to the dominant, B (cf. note to § 126).]

§ 134. *The Yearning for the Tonic and the Deduction of the Key*

The general theory according to which we need merely have a look at the opening or concluding triad in order to find the key of a composition thus does not lack reason. We merely have to consider this triad as tonic—allegedly—and immediately we can determine the key. This calculation will be correct in most cases, and our supposition will be confirmed, thanks to the evaluation of the scale-steps as we just described it. One should be wary, however, not to give to this supposition any interpretation other than the one given here. For only he who can feel exactly how the scale-step loves to show off its highest value can also understand the author when he tries to mock us, consciously and purposively, by suddenly revealing the same chord which we supposed to be a tonic as an entirely different scale-step, as we saw in the examples above. The effect of such transformations rests on the very fact that the artist is fully aware of our yearning for the tonic and flouts it consciously.

Does not Beethoven, for example, in his Piano Concerto in G major, measures 6–14, play with this, our longing for the tonic?

Example 218 (283):

How many doubts does he conjure up with this B major! Will it develop into a real B major, with all the consequences thereof, in measures 1 and 2? Then, is *B, D-sharp, F-sharp* a tonic? The major triad on E in measure 3—we shall then have to ask ourselves—is it a IV step in B major? Obviously not, as it is followed by a major triad on A, which has no place in the diatonic system of B major. Even if we admit that, under certain peculiar circumstances and with a very special significance, the major triad on A could belong in B major, we feel rather tempted to try to get by with a simpler and more natural interpretation, to wit: we could take the major triad on E for the tonic of the E major key, to which the preceding B, D-sharp, F-sharp would form the dominant, while the following harmony, A, C-sharp, E, would be its subdominant. Or we might bestow on this last triad, A, C-sharp, E, itself the honor and dignity of a tonic, which would be preceded, again, by E, G-sharp, B as its dominant and, furthermore, by B, D-sharp, F-sharp as its chromatically changed II—it would have to be recognized as such *ex post facto*. Which interpretation is the right one? The following measure 4 still does not give any concluding answer; not only does it prolong our doubts, it adds new ones, and again with the same means. When we reach the triad D, F-sharp, A, we have the feeling that this is now a tonic. The same is true when we reach the G major triad. Our feeling thus. gets confused by this continuous change of major triads, both because of their plurivalence and, in particular, because we feel tempted, step by step, to impute to each one of them the rank of a tonic. Until we understand, at the end, that the B major was nothing but a III step in G major, the triad E, G-sharp, B constituted a VI step, and the triad A, C-sharp, E was the II of the same key, so that we kept moving throughout within the same key—despite all those chromatic changes, which we will discuss later on (§ 142).

Thus Beethoven exploits our doubts in order to render his G major key richer and more chromatic than would have been possible otherwise. These doubts, however, never would have been aroused in us, had not each scale-step a tendency to appear as a tonic, if possible, or, to put it anthropocentrically, were we not ourselves inclined to ascribe to each scale-step its highest value, i.e., the value of a tonic.[2]

[2. In a later phase of his development, Schenker would have placed the main emphasis on the motion (*Zug*) which creates the unity of this whole. Cf. the elaboration of this example in Appendix I (A10); cf., furthermore, the Introduction.]

§ 135. *Precaution in Deducing the Key of a Composition from Its Opening Triad*

In other words, one may say that, in fact, most compositions begin with a tonic—as the tonic responds best to the postulate of development. We should be wary, however, of all sorts of deceptions which spirited authors have in store for us, particularly at the beginning of a work. I do not include here the beginning of Beethoven's *Symphony No. I,* which at first raised such excitement because allegedly it did not open with a tonic. For, in reality, it does begin with the tonic, even though a dominant seventh-chord is piled upon it. On the other hand, I should like to remind the reader of the opening of Beethoven's *Symphony No. IX,* of the beginning of the G minor Rhapsody by Brahms,[3] and of a good number of other examples, already quoted in § 16, etc.

[3. Cf. elaboration of Example 28 in Appendix I (A5).]

CHAPTER II

THE PROCESS OF CHROMATIZATION
(TONICALIZATION)

§ 136. *The Concept of Tonicalization and of Chromatization*

Not only at the beginning of a composition but also in the midst of it, each scale-step manifests an irresistible urge to attain the value of the tonic for itself as that of the strongest scale-step. If the composer yields to this urge of the scale-step within the diatonic system of which this scale-step forms part, I call this process *tonicalization* and the phenomenon itself *chromatic*.

§ 137. *Direct Tonicalization*[1]

How is such tonicalization effected?

First of all, the scale-step in question, without any ceremony, usurps quite directly the rank of the tonic, without bothering about the diatonic system, of which it still forms a part. Note, for example, the following passage in J. S. Bach's Italian Concerto:

Example 219 (285):

We see here how a IV step in F major (measure 2) takes the aspect of a I in B-flat major. This results from the fact that in place of the diatonic *E* there appears, under the asterisk, the *E*-flat of B-flat major. Two things should be learned from this example: first, the advantage of unfolding a scale-step more fully rather than jotting it down merely as a triad or seventh-chord; for such unfolding in a greater number of tones provides the author with the opportunity to create the aspect of a different diatonic system, i.e., to yield to the scale-

[1. Cf. notes to §§ 155 and 159.]

step's yearning for the tonic; second, the invaluable advantage which arises for the diatonic system itself from the fact that the meaning of its own tones is increased by the contrast coming from a different diatonic system. How much more beautiful does this diatonic E sound in our example, after the immediately preceding measure has introduced an E-flat and thereby, apparently, staged a B-flat major! How feeble it would sound if the diatonic E were to be heard on both occasions!

It follows that the chromatic E-flat in our example has its own deep justification, of a specifically musical nature; and if we all too often talk away such a chromatic change as a mere passing note or some such thing, this merely proves our general incapacity to follow the real meaning of the tones or, what amounts to the same thing, to hear musically.

We would show no more musical sense, however, if, for the sake of this chromatic E-flat, we were to speak of a real change of key, as if the B-flat major generated by this E-flat were a real B-flat major key, which, by a simple modulation (i.e., a transformation of the I step in B-flat into a IV in F), would subsequently be reabsorbed by the F major diatonic system. It would be cumbersome indeed to assume here an independent key and modulation, merely to concede to the E-flat the satisfaction warranted by a superficial theory. Anyone's instinct, I think, would revolt against bringing such a sacrifice to a theory; for, without this theoretical obsession, who would even think of a B-flat major key here, where the context gives neither the preconditions of this key in what precedes nor its consequences in what follows? Is not B-flat major a world quite different from that of F major? And should not B-flat major be unfolded first of all? How much simpler is our explanation. And, furthermore, it has the advantage of directing the listener to penetrate more deeply into the individuality of the tones!

Let us have a look at another example, taken from J. S. Bach, *Well-tempered Clavier*, Prelude in E-flat minor:

Example 220 (286):[2]

I - - - - - - - bII (phryg.) - - -

- V - - - - V

Here again it is a II (Phrygian) step in E-flat minor, the major triad, F-flat, A-flat, C-flat—see the B-double-flat in measure 2—that confers upon itself, without further ceremony, the rank of a tonic. It would be idle, in this case too, to speak of a real F-flat major key; much simpler is it to sympathize with the II step in its yearning for the higher value of a I step—F-flat major, as it were. Note the exquisite effect resulting from the contrast between the B-double-flat and the diatonic B-flat! The situation is the more interesting, in that the conveyer of this effect is merely a tender sixteenth-note. Further examples:

Example 221 (287). J. S. Bach, Partita II, Sinfonia:

I - - II - - V

[2. Later, Schenker corrected his interpretation of measure 3 in *Tonwille*, I, 42: "In this sense the chord in measure 27 must not be understood as the expected dominant (in its third inversion); rather, it originates in a chance coincidence of an auxiliary note with two passing notes, above a sustained bass note. A more effective and more audacious passing could hardly be imagined." Thus, again, the explanation rests on voice-leading rather than on harmony. (Cf. note to Example 259.)]

Example 222 (288). Scarlatti, Sonata, F Major:

Example 223 (289). Mozart, Piano Sonata, D Major, K. 284:

Example 224 (290).[3] Schubert, "Die Stadt":

Example 225 (291). Brahms, Trio, op. 40, Finale:

[3. This is one of those cases (cf. note to § 124) where it is dubious whether it would not be preferable to see in measure 5 a IV step with added sixth.]

— II — — — III — — — V —

§ 138. *Indirect Tonicalization*

As we saw in the previous paragraph, the scale-step is able to satisfy its yearning for the value of a tonic quite alone. Much more frequently, however, it happens that a scale-step, to satisfy such yearning, makes use of one or more preceding scale-steps. Tonicalization, in such cases, is effected *indirectly*.

To find out what chromatic change would have to be made for this purpose, we must establish, first, the relationship between the scale-step that is to be tonicalized and the preceding one: whether this is a fifth, third, or second relationship.

Since tonicalization can be effected only by a process of inversion— tonicalization being essentially a descent to the tonic!—it follows naturally that, if we divide tonicalization into three groups, according to whether it is accomplished by step progression by fifths, thirds, or seconds, we must choose, in the first two cases, only downward progression by fifths and thirds, according to the pattern V³-I (or V⁷-I) and III-I, rejecting the upward (plagal) progressions, IV-I and VI-I. In the last case, on the contrary, we must choose the upward progression by seconds, according to the pattern VII-I, since, as we saw in § 127, the inversion here in question is effected by an upward progression.[4]

4. It is true that II-I, as well, might lead to the establishment of a tonic, in so far as such progression, according to § 127, Table 4, part 2, signifies the progression II-V-I. But since the major system shows the constellation of a downward progression by a major second from a minor to a major triad not only at II-I but, another time, at VI-V, the effect of absolute tonicalization is endangered by the progression II-I. The sequence, D, F, A, to C, E, G, for instance, might be heard not only as II-I in C but, under certain circumstances, also as VI-V in F major. If, instead, we follow the other pattern, VII-I, as explained above, any danger of ambiguity is obviously avoided.

§ 139. *Tonicalization by Descending Fifths*

Tonicalization by descending fifths is effected as follows: The primary object is to find the diatonic dominant as a prelude to the scale-step which is to be tonicalized. For this purpose the preceding scale-step, the one which is to be used as a dominant, must be defined as such. This can be achieved by transforming the triad under consideration, whether this be a minor or a diminished triad, into a major triad by making either one or two chromatic changes—according to whether the new dominant is to be gained from a minor or from a diminished triad. One might ask: Why must we assume the dominant always to be a major triad, despite the fact that in the minor system, as we know, the dominant is a minor triad? The answer is simple: On this occasion, also, the artist accepts the preponderance of the natural system over the artificial (minor) system, and therefore he provides his scale-step in any case with a major dominant, no matter whether the following tonic be a major or a minor triad.[5] The VII step, for instance:

Example 226 (292):

being a diminished triad, necessitates two accidentals, a sharp at *D* and a sharp at *F*, whereupon the major triad thus gained:

Example 227 (293):

makes it possible for what was originally a VII step to function as a tonicalizing dominant. It goes without saying that these two chromatic changes can be either merely put down or fully unfolded and that the latter alternative is the more convincing one.

The minor triad, for example:

[5. Instead of appealing to the "natural" system, it would have been more correct to emphasize the necessity of obtaining a leading-tone.]

Example 228 (294):

needs only one chromatic change, at the *F* in the third; this gives rise to the major triad D-flat, *F, A*-flat and enables the original scale-step to function as a tonicalizing dominant.

§ 140. *Summary of All Forms of Tonicalization by Fifths*

[In this paragraph Schenker gives detailed schemata of the chromatic changes necessary for the tonicalization of each scale-step.[6] This schematic part is followed by illustrative examples.]

Example 230[7] (296). Beethoven, Piano Sonata, op. 31, No. 1:

6. Indirect tonicalization does not mean real modulation. Therefore Richter erroneously calls
Example 229 (295):

G: V⁷   C: V⁷   I

G major and C major, instead of simply C major: II♯₃⁷–V⁷–I.

[7. Here, as well as in Example 224, it would probably be preferable to read IV⁶⁻⁶ rather than IV–II (measures 3–4). With regard to measures 2 and 3, cf. Schenker, *Counterpoint*, I, 367.]

Example 231 (298). J. S. Bach, Chaconne, Violin Solo:

Example 232 (299). J. S. Bach, *Well-tempered Clavier,* Vol. I, Fugue, B-Flat Minor:

Example 233 (300). J. S. Bach, *Well-tempered Clavier,* Vol. II, Prelude, F-Sharp Minor:

§ 141. *Tonicalization by Descending Thirds*

In the case of progression by thirds, the relation between the III to the I scale-step, as explained in § 138, constitutes the natural foundation of the tonicalizing effect. But if we take a look at the contents of the III step in major and in minor, we find a minor triad in the former case and a major triad in the latter, both of which are trivalent, or six-valent, according to § 97. The major system, furthermore, contains a progression by a major third not only at III–I but also at VI–IV and VII–V; at VI–IV it even repeats the combination major triad–minor triad; the minor system, similarly, contains a progression by a minor third not only at III–I but at VI–IV and VII–V as well, repeating the combination major triad–minor triad at VII–V. This factor of plurivalence accounts for the very decisive difference between progression by thirds and progression by fifths, where tonicalization in most cases definitely aims at inducing the univalent V⁷ chord, with its decisive tonicalizing effect.

If we wanted to set a seventh chord on the tonicalizing scale-step where we are dealing with progression by a third, such a seventh chord, diatonically conceived, would still be trivalent (cf. § 105):

Example 234 (301):

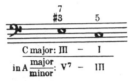

Even if it were chromatically changed into a univalent V⁷ chord, it could only induce some kind of deceptive-cadence effect (cf. § 123):

Example 235 (302):

Thus, even if we use a univalent V⁷ chord, its effect can never be so totally tonicalizing in the case of a downward progression by a third as would be the effect of that same V⁷ chord in the case of a downward progression by a fifth. In the former case, chromatic change as such lacks the ability to induce a tonicalizing effect as precise as is induced in the latter case; as it is impossible to construct on the tonicalizing scale-step a univalent chord as efficient as is that same chord in the case of progression by a fifth. This, incidentally, is explained by the fact that progression by a fifth, V–I, corresponds quite naturally to the V⁷ chord as it stands on the dominant fifth, while a V⁷ chord, if chromatically constructed, as in the case of progression by a third, remains, for this very reason, some kind of *contradictio in adjecto*.

The emphasis of the tonicalizing effect, in the case of progression by a third, thus lies less on the variable chromatic changes than on the step progression by a major or minor third in major or in minor, more, accordingly, on the psychological precedence (cf. § 133) taken by III–I over VI–IV and VII–V; the situation is different, in other words, from that obtaining in the case of progression by a fifth, where the tonicalizing effect is guaranteed by both factors, the downward progression by a fifth as well as the chromatic change inducing the univalent chord. Thus it is true that the usefulness of chromatic changes is inferior in the case of tonicalization through progression by thirds as compared to progression by fifths. It does not follow, however, that the process of tonicalization avoids or should avoid progression by thirds. Chromatic change, in so far as it returns us less precisely to our diatonic system, is the more indicated for the purpose of a real modulation. We shall come back to this later on.

Example 236 (303). Schubert, Piano Sonata, op. 53:

Example 237 (304).[8] Schubert, "Die Allmacht":

§ 142. *Tonicalization through Upward Progression by a Second*[9]

The trend and the effect of chromatic changes in the case of progression by seconds is similar to that in the case of progression by fifths. According to § 138, the pattern of tonicalization here is the sequence

$$VII^3-I^{(\natural, \flat, \sharp 3)}$$

[8. Here is an example of a progression by a third, dividing a progression by a fifth into two phases (*Terzteiler*). Cf. § 126. The chord on *A*, dividing the progression from *C* to *F*, is, furthermore, chromatically changed into a major triad. Cf. Examples 98/3*a* in *Free Composition*.]

[9. Tonicalized progression by a second in the foreground usually serves the purpose of avoiding parallel sequences of fifths and octaves, following the method, quite customary in counterpoint, of exchanging 5–6–5 (*Free Composition*, §§ 164 and 175). The tonicalizing and chromatically sharped sixth-chord is often transformed into a "root chord" (*Free Composition*, § 247). It is obvious that the usual designation "auxiliary" or "secondary" dominant, which corresponds, to some extent, to tonicalization, restricts the scope of our observation to the foreground and disregards its origin from counterpoint.]

Any progression by a second, in so far as it is to induce a tonicalizing effect, must be made to conform to this relationship, whereby it does not matter whether the tonic is subsequently a major or a minor triad. It need not be stressed that the use of the seventh chord on the VII step rather than of the diminished triad alone will increase the precision of the tonicalizing effect, just as happens in the case of tonicalization through progression by a fifth. Again we may use either the minor, the diatonic seventh, or the strictly univalent diminished seventh which results from the combination of major and minor.

Before translating the scheme into reality in a given case, we must first see whether we are dealing with progression by a minor or major second. The chromatic change will be different in either case.

1. Let us take a progression by a minor second, e.g., in the diatonic system of C major, the sequence of III (E, G, B) to IV (F, A, C). It is obvious that an accidental at the fifth, changing the B to B-flat, suffices to bring about the desired diminished triad, E, G, B-flat, which elevates the following step, F, A, C, to the rank of a tonic.

2. In the case of progression by a major second, on the other hand, the chromatic change must be such as to transform the relation between the two scale-steps in question, i.e., the major second must be replaced by a minor one if the step progression is to conform to the pattern established earlier. In other words, it is the root tone itself that must be raised chromatically.

In this second case the sharping as such produces the desired diminished triad only if we have a major triad on the scale-step in question, i.e., if in C major we want to tonicalize the sequence IV–V (F, A, C–G, B, D) and for this purpose we raise the F to F-sharp. Thereby we obtain F-sharp, A, C, which functions as a VII step in G major, and the subsequent V step appears as a I in G major (cf. § 162).

If, on the other hand, the scale-step from which we depart contains a minor triad (e.g., II–III, i.e., D, F, A–E, G, B), the sharping of the root tone is insufficient. In addition, the third, F, must be raised to F-sharp; this finally produces the diminished triad D-sharp, F-sharp, A, as a VII in E major.

In tonicalizing through progression by seconds, there are thus three alternatives: (1) to flat the fifth; (2) to sharp the root tone; and (3) to sharp root tone and third, depending on the kind of progression by a second that we are dealing with and on the kind of triad we find on the scale-step on which the diminished triad is to be obtained.

To these chromatic changes we must add eventually those others which correspond to the diatonic or diminished seventh-chords on VII.

Example 238 (305). Handel, *Messiah:*

Example 239 (306). Mozart, Piano Sonata, D Major, K. 311:

$-$ V $-$ $-$ (–) $-$ $-$ V $-$ $-$ $-$ I

§ 143. *Chromatic Change Inducing Deceptive Cadence through Upward Progression by a Second*

In dealing with step progression by seconds, a clear distinction should be made between the effect of tonicalization as illustrated in the foregoing examples and the effect of a chromatic change of the following kind:

In C major: III$_{\sharp3}^{I}$–IV; or, in notes:

Example 240 (307):

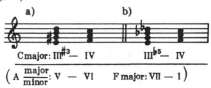

In the case of (*a*) the III step sounds like a dominant seventh-chord, V[7] of A major, which seems to relegate this case to the sphere of those chromatic changes which effect tonicalization by a V[7] chord and downward progression by a fifth. It is true that the expected tonic, as we see, is missing, and in its place the VI step, A minor, came up. This chromatic change thus reaches the effect of V[7]–VI, an effect we described as deceptive cadence in § 121. We may call this kind of chromatic change, therefore, a "deceptive-cadence chromatization." Rather than contrast the chromatic change which induces tonicalization, this kind of chromatic change forms its complement, in the sense that the deceptive cadence itself rests on the idea of the tonic which is expected; our feeling for the tonic is its precondition. Whether the progression by a second is chromatized so as to produce the effect VII–I, or following the pattern of the deceptive cadence, that of V[7]–VI, in either case the tonic is the goal of the chromatic change, with the only difference that in the first case this goal is really reached, while in the second it is replaced by a VI.

Example 241 (308). J. S. Bach, *Well-tempered Clavier,* Fugue, D minor:

§ 144. *Microtonicalization of Individual Tones*

It is not only the scale-step, as a comprehensive unit of a higher order, that strives to attain the value of a tonic; often it is an individual tone, even one of quite secondary importance. This urge, too is satisfied with the help of the preceding individual note. This is illustrated by the following example from Schumann's "Davids Bündlertänze," op. 6, No. 5:

Example 242 (309):

The harmonic note B (second eighth-note in measure 1) attracts to itself the preceding note, A, inducing a sharp (A-sharp). Our tendency always to assume the highest value thus suggests to us an analogy to a progression VII–I, although in the strict sense we certainly are not justified in assuming scale-steps here in the horizontal direction. It is true that the first eighth-note, A-sharp, also has here the function of a changing note (cf. § 167) or, if one prefers, of a suspension. This function, however, does not detract from the effect of that other service rendered.

Compare in this respect the example from Chopin, Etude in B minor, quoted in § 34. There again it is the so-called "neighboring" notes that perform, so to speak, the role of a VII step, although the notes which they thus serve are themselves but passing notes.

This shows the process of tonicalization in the narrowest confines, *en miniature*. We should be careful not to overlook these almost microscopic phenomena; they enhance the liveliness and activity of the tones on the level of the minimal, which often reveals relationships we might otherwise miss. In any case we should admire in these phenomena the omnipotence and omnipresence of the yearning for the tonic, which manifests itself more and more as a veritable miracle of Nature in our art.

Example 243 (310):

§ 145. Tonicalization as an Explanation of the Phrygian II Scale-Step[10]

The use of the so-called "Phrygian II" step, i.e., the progression from the tonic toward the minor second, was justified earlier (§ 50) by motivic considerations. This phenomenon may be explained also

[10. This paragraph is speculative, to some extent. It is corrected in § 50 and the note to that paragraph.]

with a chromatic change inducing tonicalization, as we have just seen. It is the context alone that must determine which of the two explanations is preferable. They do not collide in any way.

Let us assume that we are in D minor and imagine an inversion, descending VI–II–V–I. The diatonic content of the VI step is B-flat D, F, i.e., a major triad, while the II step contains the diminished triad, E, G, B-flat. If we avail ourselves of the possibility of combining major and minor and thus set a major triad on the dominant, our sequence takes the following aspect:

Example 244[11] *(311)*:

Let us assume further that chromatic changes effecting tonicalization be applied merely to the sequence II–V, i.e., that the V wants to become a tonic and uses, for this purpose, the preceding II; we have to change the diminished triad on II into a major triad (eventually a V[7] chord), as required by the major dominant. Upon effecting this chromatic change, we obtain the following sequence:

Example 245 (312):

When this harmonic sequence becomes an artistic reality in the D minor key—as happens almost regularly—nobody is in the least disturbed by the collision of the diatonic B-flat of the VI step and the chromatic B of the II. If we now imagine the concluding triad canceled,

11. I reproduce the contents of the scale-steps in notes but beg the reader not to think in terms of voice-leading, which I strictly reject on such occasions (cf. §§ 90 ff.). I am using notes merely for the sake of greater perspicuity.

Example 246 (313):

the remaining part of this step progression:

Example 247 (314):

looks like an A major, with the difference that the diatonic II step in A major would be *B, D, F*-sharp; in À minor, *B, D, F*, i.e., both triads would rest on the root tone *B* rather than on *B*-flat, as we have it in Example 247. In order to use the VI of D minor as a II in A $\frac{\text{major}}{\text{minor}}$, we must imagine the chromatic change to affect the root tone, *B*, i.e., to flat the *B*:

$$\text{A } \tfrac{\text{major}}{\text{minor}}\text{: } {}^{\flat}\text{II–V}^{\sharp}3\text{–I}^{\sharp, \, \natural 3} \, .$$

It is true that this step progression is heard more naturally as part of D minor, a progression which, strangely enough, does not proceed to the tonic itself but stops short at the dominant, thus inducing the effect of a half-close. This flatted II step, *B*-flat in A $\frac{\text{major}}{\text{minor}}$, with the secondary effect of a diatonic VI in D minor, constitutes the "Phrygian II."

This equation, on the other hand,

$$\text{A } \tfrac{\text{major}}{\text{minor}}\text{: } {}^{\flat}\text{II–V}^{\sharp}3\text{–I}^{\sharp, \, \natural 3} = \text{D } \tfrac{\text{major}}{\text{minor}}\text{: VI–II}^{\natural 5}_{\sharp 3}\text{–V}^{\sharp 3} \, ,$$

best explains why compositions, e.g., in A minor, most frequently conclude with the major triad, *A, C*-sharp, *E* rather than with *A, C, E*, if a Phrygian II has been used just before the conclusion. The composition thus lacks the normal closing effect which we are accustomed to enjoy in the sequence II–V–I, and, although we clearly recognize in this last step the tonic, there remains in us an afterthought, as though we were still dealing with the dominant of

D minor, to be followed still by its tonic. Cf. Chopin, Etude in A minor, op. 10, No. 4:

Example 248 (315):

CHAPTER III

ALTERATION AS A MODIFICATION
OF TONICALIZATION

§ 146. *The Origin of Alteration*[1]

Tonicalization really is the source of the so-called "altered chords."
In the conventional textbooks such phenomena either are treated
abruptly and therefore all too mystically or, in the best of cases, are
explained to some extent; but the explanations do not grasp the essence of alteration and cannot account, therefore, for all altered
harmonies in the same way. The true psychology of the altered
chords is the following:

First of all, let us place, one next to the other, a V^7 chord and a $II^{\flat 7}_{\flat 3}$
chord, e.g., on G:

Example 249 (316):

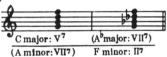

C major: V^7 ($A^\flat$major: VII^7)
(A minor: VII^7)   F minor: II^7

If for the V^7 chord in C major we set merely:

Example 250 (317):

in other words, if we eliminate the fifth, *D*, the seventh chord does
not thereby lose its meaning and character; for its univalence remains
adequately defined by the remaining elements (the root tone, the
major third, and the minor seventh of V^7 in major). Since there does
not exist another seventh-chord with just these intervals, our instinct
can be relied upon to guess the missing fifth: no tone except *D* could
fit between this *B* and *F:* that much we know at once.

We find ourselves in an analogous situation when we set only the
following three notes:

[1. From what has been said (§ 99), it is clear enough that in a later phase of his development Schenker would have relegated alteration to the sphere of voice-leading.]

Example 251 (318):

for the II♭⁷₃ in minor. There can be no doubt that the missing third must be B-flat.

Let us assume now that these two phenomena are combined somehow in such a way that to the elements which are common to both, viz., the root tone and the seventh, there is added the major third of the V⁷ in major and the diminished fifth, D-flat, of the II♭⁷₃ in minor. We thereby obtain the following construct:

Example 252 (319):

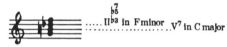

In this harmony the three notes, *G, B,* and *F,* as we have seen, induce the desire for the fifth, *D,* and the association of a V⁷ chord in C major; in a certain sense, the major third can be considered the decisive criterion of this univalent chord, as I have tried to indicate graphically in Example 252. On the other hand, our ear is tempted by the three notes, *G, D-flat,* and *F,* to supplement the minor third, *B-flat,* and thus to take this chord to be the II♭⁷₃ in F minor, so that the diminished fifth, *D-flat,* may be considered, analogously, to be the decisive criterion of this latter seventh-chord. In this sense we may say that in this harmony three elements are engaged in a struggle against three other elements—whereby it does not matter that two of these three elements are identical in either case—and while one of the litigating parties constitutes a V⁷ in C major, the other forms a II♭⁷₃ in F minor. Thus two different effects combine in a surprising unit: first of all, the effects of two different scale-steps, a V and a II, and, in addition, the effects of two different diatonic systems, the major and the minor, as the V refers us to a major, the II to a minor, system.

We are thus faced here with a combination; but, in contrast to the combinations we have considered so far (§§ 38 ff.), this one does not bring a major and a minor on the same tone (e.g., G $\frac{\text{major}}{\text{minor}}$, where the tonic is homonymous), but it unites two different keys—in our case, C major and F minor, i.e., *not* homonymous keys!—and in those keys, differing from one another by mode and tonic, it represents, to boot, two different scale-steps, a V and a II.

§ 147. Diminished Third and Augmented Sixth as Characteristics of Altered Chords

As external characteristics of such altered chords, we find here a quite new interval, which we have not encountered anywhere so far and which can only be called a *diminished third*. Its inversion brings an *augmented sixth:*

Example 253 (320):

diminished third   augmented sixth

The diminished third and the augmented sixth always indicate that we are dealing with a state of alteration.

§ 148. Alteration Brings Final Completion of Number of Intervals

The addition of these two intervals finally completes the sum total of all possible intervals.

Our tonal system does not offer any possibility of forming others, except if it were itself to undergo a change, which can hardly be expected, considering the complete conformity to Nature of our major system.

These two new intervals raise the sum of all intervals to 20; cf. § 62, where the other 18 were enumerated.

§ 149. Summary of All Univalent Altered Chords

We shall now apply the process of alteration, as described, to all the univalent chords we have met in § 108. In this we are justified by the psychological kinship, already familiar to us, of the V⁷ chord and the VII³ and VII♮⁷, ♭ chords and also by the fact that the V⁷ chord is one of the preconditions on which the process of alteration is based. All we have to do now is to transfer this same process, i.e., the new characteristic interval, to those related chords which may be substituted for the V⁷ chord.

The table of all univalent chords, in all their inversions and with alteration applied, presents itself as follows:

Example 254 (321):

1. VII^♭3

2. V^♭⁊

3. VII^♭3

While we may and must note, first of all, the effect of V in all these chords, owing to their univalent character, they acquire, through the process of alteration, a second effect, viz., that of a II. Thus the simple designation II or V which we would use in other cases to characterize a scale-step is now insufficient, and it may be preferable to use the following formula:

II+V; or, more precisely: II in F minor+V in C major.

§ 150. *Alteration in the Conventional Textbooks*

For this sum total of chords and inversions which we find applied in art, the authors of the conventional textbooks, unaware of the correlations and the origin of the altered chords, usually pick three inversions as "the most customary" (?!), viz., those in which the augmented sixth, *D*-flat, *B* (a more drastic interval than the diminished third, it is true) comes to lie on the outside. They call

Example 255 (322):

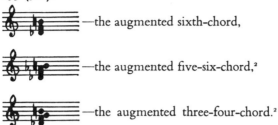

—the augmented sixth-chord,

—the augmented five-six-chord,[2]

—the augmented three-four-chord.[2]

§ 151. *The Meaning of Altered Chords in Modulation*

In the course of an inversion, we may thus make use either of the II step or, with no less justification, of the V step contained in the altered chord. It follows, for example in the following case:

Example 256 (323):

**II in F minor
+ V in C major**

that, if we assume II, we may proceed, via V, to the tonic of this key (II–V–I in F minor); or, assuming V, we may proceed directly to the tonic of C major. In other words, two ways, leading to two different keys, are possible from this altered chord:

(II F minor + V C major)–V–I in F minor,
(II F minor + V C major)–I in C major.

The first way takes off from the II step as the second fifth above the tonic, whence it descends by two fifths; it is, accordingly, the longer way. The second way is shorter because it presupposes only the first fifth above the tonic, i.e., it descends by only one fifth; but both ways are equally accessible.

§ 152. *The Psychology of Alteration*

Why does the artist need this combined effect of two steps and two keys in one harmony? The answer is: for the sake of tonicalization.

2. It is obvious that the two latter constructs are nothing but the first, with a fifth, or a fourth, added to it.

We have seen (§ 138 ff.) that, as soon as a scale-step strives to assume the character of a tonic, it can use for the realization of this aim either one or two scale-steps immediately preceding it; in the first case a V⁷ chord is to be constructed on the preceding scale-step; in the second case, such a V⁷ chord, in turn, is to be preceded by its own fifth, viz., the II step. Alteration now offers a third alternative, i.e., a combination of both methods.

The particular charm of this combination is due to the fact that the all too univalent character of the V⁷ chord seems softened by the simultaneous appearance of a II in minor; for, while the V⁷ chord brings us immediately to the tonic, the diminished fifth of the II step brings a retarding momentum; for, in so far as it is the second fifth above a tonic (of a different tonic, of course), it seems to push the goal of the tonic back some distance. Thus we feel at the same time the nearness and the remoteness of a tonic; and this creates a peculiarly suspended atmosphere. See the following examples:

Example 257 (324). J. S. Bach, Chaconne, Violin Solo:

Example 258 (325). Chopin, Mazurka, op. 30, No. 2:

Example 259 (326).[3] Wagner, *Tristan and Isolde:*

§ 153. *Psychology of the Position of Distinctive Interval*

As we saw earlier, the altered chord has only one external criterion, the diminished third. In order to forestall certain wrong notions, it is necessary to give here some consideration to the position of this distinctive interval. The origin itself of alteration, as we have described it, entails that the diminished third (*B, D*-flat in our example) be placed in such a way that its lower. component forms a major third with the root tone; the upper component, consequently, forms with the root tone a diminished fifth (in our example, *B* forms a major third, *D*-flat a diminished fifth, with the root tone *G*). As I have shown, it is this position which creates the peculiar effect of the altered chord (viz., that of a V and of a II).

If, in a practical case, we are faced with a diminished third, it is not legitimate to jump immediately to the conclusion of an altered chord, merely on account of this interval. It is obligatory, on the contrary, to consider the position of this diminished third relative to the root

[3. With regard to this example, Schenker took this position in *Yearbook*, II, 29: "Every vertical coincidence of tones as, e.g., [here follows measure 2 of Example 259] was stared at; as if music were not a meaningful sequence in time, in the sense of unfolding. . . . New chords were fancied."]

tone, because only the root tone can give us information as to the scale-step we are dealing with. Nor must we be misled by the fact that this root tone is not in all cases directly recognizable in the chord itself (Example 254, at *1* and *3*) but must be supplied mentally as a complement (this being the main point of the kinship of univalent chords). Accordingly, there are two possibilities: the root tone, either really existing (as in case *2* of Example 254) or mentally supplied (as in cases *1* and *3*), forms a third, or a diminished fifth, with the components of the diminished third; in this case, and only in this case, are we dealing with an altered chord. Or the root tone forms different intervals with those components; in this case it is simply wrong to speak of an altered chord.

The chord in the following passage of Chopin's Mazurka, op. 56, No. 3, e.g.,

Example 260 (327):

(in so far as we wish to sum up the content of this measure in one chord[4]) must be considered as an altered chord, with the root tone extant, according to case *2* in Example 254.

The fact of alteration will have to be admitted also with regard to the following example from the same piece:

Example 261 (328):

[4. Note Schenker's doubt here!]

although the root tone, C, must first be supplemented here (case 3)[5] in order to construct the scale-step.

The following passage in the same mazurka, on the contrary:

Example 263 (330):

brings a diminished third at the last beat of measure 1 (here, as an augmented sixth), C-sharp, E-flat, without offering any justification for considering this chord as an altered chord; for the C-sharp and E-flat do not form a third, or a diminished fifth, but an augmented fifth, or minor seventh, with the root tone. It should not be difficult, accordingly, to hear in this place simply a V[7] chord rather than the combined effect of a V and II step. The C-sharp, i.e., the fifth, is explained quite simply as a melodic passing note, substituting for the pure harmonic fifth, C (which is elliptically omitted); it would be possible even without such an ellipsis for C and C-sharp to follow one another, melodically, as eighth-notes.

It may be of some interest to the reader to note that this reasoning affords an explanation also for the much discussed opening chord of the Scherzo of Bruckner's *Symphony No. IX*, C-sharp, E, G-sharp, B-flat:

5. In this last example, the effect of the altered chord is further increased by the contrast with the following measures, which strictly maintain the diatonic system (IV–V in B-flat minor):

Example 262 (329):

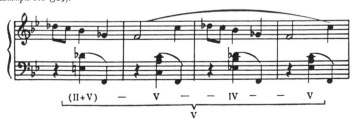

285

Example 264 (331):

In this case, too, the components of the diminished third, G-sharp, B-flat, form a fifth and a seventh, respectively, with the root tone. It is therefore impossible for our ear to hear this chord as an altered chord, with the effect of a V and a II step. We are dealing here most certainly and most simply with a diminished seventh-chord on the VII step in D $\frac{major}{minor}$ (related, by its univalence, to the V step of this same key), whose character is in no way interfered with by the chromatic change raising the fifth, G, to G-sharp. The latter must be considered as a passing note, despite the fact that it occupies so much time. This is corroborated by the sequence of the harmony D, F-sharp, or F, A (cf. score, p. 66, measure 3, and p. 67, measure 13, etc.); the *D*-sharp in the celli (measures 9 and 10) cannot be adduced as a counterargument: the unfolding of the harmony, which takes place here very fittingly, certainly admits, besides the diatonic *D*, the *D*-sharp, a creation, so to speak, of the tonic yearning of the root tone *C*-sharp.

In summing up this discussion, we may state that the diminished third (or augmented sixth) is an unmistakable indication of an alteration only when the tones of which it is composed form with the root tone a major third and diminished fifth, respectively.[6]

§ 154. *Ordinary Methods of Tonicalization Replaced by Alteration*

In concluding our theory of altered chords, we should like to emphasize that the combined effect of a V and a II step makes the altered chords as suitable for purposes of tonicalization as are the pure V and the pure II steps (that is, the II if followed by a V).

---

6. The following norm may serve as a mnemotechnical device: If in a V⁷ chord the perfect fifth is flatted, the result will be an altered chord; if it is sharped, we are dealing merely with a passing note.

CHAPTER IV

RELATIONS BETWEEN CHROMATIC CHANGE AND DIATONIC SYSTEM

§ 155. *Chromatic Change Aiding Both Nature and Diatonic System*[1]

Looking at the tonicalized scale-step, we realize that it signifies a triumph of Nature, perhaps the greatest triumph of Nature over our art: Nature, so to speak, disavows our system; all minor thirds, the diminished fifth (and, therefore, the minor triads and the diminished triad) disappear; their places are taken by major triads alone, and, although Nature takes the detour of an artistic and merely artificial means, viz., chromatic change, she achieves nonetheless the result that the root-tone quality, which she had in store originally for all tones with equalizing justice (cf. §§ 14–19), in the end manifests itself here, albeit in a different way, in the chromatically tonicalized scale-steps.

The sole criterion by which to recognize the system remains in the fact that modulation—if we feel tempted to mistake tonicalization for modulation—is not completely consummated in any of these cases (§ 137); therefore, we do not lose the feeling for the purely diatonic relationships among the scale-steps. There remains in us the expectation of a return of the artistic system; and in most cases, in fact, the minor thirds, the minor triads, etc., soon re-enter victoriously, and the triumph of the system thus alternates with the triumph of Nature. The total content of a composition basically represents a real and continuous conflict between system and Nature; and whichever of the two celebrates a fleeting victory, it will not succeed in banning the vanquished partner forever from our perception.

Accordingly, I should like to formulate the following principle:

Chromatic change is an element which does not destroy the diatonic system but which rather emphasizes and confirms it.

[1. In this paragraph and then particularly in § 157 Schenker deals with those chromatic effects which later led him to his theory of "layers" (cf. note to § 82): chromatic change in the foreground, the diatonic system in the background. Cf. *Free Composition*, § 277, where he distinguishes the scale-steps according to layers and simulated keys. The same, with regard to §§ 171–80 of *Harmony*, on modulation.]

Its point of departure is the diatonic system, whence apparently it moves away; but through the byways of a simulated tonic it returns to it. The contrasts which chromatic change—apparently a purpose in itself—can conjure up illuminate the diatonic relationships all the more clearly. It certainly is an advantage for the listener to perceive the diatonic tones as though clarified by their chromatic contrasts; the meaning of C, e.g., in the diatonic system of C major is revealed to us indirectly but all the more clearly by C-sharp and C-flat; D-sharp and D-flat likewise may serve to clarify the diatonic D, etc.

I may venture the principle, then, that for the sake of the diatonic system itself we can never write too chromatically.[2]

The harmonies behave in this respect much like the motifs. If the latter, in order to crystallize in our minds, need an association such as a simple repetition, a contrast, or any juxtaposition whatever (cf. §§ 2 ff.), the harmonies likewise welcome contrast as a most desirable means of association, and not only in the sphere of a small diatonic fragment (Example 6) but also in larger form complexes. One should note, for example, the inserted E major passage in the midst of the long E-flat major complex in the Rondo of Beethoven's E-flat major Sonata, op. 7.[3] How much greater is the effect of the E-flat major key here because suddenly we are, chromatically, in E major! Without this E major, no doubt our ear would have suffered from an overabundance of E-flat major, and the conclusion, which obviously has to be in E-flat major, would have sounded that much feebler.

A similar chromatic contrast obtains, e.g., in Beethoven's Piano Sonata, op. 106, toward the end of the development part, from B major to B-flat major; in the Scherzo of the same opus, toward the conclusion, again from B to B-flat; in Beethoven, again, *Symphony*

---

2. I am referring here only to chromatic change in the service of tonicalization, i.e., of the scale-steps of the diatonic system. That other phenomenon, currently also called "chromatic change," viz., when two homonymous keys combine as, e.g., E and E-flat in C $\frac{major}{minor}$, I do not consider to be a chromatic change but an independent principle of composition, viz., that of combination, which we have already discussed in some detail. This distinction will lead us to a better understanding of the intentions of the composer; it will not handicap our enjoyment in reading or listening.

[3. Cf. *Free Composition*, § 256]

No. IX, first movement, measures 108–16, from B major to B-flat major.

A further example is afforded by Haydn, Sonata in E-flat major, where the first and last movements are in E-flat major, while the Adagio, i.e., the central movement, shows E major (!).

§ 156. *The Limits of Chromatic Change*

It is impossible to put down a hard-and-fast rule as to the limits within which chromatization is legitimate. They depend on the particular musical and poetic intentions of each composition, and these, obviously, differ in each case. The ultimate limit, however, is set by the demand that the artist has to take heed in any case, lest any doubt arise in the listener as to the diatonic system. Considering how little it takes to suggest to the listener the diatonic system even in the greatest tumult of chromatic changes, the composer's leeway with regard to chromatic changes seems indeed unlimited. The artist who nevertheless trespasses upon the designated limit and thereby destroys the diatonic system, which—including its chromatic-diatonic elaborations—is the only natural medium for the expression of his ideas, that artist is all the more irresponsible. The least one can expect of a creative artist is that he should feel what the diatonic system means to our art, i.e., also to him. Just as a poet must under no circumstances sacrifice the primary element of rhythm to the secondary element of rhyme, even the most alluring rhyme—for without rhythm poetic language lacks "cohesion"—so the musician must never sacrifice and destroy the primary element of his art, which is the diatonic system, for the sake of a merely secondary element, that is, chromatic change. And I would not hesitate to call any composition containing such ruined diatonic systems—whatever the author's intention—simply a poor composition. If such a result was unintentional, the composer must be reproached for the inadequacy of his instinct for the art he practices. In those cases, however, where the composer unmistakably reveals his intention to ruin the diatonic system, we have not only the right but, even more, the moral duty to resent the deceit against our art and to expose the lack of artistic instinct which manifests itself here even more drastically.

§ 157. *Eventuality of Chromatic Change Calling for Precaution in Deducing Scale-Steps and Keys*

The aspect of the tonicalized scale-step occasions me to warn the reader to be cautious in deducing a key. If in a given case we are faced, for example, with a major triad, there are two possibilities: first, that we are to give to it one of the six meanings it can assume as a scale-step according to § 97 or, second, that in reality it is not what it appears to be, that perhaps it is nothing but a phenomenon affected by a chromatic change; basically, perhaps, it represents a minor or diminished triad.

The A major triad, e.g., may have the following modulatory meanings:

Example 265 (332):

    I step in A major,
    IV step in E major,
    V step in D major,
    III step in F-sharp minor,
    VI step in C-sharp minor,
    VII step in B minor.

We find, however, that the same triad—albeit unfolded—has an entirely different meaning, e.g., in the first movement of Brahms's Sextet in B-flat major, op. 18:

Example 266 (333):

When we listen to the beginning of this passage, our instinct is inclined to bet on the tonic in A major as the scale-step having the highest value according to § 133; only under certain circumstances, when some compositional criterion contradicted such a supposition, would our instinct instead assume the dominant. The subdominant could be considered only in the third place, and the scale-steps of the minor keys, being even remoter and having an even lower value, would come later still. In our case, unobstructed by any obstacle for the time being, our instinct would settle on the I step, were it not that measure 6 of our example brought a sudden turn which could hardly be integrated into A major. This turn consists in a descent by a fifth from the scale-step *A* to the scale-step *D*, which contains a minor triad. Faced with this descent, our instinct resorts to a first transformation, guided, again, by the desire for the highest possible value. In other words, we now concede to the D minor triad the rank of a tonic and, conversely, degrade the major triad on *A*, which we had supposed to be a tonic, to the lower rank of a dominant. The further step progression, however, reveals that we still have not guessed the correct value and that we shall have to effect a further transformation, viz., we have to transform in our minds what we thought to be a I step in D $\frac{major}{minor}$ into a VI step in F major, with the sequence of a V and I in this F major key. The following table may clarify this twofold transformation of values:

Original supposition . . . . I in A major
Aspect after correction of first impression . . . . V–I in D $\frac{major}{minor}$
Conclusion, after correction of second impression . . . . . . III–VI–V–I, in F major

The reader will note that what has taken place in this concrete case is a tonicalization of the VI step in F major with the help of the preceding fifth, i.e., the III step. Compare in this respect Beethoven's *Symphony No. VIII*, first movement, measures 48 ff.

It goes without saying that the same kind of precaution is indicated when we are faced with a minor triad; for a minor triad may be used for chromatic reasons on a scale-step which diatonically contains a major or a diminished triad.

§ 158. *Chromatic Change in the Service of Cyclic Technique*

We have just shown that the diatonic character of a theme is by no means destroyed by a chromatic change, wherever this may occur. But if this is so, we can exploit this fact thoroughly for the character of the theme. The example quoted earlier will best clarify this situation.

The sequence of measures we quoted constitutes the antecedent of the so-called "subsidiary" section or strain II—more correctly, we should say, of the second thematic complex. The consequent brings an enlarged repetition of the antecedent and, accordingly, a return to the tonic, F major, to conclude the whole first theme of this group. There follows the second theme of this group, which begins with the tonic, i.e., with the tendency toward a normal development. It goes without saying that for this purpose the same tonic is used which was used to conclude the preceding theme. The conclusion of one idea thus contains the beginning of the next. But the effect of this one tonic, which concludes one idea while it initiates another, and the effect, therefore, of the whole construction of this thematic complex are enhanced enormously by the fact that the first theme begins on a remote fifth rather than on the tonic itself! How monotonous it would be if both themes of this group were to open uniformly and all too normally on the tonic!

Especially in cyclic composition, where the composer is faced with the task of linking several ideas in groups, the technique, once conquered, of not developing themes uniformly from the tonic is invaluable. The tonic, being the strongest scale-step, has, more than all others, the inherent ability to mark and emphasize the opening (and, of course, the conclusion) of an idea—so strikingly that, the moment in which an idea is born, its normal development can never be missed. Imagine now a whole series of movements with such normal beginnings and developments, and test their effects. Each individual idea will turn out to be an all too complete and closed whole, and this saturated independence will kill in us the expectation of a continuation rather than inciting it. The entire series, accordingly, will make the impression of a wreath of ideas, a potpourri rather than an organic whole, such as must be formed by a cyclic composition. The fact that each turn from idea to idea is thus underlined reveals too openly the author's intention to introduce ever new sequences of thoughts—an intention which he supposes to be cyclic—and this very obviousness evokes an effect opposite to the one desired by the author.

This discussion may be summed up in the following statement: Chromatic change—disregarding for the moment its ulterior effects —not only strengthens the diatonic system by contrast but affords essential advantages to the technique of forming thematic complexes, especially in cyclic compositions.

Thus we may add the use of chromatic change as a new and important technical principle to those we described in §§ 129 ff. which the great masters apply to attain variety and complexity of contents.

§ 159. *Duration of Chromatic Change Does Not Cancel*
Effect of Diatonic System

Even where chromatic changes are applied to it, the scale-step reveals itself as the spiritual and superior unit as we defined it in its diatonic form (§ 78); i.e., the obligation to return to the diatonic system does not imply any restriction as far as the duration of the chromatic scale-step is concerned. This duration remains as variable as that of a diatonic scale-step: it vacillates between a minimum and a maximum, as far extended as we can imagine. Nor does it affect the duration of the scale-step in any way, whether such a chromatic change develops a tonic effect directly or whether it uses the preceding scale-step for this purpose. It is true that the longer a scale-step persists in a chromatic state—especially if this situation has been prepared by a more complex mechanism of tonicalization—the more easily does it arouse the impression of a real key. One should be careful, nevertheless, not to yield to the deceptive influence of this time factor; rather, we should keep present what I said in § 137 in this respect, viz., as long as the author himself maintains his diatonic system, which will always result from the diatonic scale-step following the chromatic change, we must respect his own diatonic tendency, and we must not mistake a chromatic change for a modulation.

The artistic havoc which may be wrought by such a confusion may be demonstrated by the following example: I am referring to a misinterpretation of a passage in Beethoven's Piano Sonata in E-flat major, op. 7, measures 59–93—a misinterpretation which shows the artistic sensitivity of the interpreter to be as minimal as the ingenuity of the master, manifested here with the elementary force of a vision, is gigantic.

The passage shows the second theme within the second thematic complex, i.e., within the so-called "strain" II, and as such it consists, quite normally, of an antecedent and a consequent. The antecedent leads us, in measure 67, to the dominant; the consequent brings an extension, stretching over 25 measures, and concludes with a regular cadence in B-flat major, on the tonic. (The fact that the third theme of this same complex begins with that same tonic certainly does not cancel the effect of a normal conclusion at the end of the second theme.) Considered from this point of view, this theme does not seem extraordinary in any way, as the extension of the consequent is something absolutely normal and to be taken for granted in the technique of weaving thematic complexes. But a closer scrutiny of the content of measures 81–88 of the extension brings a most unexpected surprise: A violent thunder of *fortissimo* (!) in the two preceding measures (79–80). Suddenly (!) profound *pianissimo* on a pedal point on G—already these dynamic secondary phenomena indicate something highly unusual. Add to this that the pianissimo brings a C major, apparently with all the characteristics of a real C major key. Not only do we find the tonic and the dominant of C major alternating on the pedal point; but, hedged in by these harmonies, we see a new theme arise which, although originating from one single and quite infinitesimal.motif, still undergoes a full development into antecedent and consequent in such a way that the antecedent contains the mere repetition of the motif, while the consequent brings a contrapuntal inversion and a variation of the motif. Despite this perfection in elaboration, neither the harmonic nor the motivic criteria are sufficient to suggest here a real independent C major key. The last four measures (89–93), in particular, absolutely exclude such a hypothesis. They contain a double cadence in the main key, B-flat major, with the step progression II–V–I in measures 89–90, and III–VI–II–V(–I) in measures 91–92. In the first cadence, the V step is tonicalized with the help of the II, i.e., by a chromatic change of the third (E instead of E-flat), while in the second cadence (measures 91–92) the progression III–VI is similarly tonicalized. Now I ask: Can these two cadences be considered as part of a C major? If the supposed C major key should really prove to be just that, would it not entail consequences quite different from the B-flat major key we are faced with here? As the concluding B-flat major cadences thus plainly exclude any diatonic system except that of B-flat major and the author himself, as we see, expressly maintains his main key, B-flat major, by returning to it after that C major, we obviously are not entitled to speak here of a real C major. But if it is no real C major, what else should we see in this apparent C major? Evidently nothing but a chromatically elaborated scale-step of B-flat major, with the pedal point, G, representing the VI step, while the C major triad, which appears again and again on the pedal point, elicits in our minds the association of a II step, so that the sum total of these measures must be seen quite simply as a combination of these two scale-steps in B-flat major, in a chromatically changed state. It should be noted how the first measure of the first cadence (measure 89), which, as we saw, contains that chromatically changed II step of B-flat major, follows naturally upon the chromatic change and how the continuation of the diatonic system asserts itself spontaneously, despite the chromatic changes (on the pedal point on VI and in the cadence). It seems as though with the pianissimo of the chromatic C major—signalized in advance by the powerful fortissimo—we had entered a tunnel, whose other end is indicated, to our gratification, by the cadence. Incidentally, how strikingly Beethoven characterizes, with the crescendo mark in measures 89–91, the regaining, as it were, of the possibility of breathing freely (in the regained diatonic system)!

This conception may now be confronted with the one offered by the well-known theoretician Adolf Bernhard Marx in his *Anleitung zum Vortrag Beethoven'scher Klavierwerke* (3d ed.; Berlin, 1898), p. 99. The unusual and unexpected length of the chromatic C major obviously deceived him and seduced him to write the following:

> . . . That sequence of eighth notes continues and must grow, in movement and dynamic, up to the point marked by *ff*, at which point the original movement is resumed. The subsequent strain III undulates in calm abundance and with milder motion. . . . Its continuation brings a return to the first motion, in which the phrase

Example 267 (335):

re-enters with vim.

This shows that Marx considers the inserted C major as an independent strain! This by itself belies any natural musical instinct—unfortunately, the book teems with similar misinterpretations. But one would be particularly anxious to see how he would extricate himself from the embarrassment which the return of the B-flat major diatonic system in the cadences of measures 89–93—that star witness for the character of the preceding chromatic passage—would undoubtedly create for him. He simply calls it "its continuation." "Its"? i.e., obviously "of the little melody"? How is this to be understood? His assumed strain III, is it not finished with the conclusion of the alleged C major key? Do the B major cadences form part of the C major key? Each word, each angle, betrays embarrassment. One has the impression that he would have liked to designate those few measures in B-flat major as a strain IV, had he not been deterred from such a view by the all too short duration and the unmistakable characteristics of a cadence.

Such are the errors that lurk—as we see—if we follow an external theory, based merely on sharp and flat signs, and accept for good coin whatever the eye may see, without the control exercised by our musical instinct. Earlier, in the section on the theory of intervals, I warned against taking any vertical coincidence for a real interval; and in discussing the triads I stressed the fact that not every triad represents the scale-step by which it is undoubtedly contained. Thus I do not want to omit this opportunity to make it quite clear to the reader that *not every key is in reality what it seems to be.*[4]

§ 160. *Summary of Chromatically Simulated Keys
in the Diatonic System*

I have shown with an example that, in a state of chromatic change, even a diatonic scale-step may simulate most convincingly an independent key, without, however, becoming such in reality. Let us now examine this possibility within a given diatonic system, e.g., the C major diatonic system. It may be left to the diligence of the reader to transpose this study to the remaining diatonic systems.

In order to gain all possible scale-steps, we subject the C major diatonic system, first of all, to the process of combining it with the C minor one. If, furthermore, we include the Phrygian II step as explained in §§ 50 and 145, we obtain the following scale-steps:

C	D-flat	D	E-flat, E	F	G	A-flat, A	B-flat, B
I	♭II	♮II	III	IV	V	VI	VII

There is no reason why we should not imagine on each of these scale-steps a chromatically simulated key, while each simulated key, in turn, obviously could be penetrated by the principle of combining major and minor, which, as we know, constitutes an ever present compositional method.

Obviously, we must not confuse such simulated keys, extending over larger passages, with those more modest chromatic changes applied to the diatonic scale-steps, when they are to play but a secondary role according to the pattern of tonicalization. Considering that all the simulated keys enumerated earlier do not in any way cancel the main key, we must obviously welcome them as an enormous increasing of compositional means, designed to enhance the effect of the diatonic system. In a wider sense than the one given to it in our discussion of tonicalization, I should like to repeat here the statement that the artist can never write too chromatically,

[4. This, again, anticipates the theory of the layers. Cf. note to § 155.]

in so far as it is his intention to illuminate and clarify the diatonic relations by chromatic contrasts. Also in this case, however, prudence must be the better part of valor; otherwise the author's intention may, against his will, reach the opposite effect. The ultimate limit, again, is set by the obligation not to let any doubt arise in the listener as to the diatonic system itself.

In conclusion it may be noted that the chromatic technique is an heirloom of our art; and when our turbulent young generation pretends to have introduced an innovation with this technique and therefore fancies itself to be progressive, such an attitude reveals only a lack of familiarity with our literature, as unfortunately we find all too often nowadays. In reality, that technique had been acquired by the old and oldest masters, with the only difference—redounding to the advantage of the old masters—that it was always rooted in a secure instinct and that effect and intention always remained consistent.

§ 161. *On Real Modulation*

It need not be stressed[5] that in those cases where a composer deliberately abandons a certain diatonic system we have absolutely no right to deny that a real modulation has taken place. For how could we want to defend the interest of a diatonic system that does not exist? The lack of a definite main diatonic system for whose sake we are to assume chromatically simulated keys is found more often in the so-called "development" parts of cyclic compositions. Such a lack may even be considered the main criterion of such parts, and it certainly would run counter to the author's intention if we busied ourselves trying to construct here, artificially and arbitrarily, a possibly continuous diatonic system. Since there is no interest of any particular diatonic system to defend, the only correct thing to do is to accept all keys as real, i.e., to take the modulations to be definite.

In the development of the first movement of Beethoven's Piano Sonata in E-flat major, op. 7, for example, the keys are real keys, and their sequence is: C minor, A-flat major, F minor, G minor, A minor, D minor. It would be illicit to do violence to this situation by explaining all these keys or part of them as consequences of the

[5. Cf. note to § 155.]

B-flat major diatonic system which concluded the first part of the movement. Beethoven quite intentionally uses here this change of keys, in contrast to the exposition and the recapitulation, where such unrest would endanger the definiteness of the diatonic system and of our impression.

Similar intentions of the composer, aiming at a change of keys rather than the maintenance of a certain diatonic system, may be encountered also in other kinds and other parts of compositions (i.e., not only in the development part of a cyclic composition); they are easily recognized by their haste and conciseness or by the great variety of modulatory methods (cf. §§ 171 ff.), and we are justified in calling such sections *modulatory parts.*

Ultimately it is the situation itself, the intention of the composer, not theory, that matters.

Example 268 (336). Chopin, Ballade, op. 23:

§ 162. *Usual Chromatic Changes in Cadences*

The tonicalization of scale-steps is particularly welcome in cadences. No matter whether we are dealing with full closes, half-closes, or deceptive cadences, whether they occur in the midst of a composition (e.g., at the end of a modulation) or at the very end of a composition, the composer just loves to penetrate his cadence with tonicalization.

In the already quoted treatise by J. S. Bach, in the section entitled "The Most Usual Clausulae Finales," we find, accordingly, the following formula, among others:

Example 269 (337):

For the purpose of tonicalizing the V step, G, the IV diatonic step, F, is raised chromatically to F-sharp.

Some Corollaries of the Theory of
Scale-Steps in Free Composition

CHAPTER I

ANTICIPATION

§ 163. *The Concept of Anticipation*[1]

The concept of anticipation should be explained, indirectly, in the theory of counterpoint, where it belongs in the discussion of the dissonant passing notes on the weak beat, in the so-called "second species" of counterpoint in two-part composition. It is not enough to state that a dissonant passing note must always move stepwise in the direction from which it came; but, in my opinion, it should be explained *why* this law has general validity. Since this explanation has been omitted in the available textbooks on counterpoint, I find myself obliged to offer it here, however concisely. The explanation is simply this: If a dissonance, introduced stepwise, suddenly changes direction or "leaps away," as one says in technical language, this may occasion a harmonic relationship between this dissonant passing note and the subsequent consonance, as shown in the following example:

Example 270 (338):

The bracket ⌐ clarifies to the eye the harmonic relation which thus originates between *A* and *F* (third) and *D* (fifth). This relation, joining two notes and isolating them as a particular group from all the other tones which persevere in strict neutrality, would destroy

[1. Schenker would have considered all the phenomena analyzed in this paragraph as consequences of voice-leading. The same applies to §§ 164–68.]

the equilibrium among the tones. In the theory of counterpoint, where any such disturbance is to be strictly avoided (§§ 84 ff.), this is therefore simply prohibited. In free composition, on the contrary, not only is such equilibrium not required, but variety in forming groups and joining notes into larger and smaller units is a vital characteristic: such harmonic transcendences, therefore, may and should be brought about. Free composition is thus the ground that gave rise to the phenomenon which in technical language is fittingly called "anticipation."

This is the place, then, to deal with this problem in positive terms and with some detail. For the concepts, acquired in our theory of harmony, enable us now to characterize more closely the harmonic relationships which come up in various cases of "anticipation." In the discussion of counterpoint we had to by-pass the concept of anticipation, dealing with it purely negatively, i.e., rejecting it. The possibility of saying anything more about this phenomenon was ruled out by the very vagueness of the concepts of "consonance" and "dissonance" in counterpoint; for this vagueness excludes full light, nor is it likely to instruct us adequately with regard to the situation. With the elements of the theory of harmony at our disposal, on the contrary, we may define this phenomenon in the following terms: Anticipation is to be understood as a situation in which the next harmony or scale-step is anticipated by a note or notes, either in one or in more intervals of this harmony or scale-step.

§ 164. *Various Forms of Anticipation*

Anticipations may be divided into two groups according to the manner in which they are executed: (1) completed anticipations, (2) abbreviated or elliptic anticipations.

Example 271 (339). J. S. Bach, English Suite I, Sarabande:

II (phryg.)

Example 272 (341). Chopin, Ballade, op. 38:

Another principle according to which anticipations may be grouped is the size or volume of the anticipation, i.e., the number of intervals of the next harmony which are anticipated. According to this principle, anticipations can be divided into the following groups: (1) anticipation of one single tone; and (2) anticipation of two or more tones, even of the whole subsequent scale-step.

Example 273 (342). Chopin, Ballade, op. 23:

Example 274 (343). Brahms, Intermezzo, op. 117, No. 2:

(♭♭II — — V — — I)

Example 275 (344).[2] Schubert, Impromptu, op. 90, No. 3:

Beethoven, especially during his last period, loved to anticipate the whole subsequent scale-step, and it is unfortunate that our performers usually are unable to feel such anticipations poetically with the composer and to perform them in the spirit of his original inspiration.

Example 276 (346). Beethoven, Piano Sonata, op. 109:

♯I — — II — — — — V

[2. The *D* in measure 2 must probably be considered as a suspension.]

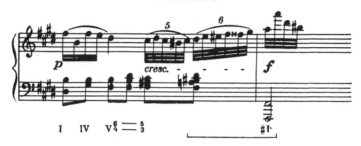

$$\text{I} \quad \text{IV} \quad \text{V}_4^6 = {}_3^5 \qquad \sharp\text{I}\cdot$$

On this occasion we wish to remember a favorite device of J. S. Bach, which consists in mixing up, in the unfolding of a part, passing notes, changing notes, auxiliary notes, and anticipations in such a way that the counterpoints which thus originate are designed to produce a strangely glimmering and fluid impression. The upper counterpoint in measure 6 of Example 241, for example, seems to grow out of the original or primary idea (*Uridee*):[3]

Example 277 (347):

passing through the intermediate state of:

Example 278 (348):

where we need, first of all, the changing note *D* in order to get a fluid transition from *E* to *C*, until we reach the final stage as given in measure 6, in which the many harmonic notes, passing notes, changing notes, and auxiliary notes flow one into the other, under the most delicate rhythmic treatment and with a continual exchange of their functions. But if we now compare this with the lower counterpoint in measure 8 of the same example, we find, first of all, that it grows analogously out of:

[3. Here Schenker uses the word *Uridee* ("primary idea") and clearly shows how free composition is a prolongation of strict composition!]

Example 279 (349):

but for one remarkable difference: in measure 6 the functions of the four sixteenth-notes forming a group of one quarter were ordered as follows: (1) upper auxiliary note (or changing note), (2) harmonic (or passing note), (3) lower auxiliary note, (4) harmonic (or passing) note. Here in measure 8, on the contrary, at the third beat this order is suddenly changed, for the sake of the D in the middle part in the theme of the fugue. The order now is the following: (1) harmonic, (2) passing note, (3) harmonic, and (4) passing note; and it is just these two passing notes (2 and 4, sixteenth-notes) which anticipate the C in the subsequent measure. For this reason, the harmonic note had to be eliminated in the intermediate stage (Example 279, *b*) in favor of the anticipating note, C.

The first aria of the *"Kreuzstab" Cantata* by the same master is particularly beautifully elaborated in this respect (cf., furthermore, Example 233, measure 2, the last sixteenth-note, D-sharp).

But let us now have a look at the following example from Beethoven's Piano Sonata, op. 57, Andante:

Example 280 (350):

It will not be difficult to recognize here the counterpart to an anticipation, i.e., the "afterstroke" of tones of a harmony.

CHAPTER II

SUSPENSION

§ 165. *The Concept of Suspension*

The so-called "suspension" is in many respects similar to the anticipation. Also the student should already have begun to get acquainted with this phenomenon in the theory of counterpoint, viz., in the fourth or syncopated species. There, in the theory of counterpoint, he should be told that it is only a consequence of two-part exercise and certain other circumstances if, for the time being, no dissonance is legitimate on an accented note unless it is both prepared by a consonant half-note on the preceding upstroke and resolved in a subsequent half-note and unless, furthermore, the syncopated note is always resolved by a downward progression, as the rule goes, never by an upward progression. This might explain why in a counterpoint, i.e., in a situation where we find only consonances which remain somewhat vague without ever reaching the rank of scale-steps, we find, correspondingly, only vague dissonances, which have to be prepared and resolved and can appear only on the accented notes in a measure.

Therefore, we speak merely of a syncopated ninth, seventh, fourth, and second in the upper counterpoint and of a syncopated second and fourth in the lower one, without gaining therefrom the impression of any more definite harmonic relationships.

The situation changes when we come to free composition; for the harmonies here may be understood as scale-steps, and the dissonances become more understandable, because we can now hear them as *suspensions* preceding this or that definite interval of a definite and definable harmony. Thus, first of all, we can establish the meaning of the harmony in question; thereafter it is quite easy to see which interval of this harmony has been suspended in the dissonance, whether it is the third, fifth, sixth, seventh, or even the root tone itself.

§ 166. *Various Forms of Suspension*

While the clear-cut harmonic conception of a chord engenders a full and easy understanding of the suspension, the suspension itself acquires such liberty that there remains, here in free composition, no restriction whatever to its use. A suspension in free composition therefore has the following characteristics:

1. It may be applied to any interval of the harmony, from root tone to seventh.

2. In so far as the number of suspended intervals is concerned, this may be either one or two or more; or even all of them may be suspended.

3. It may be applied above or below.

4. It can be resolved by upward or downward progression.

5. It may be prepared or may set in freely, without preparation.

Among the prepared suspensions I should also like to include those prepared only mentally,[1] i.e., those not explicitly set in the preceding harmony but implicitly contained therein, as, for example, in the following passage from Beethoven's String Quartet, op. 18, No. 1:

Example 281 (351):

where the suspension, *A*, must be supplemented in our perception as the third of the preceding I step, *F, A, C,* even if it was not stated there explicitly.

6. It may be resolved or not.

7. The duration of the suspension, in general, is briefer than that of the note which resolves it; but the contrary is also possible. For, as we know, the meaning of a musical phenomenon cannot be reversed by the time factor alone (cf. Example 259).

8. A chromatic change, under certain circumstances, must not deter us from assuming a really prepared suspension. All we have to

[1. With this "mentally prepared" suspension, Schenker anticipates his concept of the *Urlinie* ("primary line") and of the notes that are to be thought of as sustained.]

do is to disregard such chromatic change, and we shall immediately be able to identify the tone as a preparation.

P. E. Bach, accordingly, taught long ago, in his *Manual of Accompaniment,* § 63: "An additional accidental which flats a prepared dissonance even more does not cancel the preparation. This follows from what we said in § 11:

Example 282 (352):

All this liberty with regard to the suspension, which is adequately explained by the nature of free composition, has been familiar long since, both to practice and to theory (e.g., Examples 31 [measure 3]; 177, 187 [measure 10]; etc.; also § 124).

CHAPTER III

THE CHANGING NOTE

§ 167. *Concept of the Changing Note*

In the third species of counterpoint—where four quarter-notes are set against a whole note—we are taught that a dissonant passing note, in so far as it appears hedged in by two consonances and progresses stepwise, may also occur on an upstroke, as follows:

Example 283 (353):

But again, as in the cases of syncopation and anticipation, we are not told what the prolongation of this phenomenon looks like in free composition. And this despite the fact that nothing is easier: all we need to do is displace the bar line and put it one count before the dissonance of the upstroke, as follows:

Example 284 (354):

and we get a result which is optically most plausible: we shall understand that the so-called "changing note" is nothing but a derivation from that dissonance which was placed, in counterpoint, at the upstroke. I do not think we need waste any more words on this phenomenon.

§ 168. *Difference between Changing Note and Suspension*

Only one thing: How is this concept to be distinguished from that of the suspension, if both are dissonances on the accented part of the measure and may therefore assume an identical appearance?

The distinctive criterion is this, that the suspension strives, above all, to produce the effect of a dissonance, while the changing note has more the character of a passing note and conveys a dissonant effect only secondarily:

Example 285 (355). Chopin, Mazurka, op. 17, No. 4:

How marvelous is the effect of the changing note, *A*, which passes here, in the bass, on the accented beat of the measure, between *G*-sharp and *B* (the third and fifth of the dominant), especially as this changing note takes in tow the third, *C*, in the soprano, to reinforce its effect, as it were.

CHAPTER IV

THE PEDAL POINT

§ 169. *Concept of the Pedal Point*

There still reigns a certain confusion with regard to the pedal point, despite the fact that it is such an ancient institution (cf. § 78); it is true that, in general, this phenomenon is defined rather correctly. Since this definition, however, lacks precision, it happens rather often that a note is considered to be a pedal point even if it really is not.

For example, the holding-on of a tone as such is not a reliable criterion. For not every tone that is being held must be understood to be a pedal point, merely on account of its long duration; the time factor cannot change the meaning of a musical phenomenon—as I have already stressed repeatedly and wish to re-emphasize here. If a tone is merely a passing note, it does not matter in any way what takes place either above or below it or how long such a phenomenon, whatever it may be, may last: never will it turn into a pedal point, owing to its inherent and merely secondary character.

It is absolutely essential, on the contrary, that the tone which is to be held should, first of all, represent a scale-step. If this requirement is fulfilled, it is not always the root tone that must be held on—though this is what usually happens—but any other interval of the scale-step may be used equally well.

But even if we have a scale-step, with one of its intervals held on, it is still by no means sure that we are faced with a real pedal point; for there are other preconditions to be fulfilled: above or below the note that is being held on, the other parts must be led in certain motions.

Let us not be deceived: not even the motion that takes place above the held-on note of a scale-step is the last, decisive criterion of a pedal point; for so long as the parts, in their motion, unfold the content of only that same scale-step, e.g., in figurations, etc., we still do not have a pedal point. In the following example from Beethoven, op. 57, first movement:

Example 286 (356):

the *A*-flat, which is held on, cannot be considered to be a pedal point but merely the root tone of the dominant seventh-chord. More than that: even the famous introduction to Wagner's *Rheingold* does not represent—as is generally assumed and written—a pedal point, despite its hundred-odd measures; for all its motion, even where it is most exalted, is but the unfolding of one single chord, *E*-flat, *G*, *B*-flat. Such motion, on the contrary, must be conceived so as to express at least two different harmonies, which not only can be considered as quite independent from the scale-step represented by the held-on note but, besides, can be considered themselves as scale-steps. The final requirement, therefore, is that the tone of the pedal point must not form part of the harmony of the different scale-steps involved.

In this sense, and in this sense alone, do we get the impression of both rest and motion at the same time: the impression of rest on one certain scale-step and that of motion on two or more others.

In Beethoven's Piano Sonata, op. 28:

Example 287 (357):

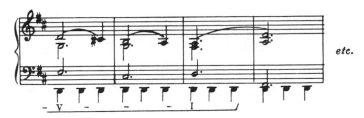

etc.

we have the impression of a calmly resting tonic, quite simultaneously with that of a lively change among the scale steps I, IV, V, I. Hence
the following definition:

A pedal point is to be understood to be a held-on tone of a scale-
step, above or below which at least two harmonies, functioning as
scale-steps in their own right, are in motion, with at least one of
them constituting a harmony different from that of the pedal point.

Example 288 (358). Wagner, *Tristan and Isolde,* Act I:

Example 289 (359). Beethoven, String Quartet, op. 59, No. 3:

§ 170. *The Psychology of the Use of Pedal Points*

The psychology of the use of a pedal point results clearly from its very definition, and there is no generally valid rule as to where a pedal point should be used. The composer must rely upon his own feeling and know himself what he wants to achieve, in a given situation, with this peculiar combination of rest and motion. Without claiming to exhaust all possibilities, however, I should like to indicate some of them.

Right at the beginning of a composition a pedal point is very useful in order to create, as it were, a certain nexus, with the effect that the tranquil continuance of the tonic—for in most cases it is the tonic we are dealing with—results in an economy of root tones, benefiting the subsequent, increasingly lively, root tones, with the further effect that, despite this tranquil continuance of the tonic, a sufficiently lively change of scale-steps takes place above the same, as is required by the exposition of the key for its own purposes (cf. § 17). The tranquillity of the tonic has its own advantage, which becomes clear by contrast with the subsequent vivacity of the root tones. On the other hand, the change of scale-steps on the pedal point has its own advantage, which manifests itself immediately in the greater precision it gives to the key (cf. Example 32; Brahms, *Symphony in C Minor*, beginning).

If the pedal point is used in the middle of a composition, its effect is different:

Example 290 (360). Chopin, Polonaise, op. 26, No. 1:

With this pedal point the composer tries to link two distinct parts (measures 1–4 and 5 ff.) as far as possible and to prevent them from falling apart and wrecking the unity of the composition.[1]

Or we find a pedal point where a brief, but nevertheless independent, theme is to be given on one single scale-step. In the development parts of cyclic compositions but also in the middle parts of other forms (e.g., the *lied* form) it happens quite frequently that the composer gains an advantage by quickly changing his keys and by constructing these quickly changing keys upon mere harmonic fragments, i.e., on very few scale-steps, sometimes on a single one. I have already warned the reader not to confuse such keys with those chromatically simulated keys which are eventually resolved in one main diatonic key. In our present case, they are always new and independent keys, according to the intention of the composer; and we may change from key to key, even if each key is represented by one single scale-step. It is obvious that in such a case the pedal point can render invaluable service to the composer, considering especially that it offers the possibility of introducing and elaborating above it some additional scale-steps of the diatonic system without sacrificing the desired effect of the individual scale-steps which are represented by the pedal point. Cf., for example, the pedal point on *B*-flat from E-flat major in the middle part, in D-flat major, of Chopin's Polonaise in C-sharp minor, op. 26, No. 1.

In other cases the effect of a pedal point in the midst of a composition may be again (as at the beginning) an economy in root tones, at the most varied occasions: for example, Wagner, *Siegfriedidyll,* measures 29–36; Beethoven, *Seventh Symphony,* second movement, measures 102–10; Beethoven, *Ninth Symphony,* first movement (after the beginning of the recapitulation), measures 327–38, etc.

At the conclusion of a composition, where a pedal point occurs most frequently, particularly on the dominant, it has the following meaning: All that had to be said has been said, at that point, by the root tones, and all that is still missing is the last concluding inversion, i.e., the fall from V to I, which is to bring the motivated and expected

1. Cf. in this respect the ingenious use of the V step in the Andante of Beethoven's *Fifth Symphony*—that V step which effects the transition to the second variation of the main theme and, at the same time, sounds as a pedal point above the scale-steps I–II–VII of that theme.

conclusion. At this moment, when the scale-steps themselves have nothing left to do, it may present a challenge to the artist to gather all remaining forces which may yet linger somewhere and to lead them, on the pedal point as the second-to-last scale-step, to a last motion, to a last struggle:

Example 291 (362). Beethoven, *Eroica,* First Movement.

SECTION I

Theory of Modulation

CHAPTER I

MODULATION BY CHANGING THE MEANING OF A SCALE-STEP

§ 171. *Concept of Modulation and Various Kinds of Modulation*[1]

Modulation means a complete change from one key to another. This change must be so complete that the original key does not return. In this lies the only essential difference between modulation and those changes to chromatically simulated keys which are changes only apparently, while in reality they are a fuller elaboration of a strictly diatonic scale-step, whereby the diatonic system must be assumed to continue.

Modulations in this strict sense of the term may be divided into three groups: (1) modulation by changing the meaning of a harmony; (2) modulation by chromatic change; and (3) modulation by enharmonic change.

[1. With regard to this paragraph and the following ones, cf. note to § 155, as well as what has been said in the Introduction about Schenker's concept of tonality.]

§ 172. *The Characteristics of Modulation by Changing the Meaning of a Harmony*

The source of modulation by changing the meaning of a harmony has been revealed in the chapters on the modulatory meaning of the intervals, as well as that of the triads and seventh-chords, and I need merely refer back to those chapters (cf. §§ 64, 65, 97).

Assuming, for example, that a triad in a certain place represents a certain scale-step, transition to another key is made possible by the simple fact that this same triad has the values of other scale-steps as well, each of which may be used *ad lib.* to effect the change. For instance, if the major triad *C, E, G,* has the function of a dominant in F major, we may either move into C major—if its value of I is taken advantage of for this change—or into G major, if it is used as a IV, etc. Such a change is at first quite inconspicuous, so to speak, silent; for this reason I should like to suggest calling it a "silent modulation." We recognize it only by its consequences, i.e., by the fact that the new key, initiated by the change of meaning of a certain scale-step, asserts itself in the subsequent harmonies, and certainly it does not yield its place to the original key. In general, a cadence in the new key has proved to be the most suitable means to fortify the new key and thus to make the modulation real and complete.

In the following example from the Courant I of the First English Suite in A major by J. S. Bach:

Example 292 (363):

- II - - - - (♯3) - V - - - VI

we see a transformation of a tonic in F-sharp minor into a VI step in A major. It is very instructive, incidentally, to note how Bach unfolds for this purpose the chord F-sharp, *A*, C-sharp in measure 2 in the sense of A major, in a rather hard and daring manner:

Example 293 (364)

(instead of the sequence C-sharp, D-sharp, E-sharp, F-sharp). This may give an idea of the great advantage afforded, for modulatory purposes also, by the unfolding of the scale-steps.

§ 173. *How To Recognize the Moment at Which the Meaning Is Changed*

If we insist that a diatonic system must not be given up until the moment at which a complete modulation to the new key simply makes it impossible to insist on the former, situations may arise, especially when we are dealing with "silent modulations," where it is difficult to fix precisely the moment of the change: we want to insist on the diatonic system, while a new key has already taken over: When did it make its appearance? At this scale-step or another one? At this triad or another one? If both triads lend themselves to a "silent change," which is the one that really initiated the modulation? Such doubts are all too real and occur quite frequently.

Let us take, for example, the following passage from the Adagio ot Mozart's Piano Sonata in D major (No. 17, K., V., 576):

Example 294 (365):

We are modulating here from F-sharp minor to A major. That much is clear immediately. But there are two possibilities: first, we may change the tonic, F-sharp, in measure 2 of our example into a VI step of A major; or, second, if we want to preserve the F-sharp minor as long as possible, we may wait until measure 3 and consider the triad *D, F, A* of that measure as the real beginning of the modulation.

The formula for the first alternative is

$$\frac{\text{F-sharp minor I}}{\text{A } \frac{\text{major}}{\text{minor}} \text{ VI–IV}^{\natural 3}\text{–V–I}}$$

324

For the second alternative,

$$\frac{\text{F-sharp minor I–VI}^{\natural 3}}{\text{A } \frac{\text{major}}{\text{minor}} \text{ IV}^{\natural}\text{–V–I}}$$

As we see, the first alternative assumes the urge to modulate to be immediate and quite natural at the end of the F-sharp minor section—why should the F-sharp minor drag along in the following measure, if the melody of the section which used that key is already extinct and if, in the following measures, we hear nothing but modulations? This first alternative, furthermore, proposes only one combination, A $\frac{\text{major}}{\text{minor}}$, whose IV step derives from the minor component. The second alternative, on the contrary, forces us to assume a further and more complicated combination in the F-sharp minor on the VI step $(D, F, A$ for $D, F\text{-sharp}, A)$.

Thus the first alternative certainly has the advantage of greater simplicity; hence the modulation should be considered to begin earlier rather than later: with the change of the I step of F-sharp minor into the VI step of the A major key.

§ 174. *Univalent Chords Excellent for Purposes of Modulation*

In so far as modulations of this kind occasionally aim at fixing the new key as rapidly as possible, it is obvious that the univalent chords (VII³, V⁷, VII⁷, ᵇ⁷) as well as the altered harmony (II^{ᵇ5}+V^{♯, ♮3}) play an important role. Whether they occur in longer cadences or in the very shortest (e.g., merely in V⁷–I, VII⁷–I), they fix the new key immediately and beyond any possibility of doubt. This explains why the current textbooks most emphatically recommend, of all the so-called "means of modulation," these univalent chords.

§ 175. *Change of Meaning Not Impeded by Combination of Systems*

Modulation by changing the meaning of a scale-step not only is not impeded by the combination of the major and minor systems; on the contrary, it is rather helped by it. This may be illustrated by the following example from Chopin's Prelude, D-flat major, op. 28, No. 15:

Example 295 (366):

We have here, at the beginning of measure 2, a tonicalized IV step in D-flat major, according to the pattern II–V–I; hence the accidental, C-flat, at the scale-steps A-flat and D-flat, which produces the effect of a II and V step in G-flat major. This IV step, which is thus elaborated, is followed, however, in measure 2 by the tonic D-flat, so that the sequence IV–I presents, as it were, a plagal turn. In this same measure, furthermore, we see the beginning of the modulation to A-flat minor. This new key is introduced here, for the time being, merely by the cadence IV–V–I; but in this cadence we see the same major triad, D-flat, F, A-flat, which had functioned as the tonic of D-flat major, taking the place of the IV step in A-flat minor, instead of the diatonic minor triad, D-flat, F-flat, A-flat. This modulation is thus based quite simply on the combination of an A-flat $\frac{major}{minor}$ key, which (like the Dorian mode) brings a major triad on the IV step, while the tonic maintains the minor character.

But what if someone wanted to assert that this step progression, such as here, indicates more clearly G-flat major than D-flat major, i.e., that we are dealing here, not with V–I–IV–I in D-flat major, but with II–V–I–V in G-flat major, and that therefore we must explain the modulation on the ground of a different change of meaning? This objection can be countered most persuasively with an argument concerning the form of the little composition: The measures under discussion initiate the middle part of the so-called *lied* form, i.e., the form in which the first part of the prelude is composed. This middle part itself falls into an antecedent and a consequent; the antecedent modulates to A-flat minor, the consequent to B-flat minor, as can be seen in the following:

Example 296 (367):

A♭minor:I	V			
(E♭minor:IV	I)			

B♭minor: IV – I - V

It is just this form that forces us inexorably to assume a real modulation at the conclusion of the antecedent also. For, to conclude an antecedent, is not a real key much more indicated than the chromatic elaboration of a single diatonic step? The more so, if the consequent uses this same key, A-flat minor, as its point of departure and thus confirms even more its reality and independence. If an analysis of the form thus excludes the possibility of considering the A-flat minor here as merely a chromatically simulated key, it follows, on the other hand, again as a consequence of formal considerations, that it is far more natural to assume a D-flat major key, which then modulates to the key of the dominant, A-flat, than to assume a G-flat major, which then should modulate to A-flat minor. With the D-flat major we maintain a connection with the diatonic system of the first part and obtain a logically consistent normal modulation, while the G-flat major, if it could be accepted at all as a true G-flat major after the preceding D-flat major, would have to be composed in a different, quite different, way, and furthermore it would entail a far less natural modulation from G-flat major to A-flat major.

To come now to the last conclusion: If the D-flat major modulates not to A-flat major, which is the diatonic key of the dominant, but rather to A-flat minor, i.e., to the homonymous minor key, which substitutes for the A-flat major key, this is simply a result of a combination of major and minor. It is proved, then, that a combination does not in the least impede the "silent modulation" in its function. Thus we may modulate from C major to G minor by simply moving toward G major and then replacing the major with a minor, by virtue of the combination. It is obvious that such combinations yield a wealth of modulations, which, however, all belong to the simplest and most natural kind of modulation. In other words, with the simplest means we may obtain a vast variety of modulations.

§ 176. *Change of Meaning Not Impeded by Chromatic Change*

"Silent modulation"—by changing the meaning of a harmony—is not impeded by a chromatic change any more than it is by a combination of major and minor. And it does not matter at all whether the chromatic change affects the third, fifth, or seventh of the root tone, or even the root tone itself; for in any case we have to disregard the chromatic change, which is disavowed by the subsequent diatonic step. The fulcrum of the modulation rests here on the root tones alone, in the scale-steps themselves.

In what concerns chromatic changes at the third, fifth, and seventh, I should like to remind the reader of what has been said in § 141 about the chromatization of a progression by a third. The modulation takes place quite independently of the chromatic change, so that this latter must be heard as a secondary phenomenon and a purpose unto itself:

Example 297 (368). Handel, *Messiah*, Recitative:

D major: III(♯3) - I - - IV - V

Example 298 (369). Schubert, Piano Sonata, B Major, op. 147:

in D major: V
in F major: III(♯3) - -

Cf. in Beethoven's *Fifth Symphony*, first movement, measures 197–208, the sequence of B-flat, D-flat, F to F-sharp, A, C-sharp (instead of G-flat, B-double-flat, D-flat) with the effect of III–I in F-sharp $\frac{major}{minor}$; or in his *Seventh Symphony*, first movement, measures 155–60, the sequence of E, G-sharp, B to D-flat, F, A-flat (instead of C-sharp, E-sharp, G-sharp) with the effect of III–I in D-flat $\frac{major}{minor}$; finally, the sequence from this latter chord to F, A, C, with the effect of VI–I in F major, etc.

This documentation may suffice to prove the following axiom: A modulation may show chromatic elements of the new diatonic system without thereby losing the character of a "silent modulation"; for the chromatic change can be explained easily as an independent phenomenon, with its own reason, which, however, already belongs in the new diatonic system.

CHAPTER II

MODULATION BY CHROMATIC CHANGE

§ 177. *The Concept of Modulation by Chromatic Change*

The second kind of modulation was called, in the previous chapter, *modulation by chromatic change*. For chromatic change is not tied ineluctably to the service of the diatonic system; rather, it may pursue its own ends as well. Thus it happens quite frequently that a chromatic contrast is used not to return to the diatonic system but rather to take definite leave of it.

It is true that the intention of the author cannot be recognized immediately, at the very moment when the chromatic change comes up. It is only the subsequent step progression that brings clarity. If after the chromatic change we see the original diatonic system returning—the one that dominated before the change took place—we shall learn from this fact that the chromatic change functioned merely in the service of the diatonic system, as was explained above. If the original diatonic system fails to return, we must assume the new diatonic system to have originated at the moment of the chromatic change; and this chromatic change must then be considered to be the means by which modulation has been effected. In this case we must take the chromatic change at its face value, so to speak; in other words, the chromatically changed harmony would come into its own right, which accrues to it from its modulatory meaning, instead of having only a simulated significance.

If, for example, in the C major diatonic system the major triad C, E, G undergoes two chromatic changes, E-flat and G-flat, we thereby obtain a diminished triad, C, E-flat, G-flat. The modulatory meaning of this chord is that of a VII step in D-flat major and of a II step in B-flat minor. It is true that, despite this chromatic change, the C major diatonic system might yet return, if the author used the chromatic change, in accordance with the principle we discussed above, for the purpose of reinforcing the diatonic system. In other cases, however, the composer may use the D-flat major or B-flat minor key, which he reaches through the new scale-step gained by the

330

chromatic change. All he needs to do is to unfold one of these keys or, at least, continue his composition, heeding the consequences of the new key, not of the original diatonic system. Of such consequences, of course, there are quite a number—and sometimes they are imponderables—e.g., when the dominant of the new key is to be developed, etc. In such cases we have a so-called *modulation by chromatic change.* Cf. J. S. Bach, *Well-tempered Clavier,* II, Prelude, E-flat major, measures 19, 35, 39, 41.

§ 178. *Difference between Modulation by Chromatic Change and Silent Modulation, Affected by Chromatic Change*

The modulation by chromatic change takes any harmonic phenomenon *literally* for what it is after the chromatic change has been applied to it, and it accepts its new modulatory meaning, while in the "silent" modulation affected by a chromatic change, this change—which is to be ascribed to reasons of its own—must be disregarded, and the root tone which is revealed by this mental operation must then be examined for its own modulatory meaning.

§ 179. *The Nature of Modulation by Enharmonic Change*

With regard to modulation by enharmonic change, i.e., the third and last kind of modulation, the reader should keep in mind what has been said in § 36 concerning the abbreviation of the perfect fifths and their temperament. Temperament introduced into music a new element of art, of artificiality, which enables us, e.g., to take *B*-sharp and *C*, *C*-sharp and *D*-flat, etc., for identical tones. If this fact is exploited in the course of a real work of art, we are faced with an *enharmonic change.*

One would think that temperament should have completely absorbed the difference between two such tones—what else would it be good for? Modulation by enharmonic change, however, is particularly well suited to demonstrate that the two tones which have undergone an enharmonic change remain basically as different as they were before the use of temperament. This is explained by the fact that, after the enharmonic change has been completed, i.e., in accordance with the new harmonic phenomenon, the diatonic sphere suddenly becomes an entirely different one, so totally different that there is no connection whatever between the keys to which the two enharmonically exchanged tones of the triad belong. It is in the access to such totally unexpected new keys that the surprising effect of this kind of modulation resides. See, for example, the following passage in Beethoven's String Quartet, op. 59, No. 1, Scherzo:

Example 299 (372):

The enharmonic change in this case consists in the transformation of the triad *A*-sharp, *C*-double-sharp, *E*-sharp, which was to be expected in accordance with the development of the keys up to that moment, into *B*-flat, *D, F,* which triad can now lead us to *G*-flat major (III–I), a key that could not possibly have been reached without recourse to enharmonic modulation. In other words, it could not have been reached with the ordinary means of "silent modulation" or modulation by chromatic change—at least, it could not have been reached so fast.[1]

The effect of a modulation by enharmonic change is, accordingly, so drastic and surprising that its use can be justified only where a particular mood, viz., a surprise, is to be given expression. "Each kind of modulation should be used at its own right place!" This axiom should be recommended warmly to the attention of the student.

It may not be superfluous to remind the reader that this kind of modulation by enharmonic change is to be clearly distinguished from those cases where the author, just in order to avoid an uncomfortable manner of notation (which perhaps would involve too many sharps or flats), steps over to a more comfortable way of notation, which, just like that modulation, can be obtained only by an enharmonic

1. Cf. Beethoven, *Fifth Symphony,* Finale, measure 77, where the *A*-flat substitutes for the *G*-sharp of measure 69 and thus leads us back to C major.

change in the way of notation. The difference between these two cases results quite clearly from the keys which only in the case of a real modulation take a different course from that permitted by the development up to that moment.

Thus Chopin, both in the polonaise and in the waltz in C-sharp minor writes the middle part in D-flat major rather than C-sharp major, which would have been indicated by the principle of major-minor combination.

But if we take a look at the Marcia Funebre in Beethoven's Piano Sonata in A-flat major, op. 26, we see that the C-flat key, which has been reached in measure 8, is followed by a B minor in measure 9. While at a first glance we might ascribe this change to a desire for simplification—for, in the long run, the notation of the C-flat minor would be cumbersome—we find ourselves surprised soon after by the full and independent consequence of this new B minor key, in the form of the D major key, whereto the B minor really modulates in measures 13–16. Thus it follows that we are dealing here with a real modulation by enharmonic change, even though the primary motivation of this change may have been a postulate of the notation, i.e., a quite external consideration.

Such an overlapping of two intentions, that of simplifying the notation and that of a real modulation which is then based upon the new notation, can be found in many works of art. See, for example, Brahms, Quintet for Pianoforte, F minor, where the C-sharp minor of the second thematic complex substitutes for the D-flat minor, resting itself on a prior enharmonic change.

§ 180. *The Four Enharmonic Changes of the
Diminished Seventh-Chord*

Current textbooks often make special reference to the enharmonic change of one or more intervals of the diminished seventh-chord of the VII step in major-minor, which seventh-chord is recommended, on account of its absolute univalence, as a prompt and secure means of modulation.

The following example may demonstrate the four possibilities of such changes. Each interval in turn becomes the root tone of a diminished seventh-chord:

Example 300 (374):

VII^b7   VII^b7   VII^b7   VII^b7

in C major / minor   in E♭ major / minor   in F♯ major / minor   in A major / minor

The Theory of Modulating and Preludizing

§ 181. *Critique of Current Methods of Teaching*[1]

The foregoing presentation of all the possible kinds of modulation should really exhaust all that need be said about the theory of modulation and its practical application, were it not that a mistaken approach, taken by the current methods of musical education, induced me to discuss here some additional points concerning practical application alone.

Theoreticians and pedagogues of music (in textbooks as well as in monographs) are wont, at this place, to connect the theory of modulating with that of preludizing, offering their students practical hints for both. There is no objection to such a connection, since a prelude without modulation is out of the question. One would expect, however, that the teacher himself at least should be in the clear as to the fact that modulating and preludizing are the free exercise of the art of composing—and they do not lose this quality merely because they are practiced not only by accomplished masters but also by still immature disciples. This quality postulates that modulating and preludizing—even in the most primitive case of a study example!—should show all the characteristics of a free composition, viz., a freely invented motif, free and variegated rhythm, as well as the harmonic tools offered by the diatonic system, the principle of combination, chromatic change and alteration, and, finally, free step progression, with its inherent peculiar psychology. But if we were to look for such criteria in the exercises offered by current textbooks, we would find ourselves badly deceived. For just as in the case of step progression, where the teacher merely taught the connection between triads and seventh-chords, a connection, so to speak, of shadows, of abstract conceptions (!), instead of conveying to the disciple the living,

[1. Cf. § 90 ff.]

motivic content of such progressions—an approach which I have already criticized in §§ 90 ff.—so do they continue here to operate with mere abstractions, with the empty shells of the tones, so to speak; which is even more regrettable, considering that we find ourselves here in an already advanced stage of study, where we are undoubtedly faced with cases of real composition! The teacher might be justified, at most, in directing the student merely to sketch a step progression—no matter whether for the purpose of modulating or of preludizing—such sketches either to be memorized or to be jotted down on paper for the sake of greater security. In so far as I am concerned, such a sketch may even take the following form, picked at random from Jadassohn's *Kunst zu modulieren und präludieren* (Leipzig, 1890), p. 160:

A:Ig:VII°⁷ C:VI

It would then be the task of the pupil to provide this sketch[2] with one or more motifs, to give varied duration to each scale-step as may be required by the motif—in other words, to create a free rhythm, etc., to give life to this sketch.

But what do we find, instead, in Jadassohn? He accords to each scale-step the identical value of a half-note, translates the scale-steps simply into triads or seventh-chords (what an obvious tautology) thus:

Example 301 (375):

A I   g: VII°⁷ C:V   I

and believes that thereby he has reached the effect of a modulation, whereas, in reality, he stopped short at his unfree sketch, although he wrote it over again.

In my opinion this way of proceeding is to be criticized all the

2. Incidentally, it is not necessary at all to assume here an A major and a G minor, as all root tones can be conceived without any difficulty as VI and ♭IV of C major, i.e., of the key which is the final goal of this sequence.

more because Jadassohn most likely knows full well that a real modulation looks somewhat different. It remains obscure to me, then, why a modulation should not look different to the student as well—in other words, why it should not be elaborated and at least be freed from the ominous shells of triads and seventh-chords. I could well imagine a textbook on this same topic which would present the plan for any modulation merely in words and numbers or, at most, in root tones (which, of course, would have to be written in the bass clef in *one* system), and I ask you: Is it necessary to mislead the student by that method?

If such a method is continued through a whole book and during a series of months, can the student be expected to grasp the true essence of modulating and preludizing, which the theoretician places before him in a few concise words in the last chapter of his work, at the very conclusion of his studies?

§ 182. *The True Nature and Aim of This Task*

Therefore, I say, the beginner should not be underrated. Whenever he begins to modulate and preludize, he should be encouraged by all means to do immediately what really has to be done. The subject itself of his studies demands this. It is better to be indulgent with his awkwardness, even his gross errors, as long as necessary than to mislead him as to the true nature of his task and to let him kill time with an absurd activity.

Who knows, furthermore, whether the method of modulating and preludizing as I conceive it would not incite the student's imagination, rendering it both more fluid and more self-reliant; who knows whether the general use of this method, extended to all students, would not create a situation where the artist would be able to improvise freely, as he was wont to do in other times. I, for one, do not have the slightest doubt that the security of the composer's technique would stand to gain by this method.

It may not be useless, therefore, to keep present good examples when we elaborate plans for modulating and preludizing—especially with regard to motif and rhythm. Such examples abound in the works of our masters, even if the composer's intention may not have been that of setting an example. May I be permitted to conclude with some such examples?

Example 302³ (376). Ph. Em. Bach, Fantasia, E-Flat Major:

3. In this, as well as in the following example from P. E. Bach, I have taken the liberty of indicating, with dotted bar lines, some measures. The composition was planned by the composer quite freely, without bar lines, in accordance with the style of a fantasia. The bar lines here indicated, however, will facilitate the understanding of the rhythm and therefore the performance of the piece.

Example 303 (377). Ph. Em. Bach, Fantasia, A Major:

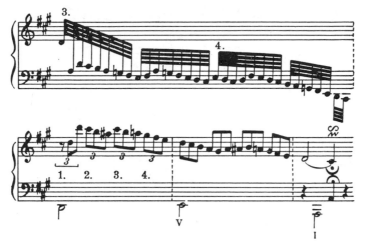

Example 304 (378). J. S. Bach, Suite E-Flat Major, Violoncello Solo:

Example 305 (379). Mozart, Fantasia, D Minor (K. 397):

I. APPENDIX TO *HARMONY*

Example A1[1] (Book, Example 2):

Example A2 (Book, Example 11):

Example A3 (Book, Example 12):

1. Examples 1 and 2 are explained adequately in the text of the book.

The sketch shows the "idea" of the melody (the "basic lineaments," as P. E. Bach said): The repetitions of the passing notes within the fourth *d–a*, in the sense of G minor, then B-flat major, and the combination with B-flat minor.

Example A4 (Book, Example 14):

On the way from the I to the II♮ step—which latter step is used as the dominant of V—the bass inverts the upward progression by a second into a downward progression by a seventh. This way is traversed step by step, and the upper part (soprano) follows in a parallel motion, a tenth higher up. When the bass arrives at G, the soprano, in turn, takes up the A-flat, as a suspension over the G. In measures 11–12, which bring the repetition, the soprano finally returns to the original A.

Example A5 (Book, Example 28):

In accordance with the rhapsodic character intended here, Brahms begins with a generous prolongation from V to I. In order to avoid the parallel octaves D–E (passing note in the bass, auxiliary note in the soprano), the tenth B–D sharp is inserted, which at the same time produces a tonicalization of the E-sound. The sixth d–b in the upper-voice (measures 1–5) is provided with chromatic passing tones; all chords are to be heard as the consequences of combinations of passing notes within G:V–I, and in no way as modulations to different keys.

Example A6 (Book, Example 38):

This sketch shows which chords are to be considered as scale-steps and which are to be considered merely as the result of voice-leading. Brahms brings the tonic in its first inversion (sixth-chord) and avoids its root position throughout, which gives to the composition its fluid character and constitutes its particular artistic charm. The B-flat (I) certainly is expected in the bass of measure 8, below the D-flat of the soprano. The bass, instead, moves on to the passing note E-flat and thus syncopates the D-flat, which then must be resolved in the C. The C, in turn, is obviously only a passing note, leading to B-flat, below which note the bass moves on to D-flat. The original sixth-chord is thus reconstituted.

Example A7 (Book, Example 79):

Instead of Schenker's somewhat cumbersome explanation, which is still based on modulations and keys—an explanation which he himself later dropped—we wish to present here his later sketch of the voice-leading. This may clarify the situation more efficiently:

The bass unfolds the C minor triad in measures 1–14. The first third, C–E-flat, is inverted into a sixth. The bass moves through this interval, chromatically until G, stepwise from there on. The upper parts move in sixth-chords above this bass; thereby the first sixth, A-flat, enters freely, the main note, G, having been omitted elliptically. A motif is thereby introduced which is then imitated by the second and first violins. The first imitation is on E-flat; the second imitation, however, changes the A-flat into an A, in order to tonicalize the subsequent sixth-chord on G (note the third inversion of the seventh-chord at the end of measure 2). As Mozart wants to maintain between each imitation the distance of a quarter-beat, the A already appears above the passing note G of the viola rather than above the F-sharp, as would have been more in agreement with the intention of the composition. Thus the A-flat and the A approach each other so closely that the ear is tempted to hear them together, and it becomes difficult to make an immediate and clear distinction between the different functions of these two tones. This difficulty, as is well known, has drawn upon this quartet the misleading name "Dissonance Quartet."

Exactly the same happens in measures 5 and 6, with regard to the G-flat and the G. From there on, the composition moves in sixth-chords toward its goal.

Example A8 (Book, § 82):

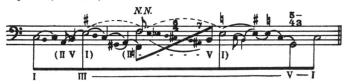

Later on, Schenker would hardly have thought of a parallel progression of triads and scale-steps. The sketch shows the arpeggio of the C triad in the bass, with the E extended, once in the sense of E major, once in the sense of E minor. The F, within the second large cadence ♭II–V–I in E minor, functions, at the same time, as an auxiliary note of E. All the chords—within the downward arpeggio E–C–A–F as well as within the transition from F to B—must be understood as consequences of voice-leading and phenomena of the foreground (see Introduction).

Example A9 (Book, Example 189):

As this sketch shows, the third, *B*, of measure 6, is still effective in measure 8 and thus prevents a real conclusion; more than that, this *B*, as an after-tremor, penetrates even into the last measures!

Example A10 (Book, Example 218):

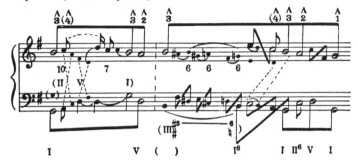

This example shows the consequent to the antecedent, which is introduced by the piano. The orchestra takes over the theme, entering, as through a mist, upon what seems to be a third step, with a process of tonicalization. However, the *B* must be understood as merely the third of the tonic, which is led, stepwise, toward the root tone; i.e., the *B* major triad is transformed into a sixth-chord on *B*. Before this sixth-chord recedes into its root position, the auxiliary note of the subject is repeated once more within an unfolded third and is provided with a IV–V progression. This is a most poetic way of introducing the orchestra, after the piano has presented itself as a solo instrument. It should be mentioned also that in an earlier sketch of Beethoven the consequent set in directly on the *G*-chord, and the *B* triad was merely touched upon in passing. The sequence of triads from *B* to *G* (a complete inversion III–VII–III–VI–II–V–I) is a phenomenon merely of the foreground, a series of chords resulting from the voice-leading. They must not be read as if they belonged to the same "layer" as the main cadence; for these chords cannot be evaluated as parts of modulations and keys.

II. APPENDIX TO INTRODUCTION

Example A11 (Figs. 1–8). J. S. Bach, Little Prelude, F Major:

Figure 1 shows the F triad in such a position that the intervals follow the order of the partials: first the octave, then the fifth, and, uppermost, the third. This is the tonal space which is expressed by this prelude.

Figure 2, *a* and *b*, transforms the chord as presented in Figure 1 into a sequence in time: vertical coincidence now becomes horizontal sequence. The soprano shows the first beginning of a melody, i.e., a horizontal line. Here we have the first appearance of voice-leading, viz., a passing note.

Figure 2, *b*, shows the pattern of the *Ursatz* ("primary structure") of the composition—in the soprano, the melodic unit; in the bass, the harmonic unit, the arpeggio. The root tone moves toward its fifth, which recedes again into the lap of the root tone.

Figure 3, *a*, shows how the point of departure, *a²*, itself is obtained only with the help of an arpeggio. In Figure 3, *b*, the space of the first arpeggio is filled with passing notes (*d²* and *e²*). The end of the second tonal space, *a²*, is adorned with an auxiliary note, *b²*. This auxiliary note returns in the auxiliary note *b²* in the second-to-last measure and thus induces the *Ursatz* to form an auxiliary note (Fig. 3, *c*).

After the insertion of the auxiliary notes, the composition takes the following aspect (Fig. 4):

And now, as to measures 5 ff.: The downward arpeggio in the sixteenth-notes in the second half of measure 2 reaches, through its repetition in measure 4, down to a lower *F*. The sounding of this low register induces a downward movement in the soprano as well. The note a^2 is transposed downward by an octave; it is "prolonged," i.e., we must think of it as though it were held on in its original position, persevering in the ear of the composer as well as in that of the listener. It follows that the auxiliary note, which at first appears in the lower position (measure 13, fourth beat), must be transposed back into the higher register, in order to reach a conclusion in the original high position (Fig. 5).

Figure 6 shows how the problem of leading the voices downward in tenths could be solved most simply.

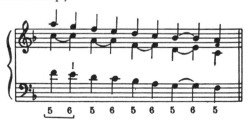

In Figure 7 the sixth-chords (resulting from passing notes) are transformed into chords in their root position (i.e., the sixth-chord on *E* into the triad on *C,* etc.; note the exclamation marks; the interval of a fifth which thus originates in the bass is filled by passing notes).[1]

At the end of this octave, when the *a*¹ is reached, there returns, in the left hand, the figure of sixteenth-notes of measure 4, as though to confirm the unity of this motion (cf. indication in Fig. 8).

In measures 9–14 the composer attempts to regain the original high position, the note *a*², which still lingers in our memory. Measures 9 and 10 represent the first

1. This example shows that chords appearing in the foreground in their root position must often be reduced to sixth-chords or four-six-chords in the background; and only thereby do they find their logical justification. Whereas Rameau suggested the reduction of all inverted triads to their root position, it is clear, then, that very often the very opposite procedure is the correct one.

phase of this attempt: the first note of the arpeggio, c^2, is reached stepwise; the second, f^2, on the contrary, by a leap. Instead of proceeding to a^2, however, we see the f^2 receding, stepwise, to the first a^1 (measures 11-13). Then a second attempt is made, this time with a new disposition of the parts: in measure 14 we reach the upper auxiliary note b^2 and the a^2 (Fig. 8).

Note the parallelism between the arpeggio in measures 1-4 and the following downward progression through one octave, and the arpeggio in measures 9-10 and the following progression through a sixth (both arpeggios are indicated by stems connected with line).

The prelude is the artistic elaboration of one single chord, projected in time. It is the expression of true tonality. Such a creation is conceivable only if it is drawn from a unitary background.

"For the Great Masters the background serves as their good memory. Such memory was enhanced and strengthened by their talent to improvise, a talent which, in turn, rests on good memory, at least to a large extent" (Schenker, *Free Composition,* p. 207).

WORKS

OF HEINRICH SCHENKER

Ein Beitrag zur Ornamentik. Vienna: Universal-Edition A.G., 1904.

Neue musikalische Theorien und Phantasien:

    Vol. I: *Harmonielehre.* Vienna: Universal-Edition AG., 1906.

    Vol. II: *Kontrapunkt, Part I.* Vienna: Universal-Edition A.G., 1910.

    Vol. II: *Kontrapunkt, Part II.* Vienna: Universal-Edition A.G., 1922.

    Vol. III: *Der freie Satz.* Vienna: Universal-Edition A.G., 1935.

Beethovens neunte Symphonie. Vienna: Universal-Edition A.G., 1912.

Erläuterungsausgaben der letzten fünf Sonaten Beethovens

    Sonata, op. 109, E dur. Vienna: Universal-Edition A.G., 1913.

    Sonata, op. 110. As dur. Vienna: Universal-Edition A.G., 1914.

    Sonata, op. 111, c moll. Vienna: Universal-Edition A.G., 1915.

    Sonata, op. 101, A dur. Vienna: Universal-Edition A.G., 1920.

Der Tonwille. 10 issues. Vienna: A. Gutmann Verlag, 1921–24.

Das Meisterwerk in der Musik (Drei Jahrbücher). Munich: Dreimaskenverlag, 1925, 1926, 1930.

Fünf Urlinietafeln. Vienna: Universal-Edition A.G., 1932.

Brahms: Oktaven und Quinten. Vienna: Universal-Edition A.G., 1934.

Instrumentationstabelle (A. NILOFF). Vienna: Universal-Edition A.G., 1908.

Bach: Chromatische Phantasie und Fuge (Erläuterungsausgabe). Vienna: Universal-Edition A.G., 1909.

Ph. Em. Bach: Sonaten (Auswahl). Vienna: Universal-Edition A.G., 1902.

Handel: 6 Orgelkonzerte (vierhändig). Vienna: Universal-Edition A.G., 1904.

Beethoven: Piano Sonatas (after the manuscripts and original editions). Vienna: Universal-Edition A.G.

Beethoven: Sonata op. 27, No. 2. Facsimile reproduction. Vienna: Universal-Edition A.G., 1921.

Also numerous articles and criticisms in various newspapers and magazines from 1890 to 1934.

INDEX OF THE MUSIC EXAMPLES

NOTE: *The numbering differs from the ones in the German edition; for reference purposes the old numbers are added in the text in parentheses.*

L. VAN BEETHOVEN

Third Symphony, EXAMPLES 133, 291
Sixth Symphony, EXAMPLE 198
Piano Concerto, G Major, EXAMPLE 218
String Quartet, op. 18, No. 1, EXAMPLE 281
String Quartet, op. 59, No. 1, EXAMPLE 299
String Quartet, op. 59, No. 3, EXAMPLE 289
String Quartet, op. 95, EXAMPLE 208
String Quartet, op. 132, EXAMPLE 47
Piano Sonata, op. 2, No. 2, EXAMPLE 207
Piano Sonata, op. 7, EXAMPLES 48, 267
Piano Sonata, op. 22, EXAMPLE 2
Piano Sonata, op. 28, EXAMPLE 287
Piano Sonata, op. 31, No. 1, EXAMPLES 80, 230
Piano Sonata, op. 31, No. 3, EXAMPLE 25
Piano Sonata, op. 53, EXAMPLE 6
Piano Sonata, op. 57, EXAMPLES 86, 87, 188, 199, 280, 286
Piano Sonata, op. 81a, EXAMPLE 132
Piano Sonata, op. 90, EXAMPLES 3, 4, 171, 215
Piano Sonata, op. 109, EXAMPLE 196, 276
Piano Sonata, op. 110, EXAMPLE 11
Diabelli Variations, op. 120, EXAMPLE 130
Variations, C Minor, EXAMPLES 93, 94

H. BERLIOZ

Symphony Fantastique, EXAMPLE 89

J. BRAHMS

Third Symphony, EXAMPLE 84
String Sextet, op. 18, EXAMPLE 266
Horn Trio, op. 40, EXAMPLES 9, 10, 225
Clarinet-Piano Sonata, op. 120, No. 1, EXAMPLE 83
Rhapsody, op. 79, No. 1, EXAMPLES 24, 85
Rhapsody, op. 79, No. 2, EXAMPLE 28
Intermezzo, op. 117, No. 2, EXAMPLES 38, 274
Chorale, op. 62, No. 7, EXAMPLE 50
Chorus, "Die Mullerin," op. 44, No. 5, EXAMPLE 52

A. BRUCKNER

Ninth Symphony, EXAMPLE 264

INDEX OF THE MUSIC EXAMPLES

INDEX OF THE MUSIC EXAMPLES

R. WAGNER

INDEX